The Birds of
WASHTENAW COUNTY,
MICHIGAN

The Birds of
WASHTENAW COUNTY, MICHIGAN

MICHAEL A. KIELB

JOHN M. SWALES

RICHARD A. WOLINSKI

THE UNIVERSITY OF MICHIGAN PRESS

Ann Arbor

Contents

Chapter One

Introduction

Background

In the summer of 1990 the three authors of this volume met for the first time to talk *seriously* about a book on the birds of Washtenaw County. One thing became clear from the start: we should not attempt a book which would also serve as an identification guide. The reasons were obvious. First, there is now an impressive array of field guides to North American birds on the market, ranging all the way from slim booklets illustrating the more common birds to technical volumes for expert birdwatchers, such as Kaufman's *Advanced Birding* (1990). Second, the inclusion of descriptions of species (plus the necessary line drawings and/or color plates) would raise the size and cost of a county book far beyond what could be considered reasonable. Third, we felt that the inclusion of such general information would detract from the *local* focus that we wanted to achieve.

In essence, we wanted to provide an up-to-date and comprehensive account of the bird-life in Washtenaw County as it was known towards the close of the twentieth century. More specifically, we wanted to provide the best answers we could to such questions as:

- When, if at all, is a particular species likely to occur in the county?
- How common (or easy to find) is that species and how does its frequency of occurrence vary during the year?
- In what kind of habitat will it be most likely to occur?
- What would be a good place in the county to look for it?

At this point someone might observe, "Why Washtenaw County?" and further comment — accurately enough — that there is nothing special about the birds of Washtenaw County. Washtenaw County is indeed, in terms of bird-life, typical of most southern Michigan inland counties. However, this is an advantage rather than a disadvantage, since an ornithology of Washtenaw County is consequently fairly representative of the avifauna in comparable counties. What makes Washtenaw County different is not so much its birds as its birders and birding history. Because of the University of Michigan, Eastern Michigan University, the Ann Arbor-Ypsilanti area and the birders attracted to these, there is an exceptionally rich vein of information extending back for a hundred years on the bird life in the county. Finally, Michael Kielb and Richard Wolinski have been recording county observations on a regular basis for almost two decades, while John Swales has been doing the same for the last six years. Together we can provide for Washtenaw County a database of more than 40,000 recent records ranging from those of very common county birds to those which are extremely rare.

We have also incorporated unusual county observations published in the Michigan Audubon Society's journal *The Jack-Pine Warbler*, as well as observations from the "Noteworthy Bird Sightings" column in the *Washtenaw Audubon Society Newsletter*, and from the quarterly *Washtenaw County Bird Survey*. Just as importantly, we have been able to draw upon the unpublished observations of numerous county birders over the last twenty years; our gratitude to them is individually acknowledged at the end of this chapter.

State ornithologies are now fairly widespread, while the number of books dealing with smaller regions is growing. Examples in Michigan include Alice Kelley's *Birds of Southeastern Michigan and Southwestern Ontario* (1978) and Eugene Kenaga's *Birds, Birders, and Birding in the Saginaw Bay Area* (1983). However, a substantial county bird book is still somewhat unusual in North America and elsewhere. Our Michigan forerunners include Cuthbert's *The Birds of Isabella County* (1963) and Walkinshaw's *The Birds of Battle Creek, Calhoun County, Michigan Area* (1978). We hope this volume will encourage the publication of others.

A powerful influence on our thinking and planning has been Kenneth Brock's *Birds of the Indiana Dunes* (1986). Like Brock, we also have tried for a style that we hope is acceptable to serious ornithologists and yet remains accessible to members of the general public with a more casual interest in birds. Further encouragement was provided in 1989 by the publication of *The Birds of Cambridgeshire* (Bircham 1989). Although this volume deals with bird-life on the other side of the Atlantic, it too represents a fairly ordinary birding area surrounding a major research university and city with strong professional and amateur interest in local bird-life. There are a number of features of this book that we have adopted.

In *The Birds of Washtenaw County, Michigan* we have aimed for a volume that is both as definitive as we can make it and of interest to a wide range of readers. Among this multiple audience we would hope to include:

- those inhabitants of Washtenaw and adjacent counties who have only a minor interest in birds and who might therefore only use the book for occasional reference

- birdwatchers of greater levels of commitment throughout south east Michigan
- participants in bird courses offered throughout the county
- visitors to the region with an interest in birds
- all those in the area with wider interests in their local natural world
- ornithologists and bird libraries in the USA and Ontario
- administrators, conservation groups, and consultants concerned with the environment and ecology of Washtenaw County

The final group of potential users (those concerned with managing the environment) brings us to a further, secondary motive for compiling this book. As local readers will know, Washtenaw County is undergoing substantial change. Shopping malls, lake cottages, residential developments, industrial parks, golf courses and many other signs of human activity have been spreading across the county, especially around the Ann Arbor-Ypsilanti area. Even in the southern and western quarters the rural character of the county is changing as woodlots mature, unused agricultural land converts to *old field* and commuters move in.

As the development of Washtenaw County's cities, townships and villages continues, some efforts are being made to preserve the natural environment. Readers of local newspapers will recollect, for instance, the recent successful moves to incorporate an extra area into Bird Hills Park and to preserve Black Pond in Leslie Park. The Washtenaw County Drain Commissioners take justifiable pride in their excellent wetland habitat by I-94 and Platt Rd. at Swift Run Pond. Additionally, there are many organizations which protect habitat important for bird-life, such as the Huron-Clinton Metropolitan Authority, local parks, the Michigan Chapter of the Nature Conservancy, the University of Michigan, and the Washtenaw Audubon Society. Even so, the county is suburbanizing around the magnet of the special qualities of Ann Arbor.

The principal aim of this book is to provide a baseline account of species occurrence in Washtenaw County during the last fifteen years. We hope that this account will be of value in gauging the possible effects of future environmental and ecological change and that it can serve as a reference for input into policy-making.

Outline of the Book

This book is arranged in five chapters. Subsequent sections of this opening chapter deal with the topography of Washtenaw County, with its ornithological history over the last hundred years, and with prospects for further collaboration and research.

Chapter two is designed to assist birdwatchers in their attempts to find birds in Washtenaw County. After an introduction, there is a one-page site-chart and two site location maps summarizing where to go and when. There are 40 sites covered, including six special "routes": three for water-fowl (two in migration and one for deep winter); two for shorebirds; and one for that arcane and mysterious activity known as "owling." The large number of locations underlines the fact that we have aimed for comprehensive coverage, even if this may mean that a visit to one of the smaller sites could prove unrewarding. For certain important locations and for the shorebirding routes, we have provided maps (prepared by Susan Kielb). We also make suggestions for bird-walks through three important sites in the Ann Arbor area: Dolph Park, Eberwhite Woods, and Nichols Arboretum.

Chapter three is the centerpiece of the volume since it contains detailed accounts of the 267 species recorded in the county between 1977 and 1991. Although many of the details of these accounts are explained in the introduction to chapter three, there are a number of features that need to be discussed in advance of chapter two.

The first is our decision to restrict the main species reports to the 1977-1991 period, i.e., the fifteen years prior to publication. This period is long enough, we feel, to even out annual fluctuations and to cope with freak movements caused by exceptional climatic or other events. On the other hand, it is also short enough to offer a snapshot of the county's avifauna towards the end of the twentieth century. Of course, it is not the case that the county has undergone no change in its bird populations since 1977 (the arrival of the House Finch saw to that), but overall changes during the last 15 years seem minor when compared to the bird-life of Washtenaw County 100 or even 50 years ago. In the remainder of the book the term *survey period* refers to the years from 1977 to 1991.

Secondly, references to the four seasons may need to be explained. The North American birding world has its own definitions for the seasons which have been influenced more by migratory movement than by climate. These definitions are as follows:

> Spring: March, April, May
> Summer: June, July
> Fall: August, September, October, November
> Winter: December, January, February

Readers should note, in particular, that in this book March is not winter and August is not summer (although both may feel like it).

The third and final feature of the species accounts that needs early explanation is the concept of *finding code*, which we have adopted — and adapted — from Brock's *Birds of the Indiana Dunes* (1986). We first give the finding codes and then discuss them.

Finding Code Definitions
(effort required)

Code	Descriptor	Single observer	All observers
1	Abundant	25 birds per hour	—
2	Common	1 bird per hour	—
3	Common	1 bird per half day	—
4	Fairly common	1 bird per day	—
5	Fairly uncommon	1 bird per week	—
6	Uncommon	1-2 birds per season	4-20 birds per year
7	Fairly rare	—	1-3 birds per year
8	Rare	—	1 bird every two years
9	Very rare	—	1 bird every five year
10	Extremely rare or vagrant	—	1 bird every 15 years

The finding code gives an indication of the chances of *encountering* a particular species in Washtenaw County for a given amount of effort spent in the field. The finding codes are based on a number of reasonable assumptions. The first is that the observer is a moderately competent birdwatcher. We do not mean by this some expert who can confidently identify an unusual sparrow by the quality of a single, short "chip" call, or a two-mile-away hawk from its flight pattern. Rather, we have in mind a person who can recognize by sight or song most county birds and who suspects something unusual when hearing or seeing it. Secondly, the observer is presumed to be in the right habitat. In other words, the finding code for, say, the Marsh Wren will not apply if the observer is trying to find it in a wood or plowed field rather than in a marsh. Finally, the finding code reflects the most favorable time (or times) of the year for encountering the species. The American Robin is therefore coded as 1 (25 birds per hour) since it is abundant from mid-March to October in many county habitats. During the winter, most robins are far south of Washtenaw County, but most years a few small parties of robins attempt to over-winter in the county. Naturally, these December-February birds are much harder to find, and so the Finding code of 1 would not apply at this time of year.

Finding codes have one distinct advantage. They offer *operational* definitions for coming across a particular species at a particular time. In the past there has often been uncertainty about what is meant by terms such as "common" or "rare." In Washtenaw County in the summer it would be entirely reasonable to conclude that both the Turkey Vulture and the Yellow Warbler are "common" species, even though the latter clearly outnumbers the former many times over. However, to a birder, especially one doing some driving around, both species fit well into a Finding code of 2. Moreover, Finding codes, as indicators of *encounterability*, have a certain realism to them since they reflect the variable degree of difficulty in actually finding a particular species. A suburban, open-spaces bird like the American Robin is easy to encounter. A Cooper's Hawk, while much larger than a robin, is a shy, typically silent, woodland bird and so harder to locate. And, in its turn, a Cooper's Hawk is easy to find compared to even more elusive species such as those that are only active at night or rarely emerge from the dense vegetation in marshes.

Chapter four completes the species accounts. It is divided into three sections. Section A describes the 30 species for which there are, in our judgment, acceptable records, but only from *before* the beginning of the survey period. This addition makes, at the time of writing, a total of 297 species on the county list. Section B discusses a number of other species that we prefer to consider of only hypothetical occurrence in Washtenaw County, while Section C briefly notes some of the sightings in the wild and exotic species that have either been released or have escaped from captivity. None of the species in chapter four is given a Finding code.

Chapter five provides annual bar-graphs for all species in chapter three with Finding codes from 1 through 8. The bar-graphs give the birdwatcher (whether expert or casual) a *generalized* overview of the seasonal occurrence and abundance of any species in an easy-to-use reference format.

The Birds of Washtenaw County, Michigan closes with a bibliography and an index. The bibliography lists all the references in the text. We have included citations of all the references known to us that deal specifically with the ornithology of Washtenaw County. The index is restricted to species names (or rarely sub-species or hybrids) and to county locations; entries in bold refer to the species accounts themselves or to the main site descriptions.

Geography and Topography

The total area of Washtenaw County is about 716 square miles, or about 458,000 acres. It is a "second tier" county as viewed from the perspective of the Michigan-Ohio state line to the south. Washtenaw County is bordered by Wayne County (which includes the city of Detroit) to the east, Oakland and Livingston counties to the north, Jackson in the west, and Lenawee and Monroe to the south. The county is divided administratively into 20 townships (see map). The current population is about 280,000 people, most of whom live in the east-central part of the county in the cities of Ann Arbor, Saline and Ypsilanti and the four east-central townships. Apart from the scattered villages of Chelsea, Dexter, and Manchester and the small city of Milan astride the southern border, the rest of the county is still largely agricultural or low-density rural-residential. The westernmost tier of four townships, along with Dexter Township in the north, proportionately contains more woodland than other areas of the county.

The main Detroit-Chicago road and rail routes traverse the county east-west. In addition to agriculture, major sources of employment are automotive manufacturing companies, a wide range of technology, research and service industries (especially in and around Ann Arbor), the University of Michigan, and Eastern Michigan University. In comparison to the rest of the state, Washtenaw County is reckoned to be relatively prosperous and to have, because of Ann Arbor-Ypsilanti and their associated universities, exceptional cultural amenities.

The geology of Washtenaw County is largely a consequence of the last major period of glaciation (some 15,000 years ago), which reconfigured the Great Lakes shorelines and provided material for the building of hills and valleys. The resulting terminal moraines (accumulations of rock debris) and the former shorelines of glacial lakes have produced a variety of landforms within the borders of the county. Two prominent moraines, the Fort Wayne and Defiance, traverse the county from northeast to southwest. They are separated by a comparatively level, but gently undulating, strip of intermoranic soils which run in the same direction. These areas serve as a natural drainage way for the adjacent uplands and hold many of the larger wetlands. The highest elevations are at Sharon Short Hills in the west (1,150 feet) and Peach Mountain in the north (1,058 feet), while the lowest portion of the county is the southeast corner. The latter flanks the eastern edge of the Defiance moraine and is composed of former beach ridges which form the margin of the Huron-Erie Plain. This continues on into Monroe County to the very edge of the present Lake Erie.

The principal river draining the county is the Huron River, generally running northwest to southeast. At Peach Mountain and around Ann Arbor it has cut through the moraines to form small valleys. The smaller Raisin and Saline Rivers, with their tributaries, drain the southern row of townships. The county has a fair number of lakes which offer a wide range of aquatic habitats for migrating waterfowl and other water-related birds. The larger natural lakes are Whitmore Lake, Portage Lake (both partly in

Livingston County), Independence Lake, North Lake, and Pleasant Lake. Most of these are associated with the moraine-dominated features north and west of Ann Arbor. Smaller lakes have often formed in *kettle-holes*, or depressions created by thick blocks of ice left behind as the glacial sheet retreated. The two lakes at Dolph Park are of this kind. In addition, several man-made impoundments have been created since settlement began in the early nineteenth century. These include Barton Pond and Ford Lake on the Huron River, Winnewanna Lake in the Waterloo Recreation Area, Four Mile Lake at the Chelsea State Game Area, and Iron Creek Mill Pond in Manchester Township.

The degree to which the natural features of the county have been changed by man is almost unimaginable, especially since there are almost no pockets of original vegetation surviving. Nearly all the land has, at one time or another, been settled, cleared and used for various purposes. Sometimes it has been abandoned, only to be re-used again at a later date. Much of the original vegetative cover was composed of forests and wetlands. An inventory of the remaining forested areas in the county was conducted using aerial photography in 1979 (*Washtenaw County Fragile Lands*, 1981). A total of 1,207 woodlots of size greater than five acres were identified. This area totalled about 60,000 acres (about 12% of the land surface), of which two thirds were privately owned and one third was under public ownership of various kinds. The higher, well-drained hills and ridges tend to be populated by *oak-hickory forest*, lower and slightly wetter ground by *beech-maple forest*, while the swampy areas may contain trees like tamarack and black ash. The quality of these wooded areas for bird habitat depends not only on size, composition and maturity of the canopy trees, but also on forest management practices. Most of the privately-owned woodlots do not reach full maturity, as they are selectively cut for timber harvest and often are used as forage areas for cattle. However, several publicly-owned woods now offer good habitat for interior forest species such as Hairy Woodpecker, Acadian Flycatcher, Ovenbird, Red-eyed Vireo and Scarlet Tanager.

Data from the Michigan Resource Information System (MIRIS) show as of 1990 about 42,000 acres of wetland remain in the county, or about 10% of the total land area. The major types of wetland are as follows:

Lowland hardwoods	21,324 acres
Scrub-shrub	14,756 acres
Emergent (marsh)	3,847 acres
Wooded wetland	1,615 acres

It has been calculated that about 91,000 acres of wetland existed in the county at the time European settlement started in the 1820s or rather more than twice the area that exists today. Wetlands have been used for rubbish disposal, have been partially filled, have been drained, or have been impacted in other ways by commercial, residential or agricultural activities. The majority of quality wetlands are now found in the western part of the county, mostly on public land.

Once the original landscape had been cleared by the harvest of timber, the upland areas were further modified by plowing for the planting of crops or used as pasture for horses, cattle and sheep. Sandy areas associated with the old glacial ridges or outwash areas, commonly referred to as *blowouts*, were singled out for further treatment. Because of their low productivity, such blowouts were viewed as worthless land in need of stabilization. This rehabilitative urge accounts for many of the plantations of various species of pines (sand-loving, fast-growing trees) located around the county on both public and private land. One avian species, the Lark Sparrow, which populated this type of sparsely-vegetated scrubby habitat, has now disappeared from the county (and all of southern Michigan) as the soils, now firmly held in place and shaded, have encouraged other plants to grow. Blowouts are also used for sand and gravel extraction.

Agriculture continues to be the largest single use of land in the county, following the construction of a system of private and county drains designed to move water rapidly off the lowlands and into streams and rivers. This drainage system dried marginal soils sufficiently to allow for the planting of crops or for the development of pasture. Historically the county had the greatest proportion of its land devoted to agriculture in the 1930s. Some land was abandoned during the Great Depression and, although there have been fluctuations since then, the farm acreage continues to decline as the human population expands and more fields are converted to residential and other uses. On abandoned agricultural land, plant succession gives rise to the important habitat known as *old field*, wherein invading species such as sumac and hawthorn begin to grow among the uncut grasses. Some habitat for birds and other wildlife is now being added onto marginal croplands as the Conservation Reserve Program allows farmers to place such acreage aside in return for subsidies. Efforts at preserving all of the remaining high quality farmland may continue to prove ineffective if development pressures from the east remain strong.

An outline of the topography of Washtenaw County should also make reference to a phenomenon known as *habitat fragmentation*, in which larger blocks of habitat are broken up into smaller pieces, such as occurs with the partial draining of wetlands and the building of houses in woodlots. Among other things, this process tends to threaten bird-life by increasing the chances of human disturbance, predation, and parasitism by the Brown-headed Cowbird. Further, a natural human concern with fire may prevent the natural fire-succession of the remaining dry oak-hickory woods, while concern with flooding may interrupt the natural development of river floodplain, bottomland and deciduous swamp communities. Although human interests and concerns will inevitably be a dominating factor in the future of Washtenaw County, an understanding of their consequences is important if Washtenaw County is to remain — as it is today — a fairly well-balanced ecosystem coping with the exigencies of humanity and the natural world.

The dramatic changes in the topography of southern Michigan, especially in the nineteenth century, have inevitably had a powerful and pervasive effect on bird-life. Here we illustrate only some of the resulting changes; a full and excellent account can be found in Richard Brewer's chapter entitled "Original Avifauna and Post Settlement Changes" in *The Atlas of the Breeding Birds of Michigan* (Brewer, McPeek, and Adams 1991).

The clearing of the forests for agriculture reduced or eliminated several species associated with extensive mature southern woods such as the Louisiana Waterthrush and Hooded and Cerulean Warblers. At the same time, other forest birds retreated north as breeding species; these include the Yellow-bellied Sapsucker, the Red-breasted Nuthatch, the Brown Creeper and a number of warblers. On the other hand, the more open agricultural habitat increased the numbers of grassland species such as several species of sparrows and the Eastern Meadowlark, while the new edge habitat favored the American Robin, the House Wren and the Gray Catbird, now three of the county's most widespread nesting species. Human structures also provided convenient nesting sites for the Chimney Swift and the Barn Swallow, and human introduction elsewhere eventually brought to Washtenaw County the House Sparrow (1879), the European Starling (1924) and the House Finch (1982). The Tufted Titmouse and the Northern Cardinal, both once rare, have benefited from climatic warming and bird feeders.

Early settlers were unconstrained by hunting regulations and were soon followed by market-hunters. The subsequent over-harvesting extirpated a number of species and severely reduced populations of waterfowl, raptors, upland game birds and shorebirds. Hunting of raptors and shorebirds is now forbidden, while the taking of waterfowl and game birds is managed and controlled by the U.S. Fish and Wildlife Service and the Michigan Department of Natural Resources. As a result of these controls, plus the conservation efforts of numerous groups — including hunting organizations such as Ducks Unlimited — many of these species have been recovering, albeit in some cases rather slowly.

It is well known that the ranges of many species of birds undergo constant change. Obviously, this phenomenon is most apparent on the edges of any particular range, for it is there that fluctuations can be most easily seen. Washtenaw County is situated on or close to the edge of a number of ranges. Among the permanent residents, the classic indicator is the Carolina Wren, a species on the northern edge of its range. Its numbers here vary from year to year depending on how many birds survive the winter. The Carolina Wren thus tells us something about winter severity from a passerine perspective. As Root states, "Temperature is the factor most strongly associated with both the distribution and abundance patterns of the Carolina Wren." (1988:181). The county also lies close to the northern limits of a number of migrants. Monitoring the occurrence of the White-eyed Vireo, the Hooded Warbler, the Yellow-breasted Chat and the Orchard Oriole may again provide ways to evaluate seasonal conditions both here and elsewhere.

An Ornithological History of Washtenaw County

Inevitably, a work of this kind is built upon the efforts of other students of Washtenaw County birds, who may have made their contributions at different times, in different ways and under circumstances quite different from our own. The main purpose of this section is, therefore, to describe and acknowledge the more important work of our numerous predecessors.

The first list of county birds, including notes on relative abundance and habitat preference, was compiled by Adolphe B. Covert and published in March 1881 as part of *The History of Washtenaw County, Michigan.* Covert listed 252 species, although not quite all of these are currently accepted (see chapter four).

The presence of the University of Michigan and Eastern Michigan University (formerly Michigan State Normal College) has, since early on, had a profound influence on the kinds and amount of natural history investigation taking place in the local area. Faculty, students and technical staff keep and publish records, maintain specimen collections, and are involved in teaching classes. For example, the two most recent distributional checklists of the birds of Michigan have been produced by faculty at the University of Michigan (Zimmerman and Van Tyne 1959; Payne 1983).

Partly as a result of this university involvement, a substantial record of the migration of birds within the county and nearby areas has been accumulated from the late nineteenth century into contemporary times. Most of the early records were summarized by N. A. Wood and A. D. Tinker in 1934. A six-year study of birds near Ypsilanti was carried out by Max Minor-Peet in the 1930s and presents detailed information on the status and habitat preferences of the birds found during that period. A nationally-important investigation into raptors by the Craighead brothers in the 1940s was largely based on fieldwork conducted in Superior Township.

Norman Wood's great work *The Birds of Michigan*, published after his death by Professor Josselyn Van Tyne in 1951, is particularly rich in information about birds in Washtenaw County, since Wood was a county resident. Edwin Burrows (1954, unpublished manuscript) extracted the data for Washtenaw County from Wood (1951) and elsewhere and brought it up to date until 1954.

From about 1950, a long series of short articles based on field-notes taken in Washtenaw County began to appear in *The Jack Pine Warbler* and elsewhere, principally by Andrew Berger, but also by H. L. Batts, R. Kirby, and others. Increasingly the JPW Seasonal Bird Surveys included unusual records submitted by professional ornithologists and local experts such as David Baker, Al Maley, Harrison "Bud" Tordoff, Josselyn Van Tyne and Dale Zimmerman. Meanwhile the Ann Arbor Christmas Bird Count had begun on a regular basis in 1948 with a small initial group of eleven observers.

During the last 15 years unusual county bird records and occasional short articles related to the county's avifauna have been published in the *Washtenaw Audubon Society Newsletter*. Local birdwatching was facilitated by the publication in 1982 of *A Guide to Bird Finding in Washtenaw County and Surrounding Areas* by D. Baker, T. Wells, and R. Wykes. This was the second revision of a guide originally authored by Al Maley. The society also helped fund publication of the *Washtenaw County Bird Survey* (1987-1990) edited by Richard Wolinski. These reports provided quarterly summaries of bird observations within the county and have contained special articles dealing with spring migration at Nichols Arboretum (M. Kielb), shorebird sightings in the county (J. Swales), and the birds of Saginaw Forest (R. Culbert).

The comprehensive survey of the county during the period 1983-1988 as a part of the Michigan Breeding Bird Atlas project added useful information on the distribution of nesting birds in the county and should form the basis for further future work. There is a particular need for information on the nesting activities of birds in the county, especially on the productivity of given species under different environmental conditions. These are topics on which this volume has very little to say, but only by being better aware of such aspects of our bird-life can we take adequate measures to protect and preserve our native bird populations and the habitats that support them.

Cooperative Endeavors and the Future

In this introductory chapter we have explained our purposes and procedures and tried to show how they interrelate. In our efforts to pull together information from both the past and the present, we have become increasingly aware of how much more needs to be done. Our final hope, therefore, is that *The Birds of Washtenaw County, Michigan* will itself serve as a stimulus to others so that the information it contains can be updated and expanded. Birding, after all, remains a largely amateur and part-time recreation and, as such, typically needs a number of focal points to ensure that individual effort is consolidated into a public record. We offer this volume as one such focal point, and in that spirit we list in the Appendix additions and changes to the species accounts resulting from observations made from January through August 1992. Reports of rare or unusual species often result in a greater number of birdwatchers searching for the bird in question, this in turn results in a greater number of sightings of additional species. The sighting of a Little Blue Heron on 15 August at Thurston Pond brought into the field a large number of birdwatchers. Intense searching for this rare species led to the discovery of two Least Bitterns and several Caspian Terns.

There are other focal points. An obvious one is the Washtenaw Audubon Society (WAS), the local chapter of the Michigan Audubon Society organized in 1944 (Beard 1944), which runs regular field trips, issues a bimonthly newsletter, holds a monthly meeting at the Matthaei Botanical Gardens and organizes the Ann Arbor Christmas Bird Count (now in its 46th year).

Another is the University of Michigan Museum of Zoology (UMMZ) on the Central Campus. The third floor provides a permanent exhibit consisting of mounted specimens of nearly all the species mentioned in this book. There is also a specialized bird library on this floor. Although it is housed in a section of the building not officially open to the public, those with a serious interest in county birds are likely to be well received. For further information contact the Bird Division (313-764-0457).

A number of organizations, such as Washtenaw Community College, the Washtenaw Audubon Society, and the Matthaei Botanical Gardens offer introductory and intermediate classes in bird identification and birdfinding. These nearly always include local field trips where participants can test their newly acquired skills. Finally, there is a Rare Bird Alert telephone tape run by the Detroit Audubon Society which provides information on rarities (updated weekly) within southeast Michigan and farther afield.

If an observer sees a less common bird (Finding code 7 or above and many with Finding code 6) it should be reported to the WAS (consult the most recent telephone directory for the current telephone number). All rare species or those not included in this book should be reported to the Bird Division (UMMZ). Of course the rarer the species, the more careful the observer has to be in eliminating more likely alternatives. Field notes are always a good idea, as is trying to get others to see the bird. As it happens, every birdwatcher (including the most famous) has had the embarrassing experience of misidentifying birds. Birdwatching remains an honor code activity and birdwatchers learn to do their honest best and to take both the kudos and the lumps as they come.

    This book would not have been possible without the help of a large number of individuals. We would like to thank Vi Benner, Susan Kielb, Robert Payne and Roger Wykes for reviewing and commenting on large sections of the manuscript. Additionally, Vi Benner provided the index for the manuscript and Mike Muha provided valuble computer assistance in retrieving the manuscript from an unreadable computer disk. We are grateful to Raymond Adams, Jr., of the Kalamazoo Nature Center for giving us access to the Washtenaw County records from the *The Atlas of Breeding Birds of Michigan* (Brewer, McPeek, and Adams 1991). We are appreciative of the support and professional help supplied by Mary Erwin of the University of Michigan Press, and of the assistance in checking records and specimens provided by Phil Chu, Janet Hinshaw, and Robert Payne. Finally, we recognize that this book would have been much weaker without the opportunity of incorporating the county records and observations of many competent birdwatchers and ornithologists who, over a long passage of years, have taken an interest in Washtenaw County birds. Therefore, to close this chapter, we list by initials and name all those people who, even sometimes inadvertently, have contributed information to this volume:

LA	Larry Anderson	ACa	Art Carpenter
SA	Sue Anderson	TC	Tom Carpenter
GB	Greg Babiarz	DC	Don Chalfant
DB	Dave Baker	AC	Allen Chartier
JB	Jim Ballard	PC	Phil Chu
EB	Elliot Bedows	TCl	T. Clark
DBe	Doris Behling	ECo	Ester Cole
WBe	Wayne Behling	EC	Ellie Cox
BB	Bob Bell	JC	Jean Cohn
VB	Vi Benner	CC	Clarence Crisp
AB	Andy Berger	RC	Robert Culbert
MB	Martin Bialecki	ACu	Alisande Cutler
MBi	Melvin Bialecki	AD	Al Danks
ABi	A. Bissell	GD	Gaylee Dean
MBr	Margaret Bradley	RD	Richard Dean
DBr	Don Brooks	PD	Paul DeBenedictis
EBu	Edwin Burrows	BD	Bill Dobbins
RB	Robert Butsch	MD	M. Donega
JCa	J. Capper	PF	Paul Favreau

CF	C. D. Fisher	DM	David Mosher
SF	Susan Ford	PM	Phil Moulton
NF	Nancy French	RM	Russell Mumford
RF	Rob French	RN	Rick Neubig
DF	Doug Fulton	TN	Tom Northrup
DG	Dorine Gapczyski	RO	Ron Orenstein
JG	Jim Gapczyski	LP	Laura Payne
FG	Frank Gill	RBP	Robert Payne
RHa	Rita Halberson	MPa	M. Parsons
WH	William Hamilton	EPa	Elizabeth Patterson
HHa	Harry Hann	MP	Mike Perrone
HH	Holly Hartman	BP	Betsy Perry
WHa	Wolfgang Hauer	SP	Sergej Postupalski
CH	Carl Haynie	CP	Curt Powell
EH	Eunice Hendrix	DP	Don Powers
DH	Dale Herter	EP	Eric Preston
MH	Matt Heumann	RP	Rick Prum
GH	Geoff Hill	JRe	Jim Reckley
JH	Janet Hinshaw	JR	Jeff Renner
SH	Steve Hinshaw	PR	Paul Rockey
SHo	Sue Horvath	BR	Bill Ross
PHo	Pam Hoskins	CR	Carol Ross
PH	Paula Hotaling	WR	Will Russell
RH	Bob Hotaling	ESa	Edwin Sanchez
KH	Ken Houser	MSc	Manfred Schmidt
RI	Rebecca Irwin	TSc	Tom Schneider
GJ	George Johnson	PS	Paul Schrodt
JJ	Jan Johnson	MS	Mike Sefton
KJ	Kay Johnson	GS	George Sexton
AK	Alexis Kielb	ESh	Ellie Shappirio
MK	Michael Kielb	NS	Napier Shelton
SK	Susan Kielb	SSl	Sarah Sloane
DL	Dale Lawson	ES	Ed Smith
DLi	D. Ligon	MSm	Macklin Smith
WL	William Lunk	SSm	Scott Smith
AM	Al Maley	SS	Sherri Smith
LM	Larry Master	TS	Tim Smart
JM	John McAree	MSt	Mary Steele
SM	Stephanie McAree	CS	Chuck Steinbach
HM	Hugh McGuinness	RS	Robert Storer
M	Meiselbach	BS	Betty Stouffer
BM	Barbara Miller	MLS	Mary Lou Stuht
SMi	Sheldon Miller	WS	Bill Swaney

JS	John Swales	TW	LaRue "Tex" Wells
ESw	Elsie Swanberg	GW	Guerin Wilkinson
BT	Barb Taylor	TWi	Tom Will
ET	Ed Taylor	RW	Richard Wolinski
DT	D. Thiry	JW	Julie Wolinski
AT	A. D. Tinker	JWo	Jean Wood
HT	Harrison "Bud" Tordoff	NW	Norman Wood
JT	Jill Trainer	BWy	Barb Wykes
TV	Tom Van't Hof	RWy	Roger Wykes
JV	Josselyn Van Tyne	KZ	Kenneth Zeeb
GV	G. Van Vliet	DZ	Dale Zimmerman
CW	C. F. Walker	MZ	Marion Zimmerman
TWa	Terry Walsh	RZ	Richard Zusi

Chapter Two

Site Guide

Introduction

In this chapter we provide detailed information on 45 birdwatching locations and birding routes in Washtenaw County. This is a large number — much larger, for example, than in the latest edition of *A Guide to Bird Finding in Washtenaw County and Surrounding Areas* (Baker, Wells, and Wykes 1982) — and of course it brings its own perils. In our search for fairly complete coverage, we recognize that we run the danger of including places that may turn out to be uninteresting on a particular visit. Partly to offset this, the site descriptions are prefaced by a chart which outlines the potential of each site or route for each month of the year. This not only offers a rough guide as to where to go when — and when not to go — but also indicates the relative level of expectation associated with a particular time and place. The key we have used is as follows:

Hot spot — Don't miss it
Good area
OK
Try some other time

We are also aware, as the first chapter makes abundantly clear, that sites are continually changing as a result of habitat growth, development, or human-aided reversion to a more natural state. This chapter therefore offers a snapshot of birding opportunities in Washtenaw County as we see them in 1991-1992. There are doubtless locations that we have missed. However, all the sites and routes listed are on property that is open to the public (at least during much of the day) or can be adequately viewed from public roadways (as at Trinkle Road Marsh). Birdwatchers should never trespass on private property to find or chase birds. It is our experience that polite requests to landowners, especially farmers, will nearly always be treated sympathetically. The sites are all indicated on a county map (see below) and are described at various length depending on their importance. Not surprisingly the longest entry is that for Nichols Arboretum since this is the one location of state-wide significance in the county.

The routes consist of suggestions for finding certain groups of species that are scattered across sections of the county or are otherwise hard to find. Three waterfowl routes are offered: one for deep winter, and two for spring/fall migration. Of course, waterfowl may occur on open water practically anywhere in the county (as some of the site locations indicate); however, the routes do offer an *organized* way of looking for them. Similarly, the shorebird route entry provides one fairly reliable search pattern and another which is somewhat more speculative. Yet again this coverage is not intended to be inclusive, especially since migrating shorebirds are known to be highly opportunistic in their resting and feeding habitats. Rather different is the Owling entry because this provides an introduction to nocturnal birding and its very different techniques.

At this point we should mention that we advocate only restricted use of tape recorders to attract birds. Certainly sparing use of recorded owl and rail calls to elicit responses from these hard-to-see species is acceptable; on the other hand, persistent playing of the songs of rare summer visitors is not, nor are clumsy attempts to find their nests, which may do no more than alert predators to their location. Birdwatching should be a low-impact and gentle activity.

Birdwatching in Washtenaw County is basically safe. There are no threatening mammals and the only worrisome reptile is the mildly venemous Massasauga Rattlesnake, but we know of no birdwatchers bitten by this shy snake. Flies and mosquitoes can be bothersome in wooded areas during summer, but they rarely attain the density and voracity for which they are feared further north. When visiting such habitat, a hat is always useful and insect repellent provides relief for some. In hot weather protection from the sun is advised and liquids should be carried on longer forays, such as in Stinchfield Woods. At all times sensible footwear is essential, as is protective clothing in cold weather. Birdwatchers should also take note of the hunting seasons (which change periodically) and are best advised to avoid dense habitat when it is open for hunting, as in the state game areas. There are plenty of alternatives in fall and winter, such as the University of Michigan properties and the metroparks. The new threat of Lyme's disease, which is caused by the bite of a deer tick, is hard to assess in Washtenaw County, but one sensible precaution is to tuck jeans into socks.

Maps and Charts
Birding in the County Month-by-Month

SITES	J	F	M	A	M	J	J	A	S	O	N	D
Ann Arbor Airport	░	░	░	░						░	░	░
Arborcrest Cemetery	░	░								░	░	░
Arkona Road Swamp	░	░	░				░			░	░	░
Barton Park	░	░	░						░	░	░	░
Barton Pond				▨	■					▨	▨	
Bird Hills Park	░	░	░						░	░	░	░
County Farm Park	░	░	░		░					░	░	░
Daly Road Pond	░	░	░		░				░	░	░	░
Delhi/Osborne Mills	░	░	░						░	░	░	░
Dexter Mill Pond	░	░	▨						░	░	░	░
Dolph Park	░	░			▨				▨	░	░	░
Eberwhite Woods	░	░			▨				▨	░	░	░
Embury Road/Park Lyndon				■	▨					░	░	
Four Mile Lake/Chelsea SGA	░	░		▨					░	░	░	░
Geddes Pond	░	░	▨							▨	▨	░
Hudson Mills Metropark	░	░	░						░	░	░	░
Huron High Woods	░	░							░	░	░	░
Independence Lake	░	░	▨						░	░	░	░
Iron Creek Mill Pond	░	░	░						░	░	░	░
M-14 Water Treatment Pond	░	░	░						░	░	░	░
Maple Road/M-14	░	░	░						░	░	░	░
Matthaei Botanical Gardens	░	░	░	■	■	■			░	░	▨	░
Mitchell-Scarlett Woods	░	░							░	░	░	░
Montibeller Twp. Park	░	░	░						░	░	░	░
Nichols Arboretum	░	░	■	■	■		■	■	░	░	░	░
Owling Sites		▨	░									
Parker Mill Area	░	░			▨				░	▨	░	░
Pioneer High Woods	░	░	░		▨				░	░	░	░
St. Joseph Hospital	░	░	░						░	░	░	░
Saginaw Forest	░	░	░		▨				░	░	░	░
Saline Wilderness Park	░	░	░						░	░	░	░
Searles Natural Area	░	░			░				░	░	░	░
Sharon Hollow Nature Preserve	░				▨	▨			░	░		
Shorebird Routes	░	░		▨	▨			▨	░	░	░	░
Southeast County Route	░	░	░						░	░	░	░
Stinchfield Woods	░	░	░						░	░	░	░
Sutton Lake	░	░	░						░	░	░	░
Swift Run Pond	░	░	░						░	░	░	░
Trinkle Road Marsh	░	░	░						░	░	░	░
Waterfowl Routes (migration)			▨	▨					▨	▨	▨	
Waterfowl Route (winter)	░	░	░							░	░	░
Waterloo Recreation Area	░		░	■	▨				░	░	░	░
Whitmore Lake	░	░	░						░	░	░	░
Wing Nature Preserve	░	░			░				░	░	░	░
Winnewanna Lake	░	░		▨			░		░	░	░	░

Hot Spot—Don't Miss it ■
Good area ▨
OK ░
Try some other time ☐

Site Locations

Washtenaw County

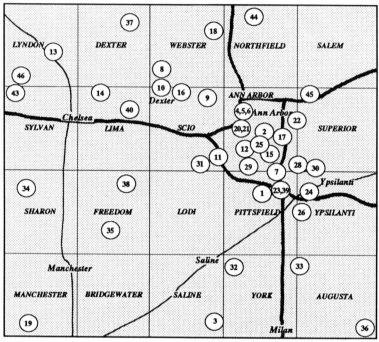

1. Ann Arbor Airport
2. Arborcrest Cemetery
3. Arkona Road Swamp
4. Barton Park
5. Barton Pond
6. Bird Hills Park
7. County Farm Park
8. Daly Road Pond
9. Delhi Metropark/Osborne Mills
10. Dexter Mill Pond
11. Dolph Park
12. Eberwhite Woods
13. Embury Road/Park Lyndon
14. Four Mile Lake/Chelsea SGA
15. Geddes Pond
16. Hudson Mills Metropark
17. Huron High Woods
18. Independence Lake
19. Iron Creek Mill Pond
20. M-14 Water Treatment Pond
21. Maple Road/M-14
22. Matthaei Botanical Gardens
23. Mitchell-Scarlett Woods
24. Montibeller Township Park
25. Nichols Arboretum
26. North Bay Park/Ford Lake
27. Owling Sites (not shown)
28. Parker Mill Area
29. Pioneer High Woods
30. St. Joseph Hospital
31. Saginaw Forest
32. Saline Wilderness Park
33. Searles Natural Area
34. Sharon Hollow Nature Preserve
35. Shorebird Route
36. Southeast County Route
37. Stinchfield Woods
38. Sutton Lake
39. Swift Run Pond
40. Trinkle Road Marsh
41. Waterfowl Routes (migration)
    (not shown)
42. Waterfowl Route (winter)
    (not shown)
43. Waterloo Rec Area
44. Whitmore Lake
45. Wing Nature Preserve
46. Winnewanna Lake

The Sites

Ann Arbor Airport

The Ann Arbor Muncipal Airport is located at the intersection of State Street and Ellsworth Road. Traditionally, the airport has offered a variety of grassfield species difficult to locate elsewhere in the county, both in summer and winter. However, several potential summer residents have not been found at this location for a decade or so, including Northern Harrier, Sedge Wren, and Henslow's Sparrow. Others continue to be at least semi-regular, such as Upland Sandpiper, Grasshopper Sparrow and Western Meadowlark. During the winter there are records of Snowy Owl, Short-eared Owl (two on the 1988 Ann Arbor CBC) and Lapland Longspur, but again not so many in recent years. As the foregoing suggests, a visit to the airport may be unrewarding. Even so, it remains the best county location for species such as the Upland Sandpiper. Enter the airport off Ellsworth Rd. (where there may be Bobolink in summer and Horned Lark in winter) and park a little to the west of the control tower.

Arborcrest Cemetery and Huron High Woods

Both located in northeast Ann Arbor, these two sites can easily be combined for a morning of birdwatching in winter. After birdwatching at these two sites it is a quick drive to Geddes Pond (see entry) where wintering ducks and gulls can usually be found.

Arborcrest Cemetery

The Arborcrest Cemetery is located on Glacier Way, east of Oak Way and west of Huron Parkway. The best birding time here is the winter, when winter finches have been reported. Check the tall stand of pines and spruces at the back of the cemetery. There is also a chance for seeing either Cooper's Hawk (which probably nests nearby) or Great Horned Owl (which nested for several years in the VA Hospital parking lot across from the cemetery). Continue east on Glacier Way to Huron Parkway then proceed south to the Huron High Woods.

Huron High Woods

Located behind Huron High School just off of Huron Parkway and Fuller Rd., these woods contain a large conifer stand and can offer some good birding in the winter including Winter Wren or Yellow-rumped Warbler. Woodpeckers and other cavity nesters are common. Great Horned Owls nest nearby and can be found roosting in the woods during the day.

Arkona Road Swamp

Arkona Road runs east from US-12 close to the southern edge of the county. Between Case and Macon, Arkona passes north of a small swamp containing numbers of dead trees and surrounded by a large private wood. Although Arkona represents something of a detour from other birding areas, it has, in our experience, proved to be the most reliable spot in the county for finding Red-headed Woodpeckers. Other likely nesting birds include Green-backed Heron, Eastern Bluebird, Tree Swallow, Eastern Phoebe, and Yellow-throated Vireo.

Barton Park

Barton Park is a low-lying tract of land on the north bank of the Huron River opposite Bird Hills Park. Until 1991 this area of *old field* was relatively inaccessible, but today there are two footbridges across the river with a connecting trail. One bridge is off Huron River Drive soon after it leaves N. Main, the other at Barton Dam. It is now possible to walk a loop across Barton Park to Barton Pond (see entry), returning via Bird Hills Park (see entry), thus exploring a wide range of habitat. At present bird records from Barton Park are rather sparse, but woodcock have been found displaying in spring and the hawthorn habitat has attracted Northern Shrike in winter. Barton Park is one of the few county locations for overwintering robins. Belted Kingfishers are permanent residents.

Barton Pond

Barton Pond is a fairly small artificial lake created by a dam across the Huron River. It lies alongside Huron River Drive a couple of miles northwest of Ann Arbor. As the map shows, there are a number of pull-offs between the dam and the Foster Bridge. Cross the railroad, follow the paths and scan the pond from the water's edge. Barton Pond attracts a good variety of waterbirds; loons and grebes are most often found in the downstream section, and ducks off "the point." (Approach the point cautiously as the ducks are often close to shore and easily disturbed.) Although Barton Pond is worth visiting during all the recommended months, the prime season is the last week in March and in April. There is probably no better time and place in the county for finding Common Loon, Horned Grebe and Red-breasted Merganser. Observers should also pay attention to the sky as well as the water: Bonaparte's Gulls are quite regular, Forster's Terns possible, and there is a chance of an Osprey. Spring rarities from Barton Pond during the survey period include two of the three records for Red-necked Grebe and one of the two records for White-winged Scoter.

Bird Hills Park

Bird Hills Park is an extensive area of woodland which lies along the Huron River to the north of Ann Arbor. Some of the slopes down to the river are quite steep, and there is a small ravine. The main entrance is located just north of M-14 on the east side of Newport Rd. There is another entrance on the west edge of the park on Bird Rd. The park is crossed by several trails. Despite its inviting name, this area seems little visited at present by birdwatchers, and not much is known about its potential for migrants. However, there are regular reports of Hooded Warbler in summer, and a Kentucky Warbler was present in June 1992. Great Horned Owls can sometimes be seen in the evening hunting from the utility poles at the edge of the freeway. This is one of the county sites which could merit further investigation.

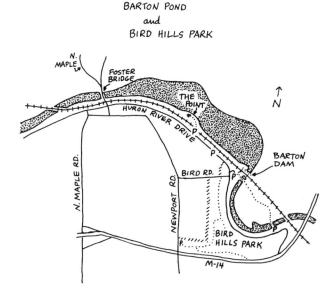

BARTON POND
and
BIRD HILLS PARK

County Farm Park

County Farm Park lies south of Washtenaw Ave. and west of Platt Rd. The main entrance and car park is off Platt Rd. County Farm Park has an extensive network of winding paths — much used by joggers and walkers — through a variety of grassy and scrubby *old field* habitats. There are also a number of nestboxes, which may attract bluebirds or Tree Swallows. A small stream, with denser vegetation, runs along the northern boundary. This is a place to visit in October for migrating sparrows or late warblers, or in April for early migrants such as the Eastern Phoebe. During the cold weather, County Farm Park also holds birds which feed on the berries and shelter in the scrub. Recent uncommon winter visitors have included a Red-shouldered Hawk and a Northern Shrike. A visit to County Farm could be added to trips to Swift Run and Mitchell-Scarlett Woods a little further down Platt Rd. The three sites offer an interesting combination of habitats all within the eastern Ann Arbor area.

Daly Road Pond

Daly Road runs east off Mast Road a little to the north of Dexter Village. The pond can be seen from the road close to the Mast intersection and from a pull-off about a quarter-mile further on. We include this pond in this section with some trepidation, because it can be a very hit-or-miss spot. Daly Road Pond is open and deep and sometimes can be almost devoid of bird-life. In April and October, however, it can host a good variety of waterfowl. It can also produce surprises. The following uncommon birds have been seen here in recent years: Greater White-fronted Goose, Red-necked Grebe, Black Tern, and Forster's Tern.

Delhi Metropark/Osborne Mills

This riparian site lies downstream of the railroad track which crosses E. Delhi Rd, south of the metropark and the canoe livery. In theory, both banks of the river should be accessible to birdwatchers, but there have been easement problems on the north bank and it is currently posted. Park by the railroad track and follow a small path south of the line, which soon joins a well-kept trail. Alternatively, park further up E. Delhi and enter by the noticeboard. This trail follows the river for most of a mile. There are no houses close to the river on this stretch, which makes for an attractive nature walk when the leaves are out. During migration a fairly good range of warblers, flycatchers and thrushes can be found; there are records for

Louisiana as well as Northern Waterthrush. Typical summer residents are woodpeckers, Scarlet Tanager, Northern Oriole, Blue-Gray Gnatcatcher, Eastern Phoebe and Belted Kingfisher. Less common but possible are Orchard Oriole and Veery. One of the two survey period records of the Black-backed Woodpecker comes from this site. Great Horned Owls nest on the northern bank.

Dexter Mill Pond

Dexter Mill Pond lies on the southwest corner of Dexter Village and can best be viewed from the cemetery off Grand St. Mill Creek runs through this marshy area, keeping an open water channel even in cold weather. The marshy areas and ponds attract ducks, geese, herons, and swallows with occasional nesting Sandhill Cranes. The trees in the cemetery collect warblers and kinglets in migration, while the willows at the water's edge often hold Palm Warblers in late April and early May. If the water levels are low, shorebirds can be found in shallow water or on any exposed mud. One of the two survey period records of White-rumped Sandpiper is from Dexter Mill Pond.

Dolph Park

Dolph Park is a 44-acre nature reserve belonging to the city of Ann Arbor. It is situated on the western edge of town east of Wagner Rd. between Liberty and Jackson Rds. There is a small parking lot off Wagner Rd. Dolph Park is a fine location for searching for migrant species in April-May and September-October, especially for less energetic or less experienced birdwatchers. Within its small confines there is an excellent range of habitat, and the extensive presence of water means that landbirds can be quite concentrated. Further, the absence of tall trees makes it easier to bird than Nichols Arboretum or Eberwhite Woods, while it involves much less walking than Matthaei Botanical Gardens.

More than 120 species have been found at Dolph Park in the last five years. Less common birds in spring have included American Bittern, Black-crowned Night-Heron, White-eyed Vireo, Olive-sided and Yellow-bellied Flycatchers, Northern Waterthrush, and Prothonotary and Orange-crowned Warblers. In fall there have been recent sightings of Osprey and Northern Pintail.

Dolph Park contains two small natural lakes: First Sister Lake (now turning into marsh) and the open Second Sister Lake, with a connecting pond and feeder streams (see map). The land habitat is mostly scrub and thicket with some taller trees, as well as remnants of *old field*. There are a number of trails and paths. A possible birdwalk during migration is the following:

1. Stroll past the interpretive panels to the overlook on Second Sister Lake.
2. Follow the small path to the left until it meets the chipped trail .and turn right towards the island bridge. This narrow section can be excellent for close views of migrant passerines, especially under growth species such as Wilson's Warbler.
3. Proceed along the path, taking the first left and then the next left to the pond overlook. Likely species along this part of the walk include migrating sparrows (skulking low in the bushes).
4. At the pond overlook a small path right goes down to the marsh. This is where the Prothonotary Warbler was seen. Retrace to the main trail.
5. At X on the map take the narrow path down to the left, moving cautiously to a dilapidated bridge over the feeder stream. This "secret spot" is the most likely location in Dolph Park for such uncommon species as White-eyed Vireo and Northern Waterthrush.
6. Retrace to the main path as far as the north slope overlook. Scan for marsh birds etc, and then take the unchipped path that circles the eastern edge of the property. The area around its junction with the main trail opposite Lakewood Drive can be productive of canopy warblers as this part of the park contains the tallest trees.
7. Take the main trail back to the parking lot.

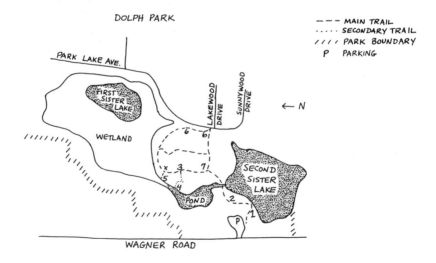

Eberwhite Woods

Eberwhite Woods is a 35-acre mature woodland situated in the heart of Ann Arbor's west side. The interesting history of the woods is well told in *Footloose in Washtenaw County* (Kraut 1990). The woods now belong to the Ann Arbor Public Schools and are scrupulously managed by the school-community "Friends of Eberwhite Woods."

The easiest access is from Eberwhite School (parking) at the end of Soule Boulevard south of West Liberty. Eberwhite contains perhaps the tallest stand of deciduous trees (maple-oak-hickory) in the county, as well as two small ponds and a small mixed area of conifer, scrub, and smaller trees.

Eberwhite is primarily a location for migrants, even though the resident species include Cooper's Hawk and Red-bellied and Hairy Woodpeckers. These impressive woods are naturally popular with the public, and relatively few species nest — one or two pairs of Wood Ducks usually try each spring but generally give up. In winter, the woodland birds find better pickings in the surrounding suburban areas (with their abundant feeders), and the woods are largely empty.

Eberwhite does not compare with Nichols Arboretum as a "migrant trap," but its small size, ease of parking, and convenient location on the west side of Ann Arbor enhance its attraction as a minor alternative. In fact, Eberwhite can offer a good range of migrating warblers, vireos, thrushes, and flycatchers in May and September. Rarer warblers recently seen include Golden-winged, Cerulean, and Mourning Warblers. Eberwhite also holds one of the very few Summer Tanager records for the county. Eberwhite can also be productive in April and October. Visits in these months provide opportunities for finding Yellow-bellied Sapsucker, Winter Wren, Brown Creeper, Hermit Thrush, and Fox Sparrow.

We offer below an itinerary for a visit during migration:

1. Park at Eberwhite school.
2. Scan the eastern edge of the wood, listening, and looking for movement (can be very productive).
3. Retrace north and take the path round the "elbow," looking for activity in the bushes and conifers (this is the densest section of the woods and attracts shier birds).
4. Enter the woods via the path crossing the open space. Proceed very slowly into the wood. The first 50 yards are typically the most productive. (If nothing much has happened by this time this is not likely to be a good day.)

5. Join the main path and follow it over the new boardwalk keeping an eye and ear open for activity in the canopy.
6. Take the small (unchipped) path that goes round the north side of the pond to the left. Concentrate here more on the ground because of the chances of sparrows, wrens, and thrushes.
7. Proceed south at the end of the pond and skirt the second pond on its east side (better light in the mornings). Look high and low.
8. Continue southwards along the western edge; join the main path and return eastwards to Eberwhite School.

EBERWHITE   WOODS

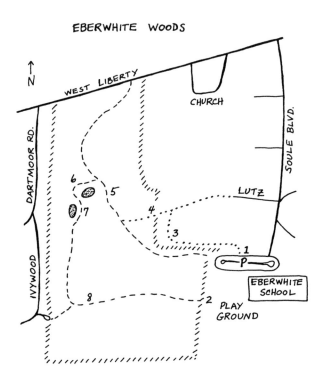

Embury Road / Park Lyndon

Situated in northwestern Washtenaw County in Lyndon Twp., this area is rich in nesting species not commonly seen in other parts of the county. A full morning of bird-watching can be most rewarding. A late evening (or early morning) visit in April or May may allow the birdwatcher to hear and see Eastern Screech-Owl, Great Horned Owl or possibly Whip-poor-will (May).

Embury Road

Embury Road runs north off North Territorial Rd. a little to the east of its junction with M-52. It forms the eastern border of Park Lyndon North in the northwest corner of the county and usually offers better birding than the park itself! Embury Rd. is one of the last truly undeveloped dirt roads in the county and contains extensive State Game Area (SGA) land on its eastern side. Blue-winged Warblers are common, having now displaced the golden-wing (see species accounts). Other summer birds are Scarlet Tanager, Yellow-throated Vireo and Ruby-throated Hummingbird. A trek inland (out of hunting season) might turn up Wild Turkey. There are also fairly recent reports of Whip-poor-will and Red-shouldered Hawk. Although an area as naturally rich as Embury Rd. will attract migrants, the variety of summer residents makes it also an interesting place to visit in June or early July. Follow North Territorial Rd. west to Park Lyndon.

Park Lyndon

This is actually two disjointed sections of one park situated in the northwest part of the county along North Territorial Rd. just west of Embury Rd. This area can host a typical variety of migrant warblers, flycatchers, and thrushes. This is another good area to hear and see Wild Turkey. This park can easily be birded when visiting Embury Rd.

Four Mile Lake / Chelsea State Game Area

Chelsea State Game Area (Chelsea SGA) incorporates a fairly large lake (Four Mile Lake), an extensive marsh to the west and some interesting wet woods in its eastern section. It thus offers a good range of habitat in one location. However, it is also a popular spot for a variety of other outdoor activities such as picnicking, fishing, canoeing, and hunting in the fall. Birdwatchers are therefore likely to meet larger numbers of people than in most places recommended in the Site Guide.

Enter the SGA along the dirt road north of Dexter-Chelsea Rd. (see map). Drive to the main parking lot at the southern end of the lake. In season scan for ducks or other waterfowl (Canvasback are traditionally more common here than elsewhere in the county). The lakeshore, wood edge and marsh may contain large numbers of other birds such as blackbirds and sparrows. Now take the west track to its end. The old marl pits may also hold a good variety of ducks, while the marshes to the east represent one of the last strongholds in the county for Marsh Wren. In migration these open parts of the Chelsea SGA are one of the better county locations for Black-crowned Night-Heron, Northern Harrier and Osprey. Return to the main track and park by the entrance to the trail through the woods. Usual summering species include Red-headed Woodpecker, Wood Thrush, Acadian Flycatcher, Ruby-throated Hummingbird and Yellow-throated Vireo. The woods also attract good numbers of migrant warblers.

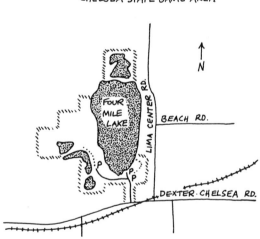

FOUR MILE LAKE
CHELSEA STATE GAME AREA

Geddes Pond

Geddes Pond refers to the stretch of the Huron River upstream of the dam at Dixboro Rd. past Gallup Park and up to the eastern end of Nichols Arboretum at Island Park. It also includes South Lake off Huron River Drive. A paved path runs along the whole stretch (much used by joggers and bikers). Although there are a number of unusual records from the Geddes Pond complex, its productivity may be declining. Certainly the recent discouragement of winter feeding (see Waterfowl in Winter) has reduced the number and variety of species at Island Park in cold weather. Even so, during migration several species of waterfowl may be present on the wider stretches, and there have been several recent sightings of Osprey. Some years Cliff Swallows nest under the Huron Parkway bridge, and Great Egrets sometimes roost on a small island in South Lake.

Hudson Mills Metropark

This large metropark lies south of North Territorial Rd. in Dexter Twp. (entrance fee required). The park has an extensive system of paved and wood-chip paths that wind their way through a variety of habitats. The paved bike-trail and the wood-chipped nature trail are equally varied, but the latter is somewhat less used. The nature trail can be accessed either from the Activity Center or from the south end of the Oak Meadows parking lot. Hudson Mills not only offers a good variety of spring, summer and fall species but has also proved fairly productive in winter (Purple Finch, Eastern Bluebird and Ruffed Grouse). Several of the Ann Arbor CBC reports of the Northern Shrike also come from this location.

Independence Lake County Park

The county park lies off Jennings Rd. north of N. Territorial Rd. in Webster Twp. In summer this park is a popular swimming and picnicking spot (entrance fee required). From October to April the entrance road is closed to cars, but birdwatchers can walk in. The clearly-marked nature trail starts from near the parking lot and loops in a circle for about a mile through varied habitat (marsh, oak-hickory woods and old field). May records include Black Tern, and a good range of summer residents can be found along the trail. The lake itself attracts an excellent variety of waterfowl in April and October through November, including the possibility of Snow Goose. There is a recent March record for a Merlin, and Northern Shrike have been seen in winter.

Iron Creek Mill Pond

This good-sized lake is located in the extreme southwest corner of the county on Sharon Hollow Rd. north of US-12. Although of historical significance (nesting American Bittern and Black Tern), today lakeshore development and recreational activities have reduced its natural character. It still hosts a variety of migrating waterfowl, and the small marsh along Wolff Run is intact. Sora and Swamp Sparrow are present, but no longer the Marsh Wren (see species account). The creek remains open in winter, and recent winter sightings include Hermit Thrush and Common Snipe.

M-14 Water Treatment Pond

The city of Ann Arbor settling pond along M-14 has always been a source of tantalizing habitat since it can only viewed from the playground of Wines Elementary School off Newport Rd. An array of ducks occur in migration. Additionally there are a great number of Killdeer. Starting in late July and continuing through early October small numbers of migrant shorebirds pass through. Greater Yellowlegs are the most frequent visitor followed by Lesser Yellowlegs, Least and Semipalmated Sandpipers. Sightings of unusual birds include White-rumped Sandpiper and Hudsonian Godwit. From this site it is easy to proceed to Bird Hills Park or the Maple Rd. / M-14 site.

Maple Rd. / M-14
(Ann Arbor Schools Environmental Study Area)

This large piece of varied habitat includes fields, secondary growth woods, several ponds with cattails and upland hardwoods. Park at the small cleared parking area and walk in to the east. In the early spring this is a good spot to find American Woodcock displaying. The ponds attract a large number of Red-winged Blackbirds and are good places to study their interesting behavior and nesting cycle. Both Sora and Virginia Rails nest in the cattails. Blue-winged Warbler, Field Sparrow, and Indigo Bunting are regular residents here. In the nearby woods there are four species of raptors nesting. Cooper's Hawk, Great Horned Owl and Red-tailed Hawk nests have been located, with Eastern Screech Owls calling in the evening. Access to this site is off Maple Rd. just north of M-14 (Maple-Miller, exit 2).

Matthaei Botanical Gardens

The site-guide chart indicates that nearly all of the locations in Washtenaw County recommended for bird-finding have periods of the year when they hold few birds. One exception to this is Matthaei Botanical Gardens. This property, which is owned by the University of Michigan, lies to the east of Ann Arbor with an entrance off Dixboro Rd. between Geddes and Plymouth Rds. Reasons for the year-round presence of birds include the mixture of deciduous and coniferous trees, fast-running Fleming Creek bisecting the property from north to south, and extensive areas of shrubs and bushes which produce an exceptional berry crop in fall. It is these features which tend to hold at least limited numbers of birds in the winter. Wintering birds include American Robin, Cedar Waxwing, Belted Kingfisher, Yellow-rumped Warbler (eating poison ivy berries), and Carolina Wren.

There are three marked trails in the gardens, all starting from the trailhead near the Conservatory: Red - 0.6 miles; Yellow - 1.2 miles; and Blue - 1.6 miles. For a short visit of an hour or so, the Red Trail may be best since it skirts the west side of productive Fleming Creek, passes through a small oakwood and returns along the edge of a wooded swamp with open grassland to the right. However, walking the longer trails and following some of the less-used smaller paths is really necessary if the full range of habitats and species is to be experienced. The Blue Trail traverses the most varied territory.

Spring migration is typically strong at the "bot gardens" with regular reports of such uncommon species as Olive-sided Flycatcher, Philadelphia Vireo, Golden-winged Warbler and Orchard Oriole. Some years a pair of Orchard Orioles will nest — a rare event in Washtenaw County. Summering Blue-winged Warblers reach their highest county density here, and their *bee-buzz* songs can usually be heard in several widely-scattered areas of the gardens. A speciality of the undergrowth around the northern end of Fleming Creek is the White-eyed Vireo; the Matthaei Botanical Gardens is probably the most northerly regular nesting site for this species in the state. The more open areas and ponds flanking the entrance road offer a range of more common species. Eastern Meadowlarks are regular in the fields in the northeast corner. Fall warbler migration can be impressive from the second half of August, especially in the vicinity of Fleming Creek; in October there will be kinglets and creepers and perhaps Purple Finch.

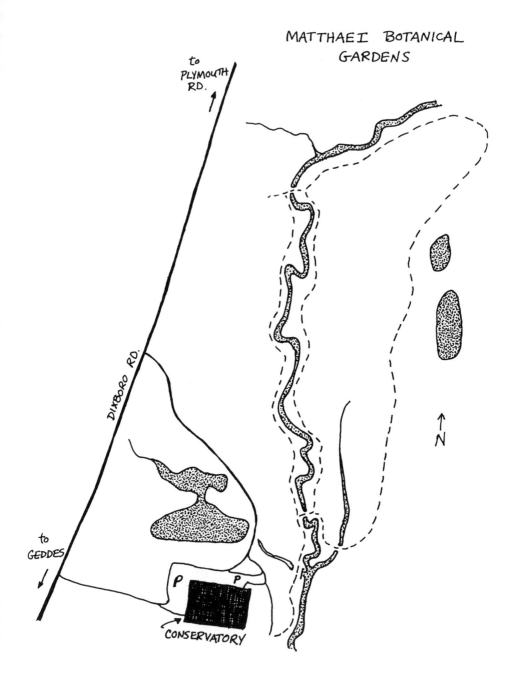

MATTHAEI BOTANICAL GARDENS

to PLYMOUTH RD.

DIXBORO RD.

to GEDDES

N

P   P

CONSERVATORY

Mitchell-Scarlett Woods

This is another of the natural areas owned by the Ann Arbor Public Schools. Access to these woods and adjacent ponds and marsh is off Lorraine St. Take Platt south of Packard to Lorraine then turn left (east) and proceed to the two schools (Scarlett and Mitchell). Park near the woods and enter at the trailhead. Birding here can be quite rewarding in the spring with 10-15 species of warblers present on good days. The trails wind their way through the woods and pass next to several ponds and a marsh (see map). Both Virginia Rail and Sora are summer residents, American Bittern is possible in spring. The fields to the east of the base-ball diamonds have had several interesting species in past years including White-eyed Vireo and Yellow-breasted Chat.

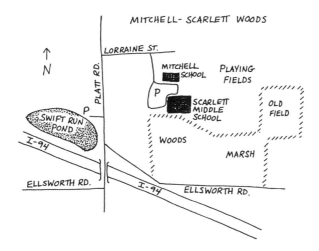

Montibeller Township Park

This small park is located in Pittsfield Twp. near the northeast corner of Ellsworth and Carpenter Rds., directly east of the Meijer Supermarket. From Ellsworth Rd. the park appears to be comprised of lawns and ball fields with typical park structures. However, at the north end of the park is a wooded area bisected by a stream. There is also a small patch of grown field associated with the smaller woods in the northeast corner.

Cross over the stream to reach the larger woods to the west and follow the trails inside the perimeter of the woods. Upon reaching the northeast corner of the woods either walk back along the stream or continue to the east into the overgrown field. The oak-hickory woods are good for spring migrants, and regular visits over the course of a year will provide a useful list of common migrant and nesting species. Summer residents include Rufous-sided Towhee, Red-eyed Vireo and, rarely, Yellow-breasted Chat (along the rear fenceline under the utility lines). The field area usually provides Field and Song Sparrow, American Goldfinch and Indigo Bunting.

Nichols Arboretum

Nichols Arboretum is the best studied ornithological site within Washtenaw County, if not Michigan. The spring migration, in particular, of birds in the Arb has been well studied over the years (Wood 1908; Tinker 1910, 1911; Barrows 1912; Wood and Tinker 1934; Wood 1951; Burrows 1954). The study of migration at this site was continued into the 1970s and 1980s with a complete survey of spring migrants, including peaks in migration, and early and late spring arrival dates (Kielb 1989). In contrast the fall migration is understudied, but there is no doubt that large numbers of migrants pass through. Even in winter interesting birds appear. In the summer, it is a nice place to take a stroll but lacks the abundance of interesting species that occur during other seasons.

Parking near the arboretum can be a problem. For those fortunate University of Michigan employees, there are parking areas near the Washington Heights and Huron River entrances (see map). For everyone else the parking situation requires a much more creative approach. Street parking off Geddes and the streets adjoining Geddes is a good strategy, provided there *is* street parking. Parking at the Fuller Pool off Fuller Rd. across the river from the Arb is another good free alternative; this, however, requires crossing the railroad tracks to enter the Arb.

In late April or early May start at the Washington Heights entrance and walk in along what was once called the "School Girl's Glen," skirting the peony garden, heading toward the ridge trail which will lead you down to the river. The ridge is a great area to observe canopy dwellers at their own level, as well as hillside loving species. It is not uncommon to have eight to twelve species of warblers, several thrushes, and flycatchers along the ridge during the first two weeks of May. Additionally, the glen to your right usually has nesting Cooper's Hawks, though occasionally they have nested well to the east of the caretaker's road. When you reach the bottom of the ridge there are three options: (1) follow the river drive to the west,

Nichols Arboretum

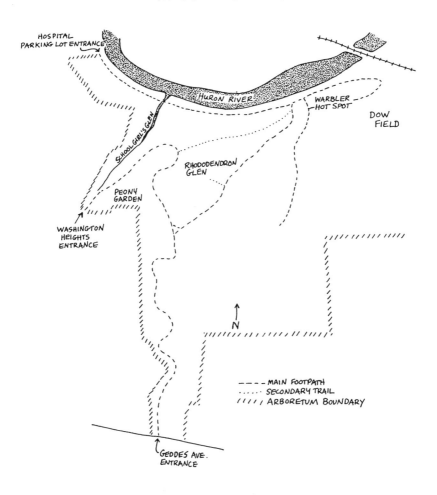

HOSPITAL PARKING LOT ENTRANCE

HURON RIVER

SCHOOLGIRL'S GLEN

WARBLER HOT SPOT

DOW FIELD

RHODODENDRON GLEN

PEONY GARDEN

WASHINGTON HEIGHTS ENTRANCE

N

- - - - MAIN FOOTPATH
· · · · · SECONDARY TRAIL
/ / / / ARBORETUM BOUNDARY

GEDDES AVE. ENTRANCE

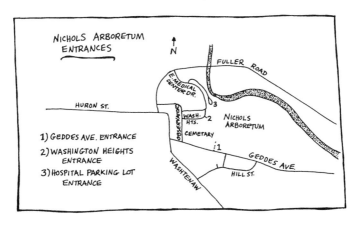

NICHOLS ARBORETUM ENTRANCES

N

FULLER ROAD

E. MEDICAL CENTER DR.

HURON ST.

OBSERVATORY

WASH. HTS.

CEMETARY

NICHOLS ARBORETUM

3

2

1

GEDDES AVE.

WASHTENAW

HILL ST.

1) GEDDES AVE. ENTRANCE
2) WASHINGTON HEIGHTS ENTRANCE
3) HOSPITAL PARKING LOT ENTRANCE

(2) follow the river drive east to the *Warbler Hot-spot*, or (3) follow the main road south past the rhododendron glen.

River Drive West

Along the river drive to the west there are sometimes skulking birds such as either Northern or Louisiana Waterthrush along the river, as well as an occasional Mourning Warbler. Warblers and thrushes are frequently quite numerous at the base of School Girl's Glen near the river entrance to the Arb. Kingfishers, swallows, Spotted Sandpipers and Chimney Swifts are all easily observed along the river. Several rarities have occurred here such as Yellow-crowned Night-Heron and American Bittern.

Warbler Hot-Spot and Caretaker's Road

Proceeding from the base of the ridge to the east you will come to the *Warbler Hot-Spot*. A loop can be made around and through these scrubby damp woods allowing you to view them from all sides. Over the years this has been one of the better areas for locating unusual birds such as the Worm-eating Warbler, Bell's Vireo, White-eyed Vireo, Brewster's Warbler, and others. Walking up the caretaker's road from the hot-spot you will have a small stream on your right; this usually floods the nearby areas and has rather dense vegetation. Both waterthrushes can be located in this area as well as Mourning, Hooded, and Connecticut Warblers. As you proceed up the caretaker's road you will ultimately come to a stand of conifers that can be excellent for winter finches (in winter). The area to the left, just before the conifers, a large open area leading up a hill, has been used for nesting by both Cooper's and Broad-winged Hawks.

Main Road South to Geddes

From the base of the ridge follow the main road south. On the left is the small stream with dense vegetation (the birds are usually the same as on the other side!), and on the right the ridge. In a little while you will come to what the local birdwatchers refer to as the rhododendron glen, another of the Arb's great birding spots. Among the many birds that have been seen in the rhododendron glen are thirty-five species of warblers and all five *Empidonax* flycatchers. Bird the length of the glen then continue up the main road. It is along the hillside areas of the main road that the greatest numbers of Connecticut Warblers have been found over the years. This rare migrant is sometimes found all the way up to Geddes and is best located by it loud song. It is, however, without a doubt the most difficult of all the Arb's migrants to observe satisfactorily; be persistent and patient.

The fall warbler migration is as spectacular here as in the spring. Realistically many of the the warblers are frequently drabber in plumage, but they are also much more numerous, and the length of their migration is more protracted than in the spring. The fall warbler migration starts in early August and continues into mid- to late October. In late August the Arb can be full of migrants.

During the winter (late November through late February) the Arb is a good area to see winter finches and species that uncommonly spend the winter in the county. Flocks of Pine Siskins are common in the winter; flocks of Evening Grosbeaks and redpolls are rare. Throughout the winter the Arb hosts wandering flocks of nuthatches, chickadees, titmice, and woodpeckers. In the denser areas of vegetation along either side of the Huron River, American Robins and Hermit Thrushes can usually be found, sometimes with large flocks of Cedar Waxwings feasting on the berry-laden shrubs scattered throughout the Arb.

North-Central Ann Arbor

The three sites below have been combined because they are all quite close to each other and can be easily visited fairly quickly.

Dhu Varren Gravel Pit

This gravel pit is located at the intersection of Dhu Varren Rd. and Pontiac Trail. It is fenced and posted, so view from the roads. Migrant ducks can be common, and Great Egret are regular during summer. If the water level is down, shorebirds are also a possibility.

Nixon Road Pond

This small pond (located on the east side of Nixon Rd. to the north of M-14) is an excellent place to observe Great Egrets through the summer and fall. Additionally there can be ducks, Pied-billed Grebe, and Common Moorhen. The only survey period sighting of Snowy Egret occurred here.

Thurston Pond Nature Center

This shallow pond and loop trail is one of several attractive natural properties belonging to Ann Arbor Public Schools. Thurston Pond lies off Georgetown north of Plymouth Rd. Outside of winter, this is one of the most regular locations in the county for Belted Kingfisher; there is also an active martin house. In times of drought, the water level can fall sufficiently to make the pond attractive to migrating shorebirds.

North Bay Park / Ford Lake

Part of this nature area will have been visible for years to eastbound travelers on I-94 as they pass over the Huron River near the Ford plant in Ypsilanti. Not visible from the expressway is what Ypsilanti Township has done with the inner lagoon. In spring 1991 the township completed work on a wide 400-yard boardwalk and a substantial observation tower. Bird records from this site are only in their infancy, but in fall 1991 the following were seen: Caspian Tern (several), Black-crowned Night-Heron, Bonaparte's Gulls and Carolina Wren. Although there is noise from the expressway and much boating activity in summer, North Bay Park has an excellent loop trail along the board walk and around the outer chain of islands. This must be one of the best locations in the county for an unusual gull. Access to the park is a little tricky. From Ann Arbor take the Whitaker Road exit off I-94, turn right at the light and then immediately left into the car pool parking lot. Proceed to the end of the lot and turn east: North Bay Park awaits.

Owling Sites

Owling is a very unusual type of birdwatching since it takes place in the dark (or at dusk or first light). It typically involves driving along quiet roads with nearby woods and stopping and listening for owl-calls. Chances of hearing owls can be improved by either imitating their calls or playing a tape. Owls that have been attracted by a taped call can sometimes be spotted with a flashlight or lamp as they perch nearby. The best times to go owling are calm nights with no rain since sounds carry farther. Most teams on the Ann Arbor CBC go owling for a couple of hours before dawn, and this is one way to get some experience. The CBC usually produces good numbers of Great Horned Owls and Eastern Screech-Owls, but rarely any other species. Reliable stretches for Eastern Screech-Owls are Cherry Hill Rd. to the east of the Matthaei Botanical Gardens, Trinkle Rd. west of

Dancer Rd., and Embury Rd. Nocturnal owling is an unusual roadside activity, and those undertaking it are sometimes subjected to questioning by local inhabitants and the security forces.

Because Great Horned Owls are too large to roost in most cavities, they can sometimes also be found in daylight. They are easiest to find in February and March when they are occupying their large nests (mostly old Red-tailed Hawk nests) in the upper branches of unleafed woodlots. For several years, a highly-visible pair nested on the median of I-94 near Ann Arbor.

Parker Mill Area

Parker Mill County Park is a new park, but an old birding area. It is situated off Geddes Rd., a little to the east of Dixboro Rd. In the winter or spring the birding here can be excellent. In either season follow the trail to the railroad tracks and cross, into the wet (usually partially flooded) woods behind the water-treatment plant. In the winter this is a haven for woodpeckers, with Downy, Hairy, Red-bellied Woodpeckers, and Flicker all commonly located, as well as the less common Yellow-bellied Sapsucker. Additional recent winter sightings include: Hermit Thrush, Yellow-rumped Warbler, Ruby-crowned Kinglet, Winter Wren, and Brown Creeper. The water in this area is always open and can hold an interesting array of waterfowl. American Coot, Tundra Swan, and all three Mergansers have been found here in the winter. Belted Kingfishers are present all year. In all seasons the park proper has become a regular place to locate Eastern Bluebirds, although there is no recent evidence of nesting. These birds may wander down from the nesting boxes in Matthaei Botanical Gardens. Recently in both spring and winter there have been several sightings of Carolina Wren.

Pioneer High Woods

The woods on the corner of S. Seventh and Stadium are owned by the Ann Arbor Public Schools and used as an environmental study area. These woods have a nesting pair of Cooper's Hawk and can sometimes hold a variety of migrants in the spring. Across from the woods, behind Pioneer High School, along S. Seventh is a large field with scrubby brush and bushes. In April this is an excellent area to observe American Woodcock make their courtship flights. Be there just before dusk. Listen for their loud, nasal, *peenting* coming from the ground. When they have begun the flight portion of their display move towards the spot they had called from and wait. Most of the time they will return to the ground within feet, if not inches, from where they took off. To the east of S. Seventh is a small willow-fringed pond, which has produced such uncommon species as Black-crowned Night-Heron and Olive-sided Flycatcher.

St. Joseph Hospital

St. Joseph Memorial Hospital (part of the Catherine MacCauley Medical Center) is located in Superior Twp., north of Huron River Dr. and east of Dixboro Rd. The hospital maintains a trail that is to the west of the main hospital and the service drive. The trail winds along the hillside that slopes down to the Huron River across from the Waste Treatment Plant. In the spring small numbers of migrants can be seen along the trail, with water-fowl present in the river. This site, however, is one of the better winter birding spots around Ann Arbor. The river remains open well after most of the other sections have frozen over. Many of the same species that occur at Parker Mill (see above) are here, since this is essentially across the river from it. Several pairs of Eastern Screech Owls are resident here. These can be found at night or early in the morning, but in addition be prepared for security guards to question your nocturnal presence; simply explain that you are looking for owls and they will usually shake their heads and depart.

Saginaw Forest

The Saginaw Experimental Forest, owned by the University of Michigan's School of Natural Resources, is located less than two miles west of I-94 along Liberty Rd. These woods consist of extensive plantings of various pines and other conifers. Among the permanent residents are: Red-tailed Hawk, Great Horned Owl, Red-bellied Woodpecker, and Carolina Wren, though this last is sporadic and irregularly found. Summer residents include both species of cuckoo, Ruby-throated Hummingbird, and others. The areas surrounding the pond and small lake can be good in the spring for migrating warblers. Recent sightings of uncommon species include Merlin and the only fall record for Whip-poor-will during the survey period.

Saline Wilderness Park

This small park is located at the intersection of Willis and Saline-Milan Rds. in south Saline. Even though called "Wilderness Park," it in fact contains several well-maintained trails. The more interesting of these skirt the pond created by the dam across Pittsfield Drain. At the eastward end of the area is a small marsh, where Sora are sometimes present.

Searles Natural Area

The Searles Natural Area, located on the north side of Bolla Rd. in Augusta Twp., is owned by the Washtenaw Audubon Society and consists of 50 acres of diverse habitat including low, wet floodplain, a creek, higher sandy area with oak-hickory forest and scattered stands of mixed hardwoods and shrubs. There is currently a project to improve the trail system in an effort to make it more accessible to birdwatchers and naturalists. This site is little birded; however, there are recent records for American Woodcock and Yellow-billed Cuckoo. To reach this area take US-23 south to Willis Rd. east, then bear left on Bolla where Willis curves to the right. The marked entrance is on the north side of the road.

Sharon Hollow Nature Preserve

The Sharon Hollow Nature Preserve lies near the central western edge of the county on Easudes Rd. near its intersection with Jacob Rd. It can be reached from Pleasant Lake Rd., then north on Sharon Hollow (briefly), and then west on Easudes Rd.

The preserve, which is owned by the Michigan Chapter of the Nature Conservancy, of mostly mature swampy woodland merits its reputation as being the prime location for spring wildflowers in the county. It also holds interesting birds, although its out-of-the-way location means that it is under-visited. According to the somewhat scant records available, probable summering birds include Blue-winged Warbler, Chestnut-sided Warbler, Ovenbird, American Redstart, Yellow-throated Vireo, Scarlet Tanager, Wood Thrush, Veery and possibly American Woodcock. In addition, Sharon Hollow is perhaps one of the most reliable spots in the county for finding nesting Acadian Flycatchers. Rare species recorded in May are Louisiana Waterthrush and Yellow-breasted Chat. The preserve would likely repay further investigation.

Shorebird Routes and Agricultural Habitat

A substantial proportion of Washtenaw County remains agricultural with considerable acreage utilized for corn, wheat, soybean, hay and sileage. Although active agriculture is widely distributed, it occurs more intensively between Saline and Manchester, along the county's southern edge to either side of Milan, and in Webster Township in the north. These areas of dirt roads, cultivated fields and small woodlots, dotted with farmsteads and isolated residences, attract the birds of the open field, hedgerow and woodland edge. Typical species are pheasant, bobwhite, meadowlark, kestrel, Horned Lark, and Savannah Sparrow. Today the agricultural areas also offer the best opportunity for finding shorebirds in the county. Much of the county lakeshore is now developed, and water levels rarely fall low enough in either the lakes or the drainage system to produce the exposed wet mud important to most shorebirds. Exceptions do occur, and in dry periods, Dexter Mill Pond, Swift Run Pond, Thurston Pond, Trinkle Road Marsh, and even the Huron River itself can all produce waders. However, better chances of finding these species lie in searching for drying-out pools in field depressions and in visiting farm ponds.

There is no escaping the fact that shorebird habitat in Washtenaw County is small-scale, patchy and highly variable from one season to the next. It is always dependent on appropriate water level and limited vegetation at the water's edge. However, despite this picture of hit-or-miss marginal pockets, an impressive total of 27 species of shorebirds has been recorded during the survey period, thus suggesting that effort can bring its (occasional) reward. This effort requires a fair amount of driving from place to place, mainly on backroads, checking out known sites and keeping an eye open for new ones. Although this kind of birdwatching may lack the physical and aesthetic satisfactions of looking for birds in wooded habitat, one compensation is that shorebirds have more extensive migration periods than most other groups. Aside from much of June, shorebirds may be migrating through the county from late March to mid-November. The second half of July and the first half of August is a good time to try a shorebirding trip, if only because the other fall migrants have not yet arrived.

In this Site Guide we offer two small areas in the county that have proved in recent years attractive to shorebirds. One is in eastern Freedom Twp. in the vicinity of Pleasant Lake; the other is Webster Twp. along N. Zeeb. Rd. Both contain at least one active farm pond and a number of low-lying areas.

Eastern Freedom Twp. Route

Approach the area by taking Ellsworth west of Parker Rd. (if traveling from Ann Arbor or Ypsilanti). Turn south on Schneider Rd. This is the start of the most productive shorebird route in the county.

1. Stop at the small farm pond next to the cowshed at the large dairy farm. In our experience, this pond always holds some water and can be quite productive, especially in fall. Scan the water's edge carefully; be patient because there may be more birds than appear at first sight.
2. Drive slowly down Schneider Rd. looking over any pools in the fields (especially in spring). Just before Pleasant Lake Rd. a mid-sized pond appears on the right. This is the celebrated Schneider Road Pond which appears so often in the shorebird species accounts. Some years there is too much water in spring, but from August on it can be highly productive. If the field to the north has been plowed, good spring shorebird habitat can occur in a depression in front of the woodlot. In 1991 "back Schneider Pond" yielded a pair of Wilson's Phalaropes.
3. Turn east on Pleasant Lake Rd. and after a quarter of a mile pull off at the entrance to the old gravel pit. Cross over the road and scan the farm pond and, in spring, check the depression in the field beyond. Viewing is awkward as Pleasant Lake Rd. carries a fair amount of fast-moving traffic, but this pond has produced Sanderling and Short-billed Dowitcher in recent years. Cliff Swallows sometimes nest at the farm.
4. Continue on Pleasant Lake Rd., turning right at the first intersection (Steinbach Rd.). Drive to the intersection of Steinbach and Bethel Church Rds. In the northeast quadrant there is usually a flooded meadow. If conditions are right, the meadow can hold good numbers of shorebirds, particularly yellowlegs and Solitary Sandpipers (Blue-winged Teal and Sora may also be present). Some springs there is similar habitat in the southeast quadrant.
5. Finally, go west on Bethel Church Rd. until it meets Schneider Rd. The flat area to the west of Schneider Rd. used to be a good location for shorebirds, but is currently rather overgrown. If it is cut or plowed, it may recover its value to shorebirds.

SHOREBIRD HABITAT
EASTERN FREEDOM TOWNSHIP

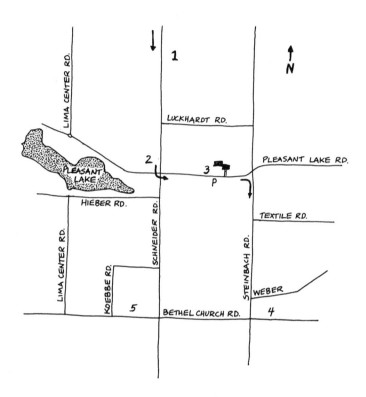

SHOREBIRD HABITAT
WEBSTER TOWNSHIP

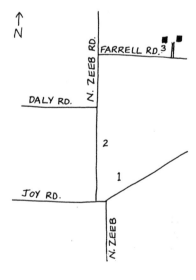

N. Zeeb Road Route

A more limited shorebirding area can be found north of the Huron River in southern Webster Twp.

1. Take Zeeb Rd. north of Huron River Drive. Stop at its intersection with Joy Rd. There is a small intermittent pond on the far side of the field to the north of Joy Rd. Migrating Common Snipe are fairly regular in its grassy fringes.
2. Continue on N. Zeeb Rd. About half a block to the north are two small ponds close to the right side of the road. Uncommon species from this site include Stilt Sandpiper, Western Sandpiper and American Pipit.
3. Turn right off N. Zeeb Rd. onto Farrell Rd. The pond at the first farm may hold shorebirds, as may a depression in the middle of the field if it holds water. Two of the five recent fall records for Baird's Sandpiper come from this field.

Finally we should mention that excellent shorebirding observations can sometimes be made at the roadside pond at a horsefarm on Scio Church Rd. one quarter mile west of its intersection with Parker Rd. Perhaps because of its nearness to the road or because the pond is surrounded by a split-rail fence, this site can offer the cautious observer remarkably close views of shorebirds. However, of late this pond appears to have been drained and has tended to be totally dry. The history of this site underlies once again the fickle nature of shorebird habitat in Washtenaw County.

Southeast County Route

In the southeastern corner of Washtenaw County, in Augusta Twp., there is a great deal of habitat that contains three species that are otherwise uncommon in the county: Orchard Oriole, Yellow-breasted Chat and Northern Bobwhite. One way of birding this area is to drive the four square mile block along Rawsonville Rd. south, Torrey Rd. west, Tuttle Hill Rd. north, Willow Rd. east, Bunton Rd. south, Liss Rd. west, then finally Tuttle Hill Rd. north. Stop on occasion to listen or look for the three species. North Bay Park is a few miles to the north.

Stinchfield Woods

Stinchfield Woods lies off Dexter-Pinckney Rd. at Peach Mountain (the WUOM radio mast is visible from a considerable distance). The property is owned and operated by the School of Natural Resources at the University of Michigan and is open to birdwatchers during daylight hours. There is very limited parking at the entrance on Stinchfield Woods Rd. and at one or two pull-off spots further west. Stinchfield Woods is a large property of 777 acres consisting mainly of conifer plantations and stands of native hardwoods (mostly oaks and hickories). Generally speaking, the conifers are close to Stinchfield Woods Rd. and the deciduous woods further in. This fine site is little visited and several hours can go by without meeting another person. Although Stinchfield can hold interesting birds during all seasons of the year, like many dry conifer plantations, it can also be disappointing. Permanent residents include Great Horned Owl, Cooper's Hawk, Ruffed Grouse and (probably) Wild Turkey. During winter there are usually Red-breasted Nuthatch and Pine Siskin. Ovenbirds are fairly common in summer. Summer rarities include Solitary Vireo, Pine Warbler and Hooded Warbler. In May 1988 a flock of 25 Red Crossbills was present. A particularly attractive and productive section is at the northwest corner close to the junction with Toma Rd. The overgrown clear-cut at the corner itself is one of the more regular locations for summering Chestnut-sided Warblers.

Sutton Lake

Sutton Lake is situated on Scio Church Rd. about two miles west of Parker Rd. Older maps and bird records refer to it as Sutton's Pond or Sutton's Lake. At one time Sutton Lake was one of the premier waterfowl sites in the county, but even by 1982 it was noted that "it no longer comes up to its former standard" (Baker, Wells, and Wykes 1982:7). The reasons for the change are not clear since the lakeshore remains only moderately developed. That said, Sutton Lake still offers a good variety of diving ducks during migration. Less common species recorded during the last five years include Greater White-fronted Goose, Double-crested Cormorant and Osprey (several records). Sutton Lake is also the most reliable location in the county for Ruddy Duck.

Swift Run Pond

Situated in southeastern Ann Arbor, Swift Run Pond is a small area to the west of Platt Rd., north of I-94. Pull into the parking area next to the Baptist Church and scan the pond. In the early spring (March and April) there is usually an array of ducks on the pond occasionally joined by American Coots, Common Moorhen, Pied-billed Grebe, and Black-crowned Night-Heron. Throughout the late spring and summer there are always Great Blue Herons, and sometimes Green-backed Herons. This is probably the most reliable inland spot in southeastern Michigan for the Great Egret, where they can be found from late April through late September. In the late spring of 1988 and again in 1990 there was an immature Little Blue Heron present on the pond. A visit to Swift Run can be combined with trips to County Farm Park and/or Mitchell-Scarlett Woods.

Trinkle Road Marsh

Trinkle Road Marsh (pronounced "trinkley") lies at the intersection of Trinkle and Dancer Rds. to the west of Parker Rd. south of Dexter and north of I-94. There is no public access, but good observations can be made from Trinkle Rd. The marsh consists of shallow open water, cattails and a stand of dead trees. During migration dabbling ducks frequent the pond, among them Northern Shoveler and occasionally Gadwall. In summer this is the most reliable county location for Common Moorhen, and in late summer it usually attracts good numbers of dispersing egrets and herons. Wood Ducks and Blue-winged Teal are regular nesting species. The trees around the marsh afford perches for raptors with recent sightings of Northern Goshawk and Red-shouldered Hawk. Rusty Blackbirds can be quite common on both spring and fall migration. Trinkle Road Marsh is often worth a stop on the way to or from somewhere else, such as Four Mile Lake.

Waterfowl Routes

Waterfowl in Winter

When the still water is frozen, overwintering waterfowl seek out open stretches of the Huron River system. One traditional location for January-February has been Island Lake Park and upstream towards Nichols Arboretum. However, the number and variety of geese, ducks and gulls has recently declined since the local authorities have posted the parking areas off

Fuller Rd. against the feeding of these birds. Other possibilities are down-stream of the Dixboro Rd. dam (Common Goldeneye are usually present) or the stretch of river below Barton Dam. But, overall, the most promising two locations for deep winter waterfowl are in the Portage Lake area on the county's northern border; unfortunately, neither provide easy or comfort-able viewing. The first is the Huron River along McGregor Rd., which can be scanned from behind the party store. The other is the channel between Little and Big Portage Lakes, where there is always some open water, sometimes stretching quite far out into the otherwise frozen lakes. If there is little snow, a car can be parked on the south side of the Dexter-Pinckney Rd. opposite a small cattail marsh. Birdwatching is awkward because the road carries a fair amount of traffic even on weekends. Either site can be rewarding — at least for January and February. There are chances of find-ing less common wintering species such as Mute Swan, Canvasback, Ring-necked Duck, Hooded Merganser and American Coot. A visit to this area can easily be combined with a walk in Stinchfield Woods (see separate entry).

Ann Arbor-Dexter Route

This route consists of four sites, three of which are discussed under indi-vidual entries: Barton Pond, Daly Road Pond and Dexter Mill Pond. If this route is run in April or before the first fall frosts, it can be combined with shorebirding along N. Zeeb Rd. (see Shorebird Routes). Start at Barton Pond. Then continue northwest on Huron River Drive, turning right on N. Zeeb Rd. After the junction with Farrell Rd., there is a small pond in a large meadow to the west of N. Zeeb. View from the road. This pond often holds several species of duck, both dabbling and diving, in good numbers. For example, American Wigeon and Redhead are often more numerous at this site than on larger bodies of water. Retrace down Zeeb Rd., turn west onto Daly Rd. and stop at Daly Road Pond; continue into Dexter and finish up with breakfast and/or a visit to Dexter Mill Pond.

North of Dexter Route

This route can be run as an extension of the Ann Arbor-Dexter Route or independently. Take Dexter-Pinckney north until Portage/Little Portage Lake close to the border with Livingston County. If necessary, check *Wa-terfowl in Winter* for parking and viewing suggestions. In spring or late fall (i.e., when there are few boats around) a range of species is possible here including American Coot, Horned Grebe and all three mergansers. Return south on Dexter-Pinckney Rd., turning right onto Stinchfield Woods Rd. and following it until reaching Silver Lake. View from the eastern shore and/or from near the parking area at the Silver Lake Rec Area (an entrance fee is required). Beware of decoys in the fall. Diving ducks should be present in season, especially Bufflehead and Common Goldeneye. Common Loon is possible, but somewhat more likely at the next site. Take Dexter-Townhall Rd. south, turn west on North Territorial, turn north at the first junction (Hankard Rd.) and then first left onto North Lake Rd. The north end of the lake can be viewed from a small roadside bluff. Scan the center of the lake for diving loons. Continue until the intersection with Goodband Rd., turn left and check Wild Goose Lake (Pied-billed Grebe etc.); turn left again on Hadley Rd. and pull off at the south end of North Lake. Check any large flocks of Canada Geese for Snow Geese. Continue south across North Territorial and then follow Island Lake Rd. to the left (this road passes West Lake but we have yet to find a decent vantage point for examining it). About two miles further on, take Lima Center Rd. Turn right and enter Chelsea SGA to finish the trip at Four Mile Lake (see separate entry).

Waterloo Recreation Area

Waterloo Rec Area extends over a considerable part of Lyndon Twp. and continues on into Jackson County. One site in the Rec Area, Winnewanna Lake, is given a separate entry. Parts of the area retain excellent mature wet woods interspersed with marshes. Some of the best of this habitat is along McClure Rd. to the west of the Recreation Area Headquarters and then north on Loveland Rd. as far as Mud Lake. Although such an area is bound to attract migrants, it is particularly noted for its summer residents. These include Veery, Ruby-throated Hummingbird, Acadian, Least and Willow Flycatchers and American Redstart. In addition, McClure-Loveland Rd. is the most reliable location in the county for nesting Cerulean Warblers. There are recent summer records for Broad-winged Hawk, Hooded Warbler and Prairie Warbler (this last from several areas).

Whitmore Lake

About half of this large lake lies within Washtenaw County, while the other (northern) portion is in Livingston County. Because of its size it is among the last of the still bodies of water to freeze over completely in winter and thus offers opportiunities to observe straggling waterfowl and gulls. Small patches of open water remain open along the west shore of the lake. These can be best viewed from the post office. Ann Arbor CBC records for

Common Loon, Lesser Scaup, Redhead, Canvasback, and Red-breasted Merganser were obtained at this location.

The lake is now heavily built-up and parking for viewing opportunities are limited by buildings and no parking signs. In the past Whitmore Lake produced a number of outstanding county records (see chapter four).

Wing Nature Preserve

The Ann and Leonard Wing Nature Preserve is owned by the Washtenaw Audubon Society and is located on the north side of Warren Rd., one half-mile east of Dixboro Rd. This small 2.5-acre wetland consists of cattail marsh, a small creek-fed pond and a smaller tamarack bog. A boardwalk takes the visitor into the center of the marsh. Typical marsh birds such as Common Yellowthroat, Red-winged Blackbird, Swamp Sparrow and others occur here. In the early spring there are occasionally Common Snipe.

Winnewanna Lake

Winnewanna is an area of marshy lake (popular for boat fishing) and surrounding woodland situated in western Lyndon Twp. It is part of the Waterloo State Recreation Area and a parking permit is required. The public access point is on Roe Rd., from which a number of paths lead along the lakeshore and through the woods. Winnewanna seems somewhat neglected by county birdwatchers, and records are incomplete. However, uncommon species noted in the last five years include Common Moorhen (summer), Black Tern (May), Bald Eagle (August) and Golden-winged Warbler (August).

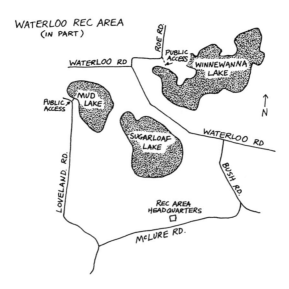

Chapter Three

Species Accounts

Introduction

This chapter is by far the longest in the book since it contains detailed accounts of the 267 species recorded in the survey period (1977-1991). These accounts are arranged in order of the forthcoming seventh edition of the American Ornithologists' Union Checklist. We have also adopted the latest AOU nomenclature for common names. In addition to the standard English and AOU nomenclature, there are also vernacular names. These would include wild canary (Yellow Warbler or American Goldfinch) and buzzard (Turkey Vulture). Finally, AOU nomenclature reflects current taxonomic knowledge and changes in taxonomy. Advancements over the years have resulted in name changes from the Sparrow Hawk to American Kestrel (a falcon not a hawk), Marsh Hawk to Northern Harrier (a harrier not a hawk), and Water Pipit to American Pipit (split from the Water Pipit). As the following examples show, the main differences between standard English and AOU nomenclature lie in capitalization.

Standard English	AOU
black-throated blue warbler	Black-throated Blue Warbler
black-crowned night-heron	Black-crowned Night-Heron
redstart	redstart
American robin	American Robin
redpoll	redpoll
common redpoll	Common Redpoll

Species of birds are grouped into orders, families and sub-families. Often we have provided general introductions to the larger groupings, such as to the waterfowl, raptors, woodpeckers, warblers, sparrows, etc. The species accounts themselves are organized in a number of regular patterns. All consist of summary data in note form followed by a paragraph. In all cases a species account opens with the English and scientific names; line two gives the finding code, and line three a brief summary of the status of the species in the county. Although the Finding codes have been discussed in the introductory chapter, we repeat the table here for ease of reference,

Finding Code Definitions
(effort required)

Code	Descriptor	Single observer	All observers
1	Abundant	25 birds per hour	—
2	Common	1 bird per hour	—
3	Common	1 bird per half day	—
4	Fairly common	1 bird per day	—
5	Fairly uncommon	1 bird per week	—
6	Uncommon	1-2 birds per season	4-20 birds per year
7	Fairly rare	—	1-3 birds per year
8	Rare	—	1 bird every two years
9	Very rare	—	1 bird every five years
10	Extremely rare or vagrant	—	1 bird every 15 years

Our working definitions of the higher codes are as follows:

Code	Number of sightings recorded during the survey period
7	At least 11
8	6-10
9	2-5
10	1

We can now see how all this works out with the first full species account in this chapter:

Common Loon *Gavia immer*
Finding code: 5 (in April)
Fairly uncommon spring and uncommon fall migrant

One point to note about the summary line is that it indicates that the Common Loon is *more* common in spring than in fall. If it had been equally common during both migration periods, the summary line simply would have stated:

Fairly uncommon migrant

The summary data in the species accounts varies according to two factors: when a species occurs in the county, and how easy it is to encounter. Both factors need a little explanation. The terms we have used for period of occurrence are as follows:

Descriptor	Definition (example)
Permanent resident	a species found in the county throughout the year (Northern Cardinal)
Migrant	a species normally found in the county only on migration to and/or from its breeding range (Common Loon)
Winter visitor	a species that spends some or all of the colder weather period in the county but does not normally occur at other times (Dark-eyed Junco)
Summer resident	a species that summers in Washtenaw County and that may nest (Yellow Warbler)
Summer visitor	a species that summers (at least in part) but does not nest in the county (Ring-billed Gull)
Vagrant	a species that is out of its normal range in Washtenaw County (Snowy Egret)

The summary data also varies according to the Finding code. For all migrants and visitors up to code 6 (and most with code 7), the summary data includes earliest arrival and departure dates plus details of the maximum numbers sighted. As an illustration, here is the remaining summary data for the Common Loon:

Spring dates: 10 March (1989) - 16 May (1979)
Spring maximum: 15 on 5 April 1978 at Barton Pond
Fall dates: 20 October (1989) - 18 December (1983)
Fall maximum: 5 on 5 November 1990 at North Lake

Readers should note that the dates given are the *extremes* recorded during the last 15 years. Generally speaking, birds are much more likely to occur in numbers in the mid-sections between the extremes. Thus most spring loons will be seen in April and most fall migrants in November. The "normal" periods of occurrence are therefore more accurately indicated by the bar-graphs (chapter five) or by the histograms (if they have been provided). Similarly the maximum numbers are also extremes and may represent flocks or congregations far larger than normal.

For the rare species (codes 8-10) no periods of occurrence are given since the records are few and sporadic. Instead, all the known survey period sightings are listed at the end — or towards the end — of the commentary. These individual records include the initials of the observer or observers. In cases where a rarity was seen by a large number of people (five or more), we have used the standard abbreviation of "MObs" for many observers. A full listing of all those who have contributed records (including early or late dates and maxima as well as individual sightings of rare species) was given at the end of chapter one. We have also provided individual records for all or part of the survey period for some of the more interesting Code 6 and 7 species. A good case in point would be the Bald Eagle. Because of the special status of this national symbol, we have listed all 20 known sightings during the last 15 years.

As explained in the introductory chapter, we have included histograms for 28 of the migrant/visiting species. Useful histogram data relies essentially on regular observations rather than raw numbers *per se*. For that reason the histograms are based on the extensive records of the authors collected over much of the survey period rather than on exceptional sightings in the literature or on the Christmas and May bird counts where intensive effort distorts the picture. Histograms usefully represent the general pattern of migration over a number of years, but by doing so they disguise the variation that can occur from season to season. For example, we provide a histogram for the Lesser Yellowlegs in the species accounts. This shows an impressive rise-peak-fall for both migrations. However, the annual migrations show a somewhat different story. Below are the fall migration numbers for the Lesser Yellowlegs by month over the last four years:

	1988	1989	1990	1991	Total
June	-	-	-	1	1
July	6	5	12	45	68
August	9	196	41	39	285
September	1	46	2	3	52
October	1	34	2	-	37
November	-	2	-	-	2
Total	17	283	57	88	445

Although the right-hand column represents the histogram, it disguises a number of facts. As can be seen, the fall migration of the Lesser Yellowlegs can be quite variable. In terms of totals, there is an order of magnitude difference between 1988 and 1989. Further, the strong migration in 1989 extended well into October, while the average migration in 1991 peaked early in July and was largely over by the end of August.

On the other hand, histograms have the peculiar merit of showing the onset of migration for species that summer or winter in the county in reduced numbers. In some cases, for example, it is possible to tell whether a September bird is a resident or a migrant. September Veerys in Eberwhite Woods are migrants since they are not recorded there as a summer resident. In other cases individual birds are not so easy to characterize, but the histogram will show the general trend of incoming migrants.

As an illustration, here is the histogram for the Great Blue Heron.

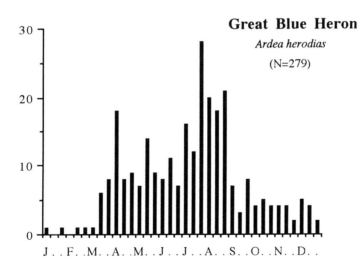

Great Blue Heron

Ardea herodias

(N=279)

Like most histograms in this book, each month is divided into three ten-day periods indicated by " J . . F . . etc." Thus the horizontal scale refers to the passing of the calendar year, while the vertical scale indicates the numbers recorded in the data-base for any ten-day period. The number under the name (e.g., N = 281) represents the total number of observations. The histogram of the Great Blue Heron can be interpreted in the following way. Herons start arriving in the second half of March with many birds remaining in the county as summer residents. From the end of July these numbers are augmented by birds undergoing what is known as "post-breeding dispersal." The histogram then seems to indicate that most of the birds in the county depart south as soon as early September, leaving a small and diminishing number of Great Blue Herons attempting to overwinter.

A few histograms, such as that for the Osprey, are given in monthly intervals (1-12), while some of the passerine migration patterns are displayed in five-day intervals.

We also need to add a comment about the verbalizations of birdsongs given in some of the species accounts. While birders' ears may all be hearing the same song, it happens that most individual attempts to reflect what has been heard in words turn out to be strangely different. For some reason mind predominates over matter. The verbalizations we offer are therefore best considered as subjective.

Abbreviations

ABBM	= Atlas of the Breeding Birds of Michigan
CBC	= Christmas Bird Count
DNR	= Department of Natural Resources
JPW	= The Jack-Pine Warbler
LP	= Lower Peninsula
NC	= Nature Center
NWR	= National Wildlife Refuge
Rec	= Recreation
SGA	= State Game Area
Twp.	= Township
UMMZ	= University of Michigan Museum of Zoology
UP	= Upper Peninsula
WAS	= Washtenaw Audubon Society

Species Accounts

Family Gaviidae (loons)

Red-throated Loon *Gavia stellata*

Not seen during the survey period; see chapter four

Common Loon *Gavia immer*

Finding Code: 5 (in April)
Fairly uncommon spring; uncommon fall migrant
Spring dates: 10 March (1989) - 16 May (1979)
Spring maximum: 15 on 5 April 1978 at Barton Pond
Fall dates: 20 October (1989) - 18 December (1983)
Fall maximum: 5 on 5 November 1990 at North Lake

The Common Loon breeds in the northern part of the state of Michigan as well as further north. Small numbers pass through the county on both north- and south-bound migration, when it is most likely to be found on larger bodies of water such as Four Mile, North, Silver and Independence Lakes, and Barton Pond. A preponderance of spring records comes from this last site in the first ten days of April, although this may be partly an observer effect since Barton Pond in April is a favorite spot for searching out water birds. Common Loons seem scarcer in the fall (at least finding code 6), and only single birds are usually seen at widely scattered locations. The earlier literature refers to county nesting records in the 1920s and 1930s, and even in the 1970s double-figure groups of migrants were occasionally seen (TWi). Today, however, the Common Loon remains a fairly uncommon migrant. Additionally, on migration it tends to be silent and occupy the central portions of larger bodies of water, where it frequently dives. It can be hard to find. During the survey period, there is a single summer record of an immature bird on Four Mile Lake on 27 July 1991 (RW, JW).

Family Podicipedidae (grebes)

Pied-billed Grebe *Podilymbus podiceps*

Finding Code: 3
Common migrant and uncommon summer resident
Spring dates: 27 February (1980) - 7 May (1988)
Spring maximum: 10 on 9 April 1978 at Barton Pond
Fall dates: 27 August (1988) - 9 December (1989)
Fall maximum: 6 on 22 October 1988 at Wild Goose Lake

The small Pied-billed Grebe is a widely-distributed visitor to the county, especially in April and October (see histogram). It may be found on open lakes or small ponds or in clear channels through marshes during these periods — although it has the habit of sinking mysteriously from sight as the observer watches. The spring and fall arrival and departure dates are somewhat obscured by the fact that a small number of "PBGs" summer in Washtenaw County and, less regularly, attempt to over-winter. For example, Pied-billed Grebes have been recorded on four of the last 15 Ann Arbor CBCs. In 1988/1989 two birds spent most of the December-February period in the open water just downstream of Barton Dam. Most summer records in recent years have been of adults, although chicks have been seen on one or two occasions (DC). The number of nesting pairs in the county is uncertain but is probably quite small.

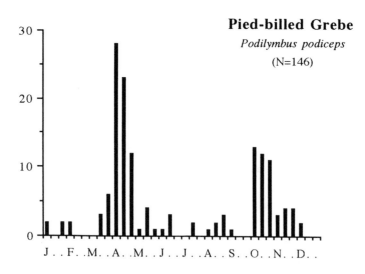

Pied-billed Grebe
Podilymbus podiceps
(N=146)

Horned Grebe *Podiceps auritus*

Finding Code: 5 (in April)
Fairly uncommon migrant
Spring dates: 6 March (1988) - 11 May (1991)
Spring maximum: 40 on 14 April 1978 at Barton Pond
Fall dates: 10 September (1988) - 5 December (1987)
Fall maximum: 2 on 14 November 1987 at Gallup Park

The Finding code of 5 represents something of an annual spring average for this species, as its frequency on migration through the county varies considerably from year to year. In April 1988 there were numerous reports of Horned Grebes (especially from the Portage Lakes), while in all of 1990 not a single sighting was reported. March records are usually of birds in gray winter plumage, but most April birds show the "golden horns." The bird found in a small pond off Waters Rd. on 11 May during the 1991 May Bird Count was exceptionally late.

Red-necked Grebe *Podiceps grisegena*

Finding Code: 9
Very rare spring migrant

This large grebe is rarely found inland in southern Michigan, and Washtenaw County is no exception. The three records of single individuals during the survey period are all in April:

1. 7-10 April 1985 at Barton Pond (MObs)
2. 4 April 1986 at Daly Road Pond (RW)
3. 10-11 April 1987 at Barton Pond (EB)

Eared Grebe *Podiceps nigricollis*

Finding Code: 10
Vagrant

There is only one survey period record in Washtenaw County for this rare western visitor to Michigan. A winter-plumaged bird was observed on Sutton Lake on 28 October 1979 (TWi, HM, JT).

Western Grebe *Aechmophorus occidentalis*

Finding Code: 10
Vagrant

The elegant Western Grebe rarely ventures into the central Great Lakes region, although it is a fairly common species in the western Great Plains states. During the 1977-1991 survey period, there is only one record of one bird, on 18 April 1988 in southwest Ann Arbor (MK).

Family Pelecanidae (pelicans)

American White Pelican *Pelecanus erythrorhynchos*

Not seen during the survey period; see chapter four

Family Phalacrocoracidae (cormorants)

Double-crested Cormorant *Phalacrocorax auritus*

Finding Code: 7
Fairly rare in the spring, summer and fall
Spring arrival: 22 April (1989)
Fall departure: 13 October (1990)
Maximum: 23 on 13 May 1990 along the Huron River

This species is the only cormorant likely to be seen in Michigan. After a long period of decline, it has been making a comeback since the 1980s, particularly around the Great Lakes. Summering cormorants can now, for example, be found in large numbers in the western Lake Erie area. It is likely that a small fraction of this growing population is starting to make forays into small inland waters, presumably in search of food. Apart from an isolated record from 28 September 1976 at Ann Arbor (PH, RH), there were no county sightings of this resurgent species until 1988. Since then the following ten records have been reported (single birds unless otherwise noted):

1. 21 May 1988 at Winnewanna (SH)
2. 22 April 1989 two at Winnewanna (JG)
3. 17 August 1989 at Iron Creek Mill Pond (MB)
4. 13 May 1990 23 along the Huron River in Ann Arbor (MObs)
5. August - 15 September 1990 two birds at Loch Alpine (MObs)
6. 4 October 1990 at M-14 and Curtis Rd., Superior Twp. (BP)
7. 13 October 1990 two at Sutton Lake (VB, JS, RW)
8. 29 June 1991 at Schasser Lake (SK, MK)
9. 15 July 1991 six along the Huron River at M-14 (MK)
10. 21 September - 3 October 1991 at Daly Road Pond (VB, JS, RW)

Order Ciconiiformes (herons, egrets, bitterns, and New World vultures)

Family Ardeidae (herons, egrets, and bitterns)

These marsh birds have long dagger-like bills, which they use to capture fish, frogs, or other organisms. Herons are colored (mostly gray, blue, and green), most egrets are dazzling white (with the exception of the Little Blue Heron, an *Egretta*) while bitterns have a cryptic brown plumage which hides them in the marsh. Most members of this family are tall and stately and can often be seen waiting patiently in the water for a food source to come within striking distance. They fly with "kinked" necks. Six of the ten species are uncommon to rare in Washtenaw County.

American Bittern *Botaurus lentiginosus*

Finding Code: 7
Fairly rare migrant
Spring dates: 1 April (1988) - 16 May (1988)
Spring maximum: 2 on 12 May 1991 in Nichols Arboretum
Fall dates: 4 September (1989) - 25 October (1987)
Fall maximum: only single individuals reported

The "thunder-pumping" calls of the American Bittern are more often heard than the birds themselves are seen. The American Bittern was once a common summer resident in many of Michigan's marshes, including those in Washtenaw County. Thirty years ago, for example, they were regular residents at Iron Creek Mill Pond (MB). With the dramatic decline in wetlands in southern Michigan there has been a parallel decline in the American Bittern. In Washtenaw County a small number now occur almost annually as spring and/or fall migrants. In the marshes to the west of the Waterloo Rec Area in adjacent Jackson County a small number of American Bitterns can still be found in the summer. County sightings during the last five years are:

1. Summer 1986 in Lyndon Twp. (ABBM)
2. 13 April 1987 at Mitchell-Scarlett Woods (JS, VB)
3. 25 October 1987 at Saginaw Forest (JWo)
4. 1 April 1988 at the Huron River and Wagner Rd. (JS, VB)
5. 14 May 1988 at Dolph Park (CC)
6. 16 May 1988 along M-52 in Lyndon Twp. (RW)
7. 4-6 September 1989 at Schneider Road Pond (RW, JW)
8. 12 May 1991 two in Nichols Arboretum (MK)

Least Bittern   *Ixobrychus exilis*

Finding Code: 8
Rare summer resident

The Least Bittern is a secretive marsh bird usually detected only when it makes occasional short flights just above the cattails, often showing its white wing patches. Numbers declined in lower Michigan in the 1960s and 1970s (ABBM), and there are only seven confirmed county records during the survey period. As the details suggest, there are no reliable sites; all records except one are of single individuals:

1. 24 July 1977 at Sugar Lake (TSc)
2. 23 June 1984 at Joslin Lake (TWi)
3. 2 July 1984 at Silver Lake (HH)
4. 6 June 1986 at Four Mile Lake (TC)
5. Summer 1986 two in Superior Twp. (BW)
6. 15 August 1987 along the Huron River (JS, VB)
7. 22 July 1989 along the Huron River (JS, VB)

Great Blue Heron *Ardea herodias*

Finding Code: 2
Common migrant and summer resident, uncommon in winter
Spring arrival: 5 March (1988)
Spring maximum: 40 on 28 March 1987 at a nesting colony

The Great Blue Heron is one of the most widely recognized species in Washtenaw County and even non-birders are familiar with this large water bird. While the Great Blue Heron is most common in the spring through fall period, a small number spend at least the early part of the winter in the county when streams remain open as potential fishing sites. The difficulty of separating fall migrants from early wintering birds has, in this rare case, precluded us from offering a fall departure date (see histogram). The Great Blue Heron has been recorded on seven of the last 15 CBCs. Migrants typically begin to arrive in mid-March and begin to depart around the end of August. At the present time two rookeries are being used in the county, but as nesting Great Blue Herons are easily disturbed their locations are not disclosed.

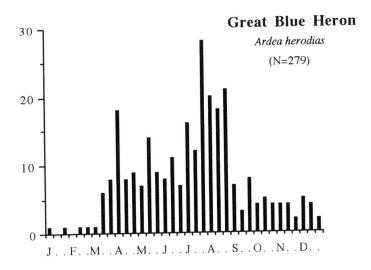

Great Blue Heron

Ardea herodias

(N=279)

Great Egret   *Casmerodius albus*

Finding Code: 4
Fairly common migrant and summer resident
Spring arrival: 24 March (1987)
Spring maximum: 30 on 20 May (1989) at Swift Run Pond
Fall departure: 23 October (1987)
Fall maximum: 22 on 14 August 1991 at the Trinkle Road Marsh

The Great Egret is the common large white marsh bird seen in Michigan. Indeed, evidence from the survey period suggests that Great Egrets have been slowly increasing in numbers in the county. They are quite widely distributed in the summer found in shallow water on ponds, lakes, and along the open stretches of streams and rivers, being most regular at Swift Run Pond. They nest in adjoining Monroe County. The relatively high maximum counts for spring and fall show migration and post-breeding dispersal peaks. There is one very unusual winter record: 16 December 1990 at Dhu Varren Road Gravel Pit (MK).

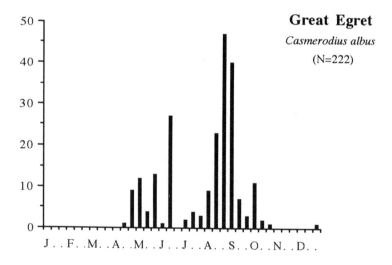

Great Egret

Casmerodius albus

(N=222)

J . . F . .M . .A . .M . .J . .J . .A . . S . . .O. . .N . .D . .

Snowy Egret *Egretta thula*

Finding Code: 10
Vagrant

The Snowy Egret is smaller and more slender than the Great Egret. There is a single record of this dainty "yellow-slippered" southern visitor: one was found with five Great Egrets at the Nixon Road Pond on 13 August 1984 (MK). This sighting is apparently the second for the county since there is a specimen collected in Ann Arbor on 10 May 1889 (UMMZ). As small numbers have recently become more regular at Pte. Mouillee, Monroe County, there may be a chance of future sightings in Washtenaw.

Little Blue Heron *Egretta caerulea*

Finding Code: 9
Very rare visitor

During the survey period there are three records in Washtenaw County for this southern heron. This matches the three records (1930-1938) listed in Wood (1951). There are two additional pre-survey records, an immature from Ford Lake (5 August 1969, MH), and a bird from Ann Arbor (27 May 1974 BB). Four of these earlier records plus the first record of the survey period are all from August and clearly reflect post-breeding dispersal. The two May records of individuals at Swift Run Pond were of immature birds in almost all white plumage with few blue feathers:

1. 2 August 1982 in Superior Twp. (MK)
2. Week of 20 May 1989 at Swift Run Pond (MS, MK)
3. 7-14 May 1990 at Swift Run Pond (MObs)

Cattle Egret *Bubulcus ibis*

Finding Code: 9
Very rare spring visitor

This small southern egret is becoming more common along the eastern Great Lakes coast of Michigan, but it is still a rare species inland in the southeastern part of the state. There are only five records of single Cattle Egrets in Washtenaw County; two from the 1960s, one in 1972 (AM, GV) and two from towards the end of the survey period :

1. 11 May 1988 at Werkner Rd., near Chelsea (DBr)
2. 17 May 1991 southwest of Ann Arbor (ES)

Green-backed Heron   *Butorides striatus*

Finding Code: 4 (in migration)
Fairly common migrant and fairly uncommon summer resident
Spring arrival: 28 April (1984)
Fall departure: 30 September (1979)
Maximum: 5 on 18 August 1988 off Wellwood Rd., Manchester Twp.

This small heron is a fairly common migrant in the county but is somewhat uncommon as a nesting species. It typically nests in shrubs or dense trees in or adjoining wetlands. In suitable county habitat, such as Dolph Park, Trinkle Road Marsh, or the Chelsea SGA, one or two summering pairs can usually be seen. The Green-backed Heron does not usually arrive in the county until the first days of May and departs south in September.

Black-crowned Night-Heron   *Nycticorax nycticorax*

Finding Code: 6
Uncommon spring and fall migrant
Spring dates: 22 March (1987) - 18 May (1982)
Spring maximum: 2 on 11 May 1988 at Dolph Park
Fall dates: 22 July (1982) - 30 September (1987)
Fall maximum: 3 on four separate occasions

The Black-crowned Night-Heron is currently listed as a species of special concern in Michigan; only 3% of the townships across the state provided any evidence of nesting during the Atlas Survey period (ABBM). At present nesting night-herons are largely confined to marshes adjoining Lake Erie in Monroe County and around Saginaw Bay. Consequently this species is an infrequent visitor to the county, perhaps most likely to be found during August or early September when post-breeding dispersal occurs. There are no reliable locations. Brown juvenile birds are nearly as common as adults in the fall.

Yellow-crowned Night-Heron *Nycticorax violaceus*

Finding Code: 9
Very rare spring visitor

The Yellow-crowned Night-Heron is a rare species anywhere in Michigan. In the late 1970s and early 1980s there was a small colony nesting in nearby western Wayne County. This may have been the source of the two county sightings during the early part of the survey period. Both sightings were along the Huron River in Nichols Arboretum in Ann Arbor:

1. 30 April 1981 (MK, TWa, TWi)
2. 16 April 1982 (WH)

Family Cathartidae (New World vultures)

Recent biochemical work with DNA-DNA hybridization has shown that the New World vultures are most closely related to the stork family (Sibley and Ahlquist 1983, 1988). These data agree with earlier work on bone structure (Ligon 1967) and feather tracts (Jollie 1976, 1977), which had shown the same similarities. Because of these relationships, the forthcoming edition of the AOU checklist places the Cathartidae in the same order with the storks, Ciconiformes.

Turkey Vulture *Cathartes aura*

Finding code: 2
Common migrant and summer resident
Spring arrival: 26 February (1989)
Spring maximum: 56 on 4 April 1989 over Dolph Park
Fall departure: 5 December (1990)
Fall maximum: 29 on 6 October 1990 at Zeeb and Farrell Rds.

The Turkey Vulture is a common migrant and summer resident (see histogram). Turkey Vultures are frequently seen over open farm fields and in migration may form large communal roosts consisting of up to 20-40 birds. The roosts are often in large dead trees adjacent to both woods and fields.

In Washtenaw County the Turkey Vulture typically nests in stumps of dead trees in secluded woods, though they sometimes will use abandoned barns or other buildings.

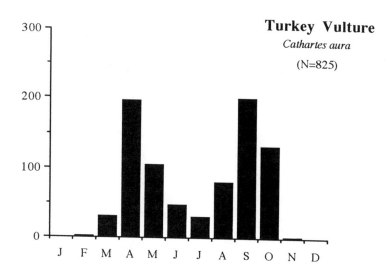

Order Anseriformes (swans, geese, and ducks)

The web-footed, aquatic waterfowl include swans, geese, and ducks. Although they differ in size, color, and behavior, many members of this large group are easily recognized. On water they typically remain relatively motionless long enough to be identified by the novice birder and yet supply an interesting array of color and plumages to keep the most experienced observer coming back for another look. They have also been of interest to the hunting community as sport and meat for the table. Swans and geese represent two fairly consistent groups in terms of their feeding behavior, while ducks show a greater diversity.

In Michigan, ducks are usually separated into two major groups based on their foraging behavior: the puddle (or dabbling) ducks and the diving ducks. Puddle ducks, like the Mallard, feed from the surface of the water and are often seen "tipped up" with head and neck submerged. These ducks are also comfortable on semi-flooded areas and can walk on dry land fairly easily. When frightened, puddle ducks spring directly into the air. The diving ducks feed by submerging their entire bodies underwater to reach plants, invertebrate animals, or fish, often remaining hidden from view for up to a minute. These ducks require a running start across the water to become airborne. A common county diving duck is the Lesser Scaup. Diving ducks are birds of the open waters of lakes and of wider stretches of the Huron River. Their plumage consists of bold patterns of black and white or large areas of contrasting colors. The wing patterns of diving ducks in flight exhibit patches of white and gray, whereas puddle ducks have a colored speculum along the trailing edge of the secondary flight feathers.

Twenty-seven species of waterfowl have been recorded in the county during the survey period. Of this large group only five (Mute Swan, Canada Goose, Wood Duck, Mallard and Blue-winged Teal) regularly nest in Washtenaw County. The others over-winter or pass through to or from their breeding grounds further north, typically in Canada. The best months for observing migrating waterfowl are March-April and October-December.

Family Anatidae (swans, geese, and ducks)

Tundra Swan *Cygnus columbianus*

Finding code: 7 (in November)
Fairly rare fall migrant, rare in spring
Spring dates: 21 March (1987) - 14 April (1987)
Spring maximum: 20 on 21 March 1987 at Little Portage Lake
Fall dates: 30 October (1984) - 17 November (1989)
Fall maximum: *c.* 2,100 over Noggles Rd. on 17 November 1989

These large migrants can occasionally be observed during fall migration as they fly high over the county in "V" shaped flocks. The exceptional record of over 2,000 birds flying over Manchester Twp. represents a very unusual sighting, possibly traveling due south from the regular staging area at the Shiawassee NWR. This flight lasted for nearly four hours (MB). More typically, however, county observations on local bodies of water or in fields have been of individuals or pairs. Usually these birds remain for only brief periods, a day or less, and then continue their migratory journey. There are no reliable locations. Most recent sightings have been in November.

Mute Swan *Cygnus olor*

Finding code: 3
Fairly common permanent resident
Maximum: 14 on 6 January 1991 at Big Portage Lake

This large introduced species of swan has become a member of the county avifauna relatively recently, first being recorded on the Ann Arbor CBC in 1974. This swan was introduced into the state in the Traverse Bay area in the 1920s and has since spread throughout much of the Lower Peninsula, boosted by further releases in Kalamazoo and Oakland Counties (ABBM). Although the Mute Swan is only fairly common in Washtenaw County, it has been given a finding code of 3 because of its high visibility even at great distances. Currently several pairs nest in the county on some of the larger lakes (Pleasant, Horseshoe and North), along the Huron River and more recently at the Loch Alpine subdivision. Most observations are of single birds or of family groups. These swans tend to drive off other waterfowl species from their large territory during the nesting season, and at this time they can also be aggressive towards encroaching humans. Larger groups are recorded during the winter months when the birds become concentrated in remaining pockets of open water.

Greater White-fronted Goose *Anser albifrons*

Finding code: 9
Very rare visitor

This goose nests in central and western Canada, and the few birds seen in Michigan on migration are presumed to be eastern vagrants. During the survey period there are only two confirmed records, both of single individuals mixed in with a flock of Canada Geese. On both occasions the Greater White-fronted Goose stayed for several days. The details are:

1. 18-31 October 1987 at Sutton Lake (MObs)
2. 18-22 March 1989 at Daly or Zeeb Road ponds (RW, VB, JS)

These geese may be more common on migration than county records indicate since their relatively small size makes them difficult to find in the large flocks of Canada Geese with which they associate.

Snow Goose *Chen caerulescens*

Finding code: 7
Fairly rare migrant
Spring dates: 28 March (1989) - 15 April (1989)
Spring maximum: 45 on 15 April 1989 in Sylvan Twp.
Fall dates: 4 October (1988) - 30 December (1979)
Fall maximum: 50 on 28 November 1989 at Independence Lake

This attractive, docile-looking goose nests in the high Arctic and is an uncommon visitor on migration to the county, sometimes as individuals and sometimes in flocks of up to 50 birds, and often in association with Canada Geese. The Snow Goose is only marginally a code 7 species as it is not quite recorded annually. For example, during the last five years there was one record in 1987, four in 1988, four in 1989, one in 1990 but none in 1991. Seven of these ten records were in fall. White and blue color phases seem about equally common. Snow Geese records have been spread widely and erratically across the county, and no reliable locations are known.

Canada Goose *Branta canadensis*

Finding code: 1
Abundant migrant and common permanent resident
Maximum: 669 on 17 October 1990 at Daly Road Pond

The Canada Goose rivals the Mallard as the most common species of waterfowl in the county during any time of the year. Close inspection of flocks of geese in fall and spring may reveal geese of different sizes. The large geese are the resident introduced subspecies, the Greater Canada Goose. Any smaller forms will be geese that have migrated south from much further north. Canada Geese nest throughout the county in both rural and urban habitats, and family groups are a familiar sight on lawns, parks and golf courses wherever water is available. The geese winter along portions of the Huron River and on open patches of water in otherwise frozen lakes. Indeed, it is often continued goose activity which keeps these patches from freezing over. Only occasionally do harsh weather and snowcover force the winter population to move further south in search of food. Large flocks of Canada Geese should always be examined since less common waterfowl species sometimes join the flocks to forage or to loaf in pockets of water kept open by the geese.

Brant *Branta bernicla*

Finding code: 10
Vagrant

On 2 November 1980 two of these rare migrants flew in to decoys at Iron Creek Mill Pond. One was shot and reported to the DNR (MBi, JRe).

Wood Duck *Aix sponsa*

Finding code: 2
Common migrant and summer resident, rare in winter
Spring arrival: 6 March (1988)
Fall departure: 19 December (1990)
Maximum: 130 on 20 August 1985 at Wellwood Rd., Manchester Twp.

The beautiful Wood Duck was once uncommon in southeastern Michigan, its numbers much reduced by hunting and the cutting of the woods in which it nests. Today it has made a dramatic comeback helped by conservation measures, nestboxes and the maturing of woodlots. For nesting, it requires trees large enough to provide suitable cavities, and nearby water. Although the number of nesting pairs in the county is not known, it is certainly both substantial and increasing. Dexter Mill Pond and Trinkle Road Marsh are two of several reliable locations. Numbers build in the fall as migrants join the resident population. A few Wood Ducks linger in the county during mild winters on the Huron River or other open streams. It has been found on 13 of the last 15 CBCs, although in very small numbers.

Green-winged Teal *Anas crecca*

Finding code: 4
Fairly common migrant
Spring dates: 17 March (1990) - 6 May (1989)
Spring maximum: 30 on 26 March 1990 in Freedom Twp.
Fall dates: 21 August (1990) - 23 November (1989)
Fall maximum: 30 on 28 October 1979 on Sutton Lake

This small dabbling duck is a somewhat irregular spring and fall migrant through the county; in some migration periods it seems quite common, but in others very hard to find. Like the Blue-winged Teal, it usually occurs in emergent wetland habitats containing pools of open water, in flooded farm fields or along the fringes of the Huron River, often in the company of other puddle ducks. According to the ABBM, the Green-winged Teal is a rare breeding species throughout the state. There are no recent summer records for Washtenaw County, although there are at least two for Lenawee County to the south. Winter records are very scarce, but one was found on the 1990 CBC and remained in the Gallup Park area at least until the end of February.

American Black Duck *Anas rubripes*

Finding code: 3
Common migrant and winter visitor, rare in summer
Fall arrival: 15 September (1990)
Spring departure: 25 April (1989)
Maximum: 63 on 4 January 1990 at M-52 and Jersusalem Road

The American Black Duck has decreased in numbers through its range during the past three decades, and observations within the county reflect this trend. Indeed, it could be argued that the Black Duck is now a code 4 species. A few Black Ducks can sometimes be found in much larger groups of Mallard, from which they can be distinguished by the contrast between their darker bodies and lighter heads. However, the county picture of the Black Duck is confused by the presence of semi-domesticated Black Duck x Mallard hybrids. The increasingly disproportionate abundance of these two species is borne out by the CBC data: during 1985-1990 observers found an annual average of 1,400 Mallards, but only 25 Black Ducks. There is one confirmed nesting record for the survey period — in 1986 in Salem Township (ABBM).

Mallard *Anas platyrhynchos*

Finding code: 1
Abundant permanent resident and migrant

When most people refer to ducks they are referring to Mallards, just as they associate duck calls with the *quack quack* of this ubiquitous bird. The Mallard is the most common duck in the county and can be found in both rural and urban settings throughout the year. As a breeding species, it nests in or near a wide variety of wetland habitats. Ducklings are common from mid-May through July. Larger numbers occur during the fall when migrants join the local resident flocks. Winter distribution is somewhat confused by the presence of semi-domesticated birds in urban centers.

Northern Pintail *Anas acuta*

Finding code: 7
Fairly rare migrant
Spring dates: 4 March (1990) - 3 April (1988)
Spring maximum: 10 on 24 March 1990 at Fletcher Rd. and I-94
Fall dates: 18 September (1990) - 30 October (1988)
Fall maximum: 4 on 2 October 1982 at Mulvaney Rd.

The elegant long-necked Northern Pintail is much more common in the western U.S. In Michigan a few pairs nest in the major lakeshore marshes (ABBM). Inland, at least as far as Washtenaw County is concerned, it is the rarest of the regular migrants, and typically only one or two individuals or pairs are recorded each year. It can occur on the larger lakes like Sutton or Four Mile or in wetlands or flooded fields. There are two winter records during the survey period: 18 December 1977 on the Huron River in Ann Arbor and 21 January 1991 at Dexter Mill Pond.

Blue-winged Teal *Anas discors*

Finding code: 4
Fairly common migrant; fairly uncommon summer resident
Spring arrival: 18 March (1989)
Fall departure: 13 December (1989)
Maximum: 28 on 15 September 1979 at Swift Run Pond

The Blue-winged Teal is usually the last duck species to arrive in the spring and the first to depart in the fall; most have left by the beginning of October (see histogram). It was once a common nesting species found on small field ponds and marshes throughout much of the county. Today it is less common as a summer resident, although it can still be found in secluded small ponds in abandoned pastures and in more open marshes. Most years more than one pair nests at Trinkle Road Marsh. Ducklings have been seen from early June. During the short fall migration the Blue-winged Teal is close to being a code 3 species.

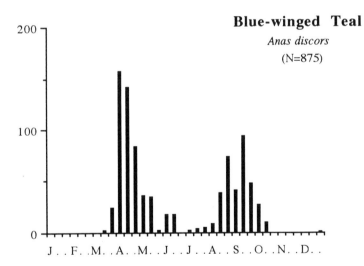

Blue-winged Teal
Anas discors
(N=875)

Northern Shoveler *Anas clypeata*

Finding code: 4
Fairly common migrant
Spring dates: 4 March (1986) - 7 May (1988)
Spring maximum: 16 on 7 April 1991 at Daly Road Pond
Fall dates: 17 October (1987) - 5 December (1989)
Fall maximum: 7 on 1 November 1989 at Pierce Lake

The male shoveler is one of the most attractive of the waterfowl which migrate through the county. The female shoveler on the other hand can easily be overlooked amid a crowd of Mallards unless the outsize bill is noticed. The Northern Shoveler is a classic puddle duck and is normally only found in flooded fields, shallow ponds or marshes with an abundance of vegetation and some open water. It can be a late migrant lingering into early May; in the county the fall migration period would seem to be rather short.

Gadwall *Anas strepera*

Finding code: 7
Fairly rare migrant
Spring dates: 1 April (1989) - 11 April (1989)
Spring maximum: 2 on several dates
Fall dates: 9 October (1987) - 23 November (1989)
Fall maximum: 20 on 28 October 1979 on Sutton Lake

The number of sightings of this gray dabbling duck is slightly higher than that of the pintail, but since 1979 the numbers seen on any one occasion have consistently been very low. It can occur in any puddle duck habitat; there have been recent sightings at Trinkle Road Marsh and along the Huron River upstream of Barton Pond. The inconspicuous plumage of this duck, combined with its relative scarcity, make it difficult to find in the county. It occurred on Ann Arbor CBCs in 1978 and 1989.

Eurasian Wigeon *Anas penelope*

Not recorded during the survey period; see chapter four

American Wigeon *Anas americana*

Finding code: 3
Common migrant, rare summer straggler
Spring dates: 12 March (1988) - 6 May (1989)
Spring maximum: 27 on 25 March 1989 at a pond on N. Zeeb Rd.
Fall dates: 21 August (1989) - 26 December (1989)
Fall maximum: 27 on 27 October 1989 at Pierce Lake

The American Wigeon or "Baldpate" is an attractive small puddle duck which also occurs in migration on some of the larger lakes. It is a rare and local nesting species in Michigan, but occasional non-breeding summer stragglers can turn up in various parts of the state. During the survey period there were several records up to the last week of June and one July record — an adult male at Trinkle Road Marsh on 20 July 1991 (VB, JS). There are several December-January records of birds sighted on flowing open water, including two on CBCs in 1978 and 1989.

Canvasback *Aythya valisineria*

Finding code: 4
Fairly common migrant, uncommon winter visitor
Spring dates: 12 March (1988) - 27 April (1988)
Spring maximum: 136 on 4 April 1989 at Chelsea SGA
Fall dates: 27 October (1990) - 1 December (1991)
Fall maximum: 6 on 11 November 1989 at Sutton Lake

This large and handsome diving duck passes through the county on its migration from the Atlantic Coast to the central prairies and on its return journey. Migration peaks in the second half of March and in November, with some birds staying into the winter if the larger lakes remain partly open. This is a bird of the open water, and large numbers sometimes winter on the Detroit River. Inland it seeks out the more expansive county lakes. The largest concentrations are usually at Four Mile Lake in the Chelsea SGA.

Redhead *Aythya americana*

Finding code: 4
Fairly common migrant, uncommon winter visitor
Spring dates: 5 March (1988) - 13 May (1989)
Spring maximum: 16 on 8 April 1989 at Sutton Lake
Fall dates: 8 October (1988) - 19 December (1987)
Fall maximum: 51 on 15 December 1988 at Four Mile Lake

The Redhead looks similar to the Canvasback (except for back color, headshape and bill), can be found in the same places as the Canvasback on county migration and occurs in comparable numbers. It differs perhaps in having a longer spring migration period. Redheads have been found on six of the last 15 CBCs.

Ring-necked Duck *Aythya collaris*

Finding code: 2
Common migrant, fairly rare winter visitor
Spring dates: 27 February (1980) - 6 May (1989)
Spring maximum: 85 on 9 April 1988 at Winnewanna
Fall dates: 8 October (1988) - 14 November (1978)
Fall maximum: 274 on 8 November 1989 at Pierce Lake

This duck is unhelpfully named, for the birdwatcher can rarely see the neck collar. A better name would have been Ring-billed Duck. This black and white diving duck can be distinguished from its squat look-alike, the Lesser Scaup, by its longer neck and elegant carriage of the head. The ring-neck is a common migrant in both spring and fall on lakes, ponds and the wider stretches of the Huron River. A few winter records exist of birds at the Little Portage-Portage channel. It has been found in very small numbers on five of the last 15 CBCs.

Greater Scaup *Aythya marila*

Finding code: 8 (in April)
Rare spring migrant

Separating the two scaup species is one of the most difficult identification problems among the waterfowl. The Greater Scaup is essentially a coastal duck in winter and tends to stop on migration on the Great Lakes. The presumption is that all scaup seen in Washtenaw County are Lesser Scaup until shown to be otherwise. Most of the recent records have occurred in April. These include:

1. 14 April 1982 two at Geddes Lake (MK)
2. 8 April 1988 two at Four Mile Lake (RW)
3. 5 November 1988 two on Silver Lake (JS, VB)
4. 4 April 1989 one at Matthaei Botanical Gardens (BP)
5. 15 April 1989 two at Iron Creek Mill Pond (VB, JS)

Additionally, there is a 1979 CBC record of a group of 15, but the details are not known to us.

Lesser Scaup *Aythya affinis*

Finding code: 2
Common migrant, sometimes abundant
Spring dates: 12 March (1988) - 4 May (1988)
Spring maximum: 260 on 9 April 1989 off Willis Rd.
Fall dates: 26 September (1987) - 4 December (1989)
Fall maximum: 33 on 10 November 1987

The Lesser Scaup is probably the most common diving duck in the county with occasional large accumulations at locations such as Four Mile Lake, Sutton Lake or Portage Lake. Unlike Ring-necked Ducks, Lesser Scaup usually stay well away from the shoreline. On the 1990 CBC Whitmore Lake was free of ice, and 35 Lesser Scaup were found there, this being the only CBC record during the survey period.

Oldsquaw *Clangula hyemalis*

Not recorded during the survey period; see chapter four

Surf Scoter *Melanitta perspicillata*

Not recorded during the survey period; see chapter four

White-winged Scoter *Melanitta fusca*

Finding code: 9
Very rare visitor

The White-winged Scoter is normally associated with larger bodies of water such as Lake Erie, but even there it is uncommon. Inland it is scarce anywhere in Michigan. There are two records during the survey period:

1. 30 December 1979 - 1 January 1980 an adult male at Gallup Park on the Huron River (MSm)
2. 25 March 1989 a female or immature at Barton Pond (VB, JS)

Common Goldeneye *Bucephala clangula*

Finding code: 2
Common winter visitor
Fall arrival: 28 September (1991)
Spring departure: 16 April (1987)
Maximum: 150 on 13 February 1988 at the Little Portage/Portage channel

Most goldeneyes arrive from the north in November and depart in March (see histogram). During this time these hardy ducks can be the third most numerous waterfowl species in the county, occupying any large stretch of open water. The CBC average for the last 15 years is 30 birds. They can also be detected in flight by the whistling sound of their wings. In early spring male goldeneyes can be seen rearing their heads backward in courtship display.

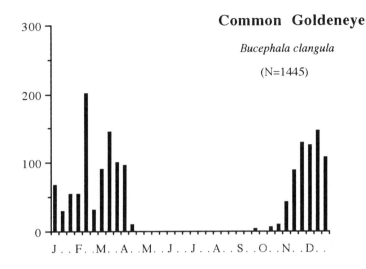

Common Goldeneye

Bucephala clangula

(N=1445)

Barrow's Goldeneye *Bucephala islandica*

Not recorded during the survey period; see chapter four

Bufflehead *Bucephala albeola*

Finding code: 2
Common migrant, uncommon early winter visitor
Spring dates: 27 February (1980) - 29 April (1989)
Spring maximum: 32 on 17 April 1988 at Silver Lake
Fall dates: 29 October (1988) - 1 January (1991)
Fall maximum: 51 on 24 November 1989 at Silver Lake

This diminutive diving duck arrives in late fall with colder weather, remaining briefly before departing southward only to return in early spring
with the opening up of rivers and lakes. Buffleheads are seldom found on
the smaller ponds of the county, being usually confined to larger bodies of
water. For some reason Silver Lake is a favorite county location for this
species. Few Buffleheads attempt to overwinter, although 1-3 birds were
found on the 1979, 1983 and 1990 CBCs.

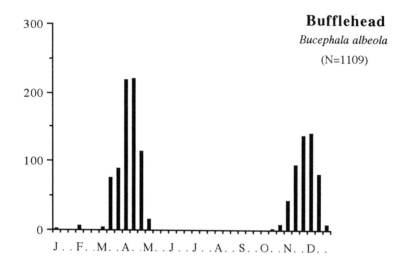

Bufflehead
Bucephala albeola
(N=1109)

Hooded Merganser *Lophodytes cucullatus*

Finding code: 4
Fairly common migrant, rare in winter
Spring dates: 19 March (1982) - 29 April (1988)
Spring maximum: 12 on 8 April 1988 at Daly Road Pond
Fall dates: 3 September (1989) - 16 December (1990)
Fall maximum: 19 on 17 November 1991 at Barton Pond

According to many observers the male Hooded Merganser is the most beautiful of all North American waterfowl. Hooded Mergansers are cavity-nesting ducks, and they breed sparingly in Michigan in their preferred habitat of secluded, heavily-wooded, fast-flowing streams. There are no confirmed records of nesting in Washtenaw County. Hooded Mergansers migrate through the county in fairly small numbers, mostly in April and in October-November. They are somewhat irregular, common some years and uncommon in others. Several of the recent observations have come from Barton Pond and Four Mile Lake. Sometimes a few birds linger into winter, but there are no February records.

Red-breasted Merganser *Mergus serrator*

Finding code: 5
Fairly uncommon spring migrant, fairly rare at other times
Spring dates: 19 March (1989) - 20 April (1988)
Spring maximum: 80 on 1 April 1978 on Barton Pond
Fall dates: 28 October (1990) - 5 December (1989)
Fall maximum: only single individuals

This merganser is smaller than the Common Merganser; even so, separating the females of the two species can be problematic under poor viewing conditions. The Red-breasted Merganser is rarely seen on spring migration except in late March and early April. As a spring migrant, it is also rarely found away from certain larger lakes such as Independence Lake, Pleasant Lake, Barton Pond, and Portage Lake. It is even less common in the fall, and all of the 30 or so records have (surprisingly) been of single individuals. As with many other duck species, a few individuals attempt to overwinter; it has been recorded in small numbers on four of the last 15 CBCs.

Common Merganser   *Mergus merganser*

Finding code: 2
Common winter visitor
Fall arrival: 20 October (1989)
Spring departure: 24 April (1991)
Maximum: 84 on 19 March 1989 at Barton Pond

This species is the largest of the three fish-eating mergansers of North America. As the Finding code indicates, it is also the most common merganser in the county. During migration, it can occur in groups of up to 30-40 birds on lakes and ponds of various sizes and on the Huron River. As January approaches, the number of Common Mergansers diminishes as the lakes freeze. However, like the Common Goldeneye, the Common Merganser continues to winter in the county, seeking out open water along the Huron River system.

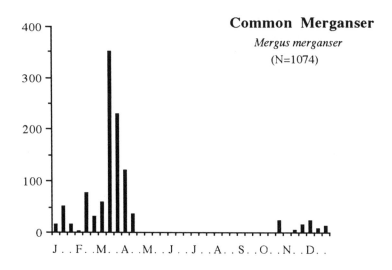

Common Merganser

Mergus merganser

(N=1074)

Ruddy Duck *Oxyura jamaicensis*

Finding code: 4
Fairly common migrant
Spring dates: 23 March (1986) - 31 May (1987)
Spring maximum: 14 on 16 April 1986 at Sutton Lake
Fall dates: 30 September (1989) - 21 November (1989)
Fall maximum: 23 on 17 October 1987 at Sutton Lake

Small groups of these torpid ducks can occasionally be found on larger bodies of open water throughout the county. However, the most reliable location for finding Ruddy Ducks in both spring or fall continues to be Sutton Lake. Ruddy Ducks nest in the prairie pothole regions, and there are only a handful of recent Michigan nesting records (ABBM). Some summers Ruddy Ducks have been found at Thorn Lake just across the Jackson County line, but these are not thought to be nesting birds.

Order Falconiformes (diurnal birds of prey)

Family Accipitridae (hawks, harriers, eagles, and Osprey)

There have been profound changes in the status of the nesting species among the Accipitridae in Washtenaw County over the last 40 years. The initiating factor in producing these changes was the introduction of DDT, with changes in farming practices in the years following, and the cutting of larger woodlots and filling of wetlands. In their classic study of raptor populations in Superior Twp., the Craighead brothers found that the Northern Harrier (7-9 pairs/township), Cooper's Hawk (6-8 pairs/township), Red-shouldered Hawk (14-19 pairs/township) and Red-tailed Hawk (5-6 pairs/township) were the most common nesting raptors in the county (Craighead and Craighead 1956). Since that time the changes in these populations have been dramatic. By the beginning of the survey period the Red-shouldered Hawk had virtually disappeared from the county as a nesting species while the Cooper's Hawk and Northern Harrier populations had dwindled to a small number of pairs countywide. By the mid-1980s the Northern Harrier had also vanished from the county as a nesting species. At the same time the Red-tailed Hawk population was growing steadily. This large raptor has apparently beneftted from the recent fragmentation of woodlots and the depletion of marshy edges to lakes. Since the time of the Craigheads the Red-tailed Hawk has totally replaced the Red-shouldered Hawk as the common buteo nesting in the county (or southeastern Michigan for that matter). By the late 1980s the Red-tailed Hawk population in Washtenaw County had reached 10-20 pairs per township. At the same time the Cooper's Hawk population was recovering. In 1991 in Ann Arbor there were seven pairs of Cooper's Hawks with less than half of the potential habitat filled with pairs (as of 1992 this has grown to 11 pairs). The reason why this species has rebounded while the Red-shouldered Hawk and Northern Harrier remain absent from the county seems to lie in the maturing of the remaining small woodlots and the apparent tolerance by Cooper's Hawks of nearby human activities. In fact, many of the Cooper's Hawk nests located have been on parklands and in residential areas with tall oak-hickory woods, all areas that were essentially protected but at the same time small. The Northern Harrier may never return to Washtenaw County as a nesting species following the increase and dispersal of the county's human population. The situation with the Red-shouldered Hawk is puzzling. There are woodlots countywide that have matured to the point where they are suitable for this species, but they are not being used. Instead, they are being colonized by Broad-winged Hawks. The four Broad-winged Hawk nests discovered between 1987 and 1990 are as many as had been located between 1890 and 1980. One likely explanation is that there is a potentially larger population of Broad-winged Hawks statewide from which to draw than there is for Red-shouldered Hawks. The current nesting status of the Accipitridae in Washtenaw County can be summarized as follows:

Northern Harrier	extirpated
Cooper's Hawk	fairly common and increasing
Red-shouldered Hawk	extirpated
Broad-winged Hawk	rare, but increasing
Red-tailed Hawk	common, stable or slightly increasing

Osprey *Pandion haliaetus*

Finding code: 6
Uncommon migrant
Spring dates: 14 April (1985) - 6 June (1986)
Spring maximum: only individuals
Fall dates: 30 August (1991) - 20 November (1986)
Fall maximum: 2 on several dates in October 1989

The Michigan population of Ospreys topped 169 pairs in 1989 (Evers 1992). In Washtenaw County the Osprey is a fairly rare spring migrant, and somewhat more common in the fall (see histogram). Ospreys, as fish-eating birds, are most commonly seen along the Huron River or at any of the larger lakes in the county. In the early part of the survey period the Osprey would have been given a finding code of 7, but 28 sightings in the past five years have accounted for its current status.

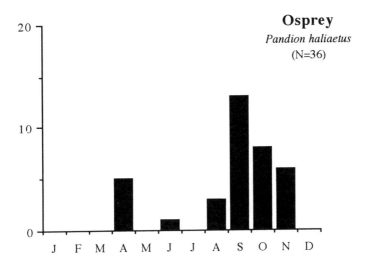

Osprey
Pandion haliaetus
(N=36)

American Swallow-tailed Kite *Elanoides forficatus*

No sightings during the survey period; see chapter four

Bald Eagle *Haliaeetus leucocephalus*

Finding code: 7
Fairly rare visitor in migration, very rare in the summer

Like the Osprey, the Bald Eagle nests most extensively in the northern half of the state. There is, however, a nest within an hour's drive of Washtenaw County, in Monroe County. Additional Lake Erie nests are located in nearby Ohio and Ontario. As the Bald Eagle has slowly recovered from the effects of DDT, which hampered its reproductive success, so the number of county sightings has increased. For much of the early portion of the survey period the Bald Eagle would have been a code 8 bird, but today it has increased to code 7. Small numbers occur irregularly throughout the county, either along the course of the Huron River or at the larger lakes. As the following list of sightings indicates, a Bald Eagle may turn up at almost any time in the county, although it is somewhat more likely to be encountered during migration.

1. 8 October 1977 an immature at Sutton Lake (RWy, BWy, ACu)
2. 19 March 1980 in Ann Arbor (DL)
3. 21 March 1981 at Four Mile Lake (ET, BT)
4. 29 March 1981 at Dexter (CS)
5. November 1983 at Curtis Rd. (MPa)
6. 21 December 1983 at Strawberry Lake (DT)
7. 28 January 1987 at Whitmore Lake (RI)
8. 4 June 1987 at Pierce Rd. (ESw)
9. 24 May 1988 at Winnewanna (TW)
10. 24 May 1988 at Chelsea SGA (TN)
11. 16 August 1988 an immature over northwest Ann Arbor (MK)
12. 14-19 August 1988 at Winnewanna (TN)
13. 19 November 1988 an immature along the Huron River (JS,VB)
14. 30 November 1989 at Noggles Rd., Manchester Twp. (MB)
15. 17 January 1990 at Portage Lake (MB)
16. 17 June 1990 first year bird in Northwest Ann Arbor (MK, SK)
17. 3 January 1991 an adult just north of Ann Arbor (MK, SK, AK)
18. Spring 1991 an adult along the Huron River (MObs)
19. 16 September 1991 at North Lake (DBr)
20. 14 December 1991 on the Ann Arbor CBC (WF)

Northern Harrier *Circus cyaneus*

Finding code: 6
Uncommon migrant
Spring dates: 24 March (1990) - 27 May (1989)
Spring maximum: only individuals
Fall dates: 7 August (1979) - 19 December (1987)
Fall maximum: only individuals

The Northern Harrier was once a fairly common nesting species throughout Washtenaw County, but the last verified nesting was in the early 1980s. Currently, the Northern Harrier is an uncommon species in migration and a rare winter visitor. Single birds have been recorded on six of the last 15 CBCs. As is typical in most areas, gray males are much less common than the brown females or immatures. Fall migrants often show the orange-tinged breasts of first-year birds.

Sharp-shinned Hawk *Accipiter striatus*

Finding code: 5 (in September)
Fairly uncommon migrant, fairly rare winter visitor
Spring dates: 19 April (1987) - 13 May (1989)
Spring maximum: 2 on several occasions
Fall dates: 24 August (1991) - 10 October (1988)
Fall maximum: 2 on several occasions

The Sharp-shinned Hawk is a fairly uncommon species in the county in migration, absent in the summer and fairly rare in the winter. Because of published accounts (at migration stations) stating that Sharp-shinned Hawks are much more common than Cooper's Hawks, many people believe that they have little chance of seeing the latter; therefore nearly all accipiters are quickly called "sharpies." In fact, the county records indicate that the only month of the year in which there are likely to be more sharpshins than Cooper's Hawks is in September. Small numbers of sharpies winter in the county, sometimes preying on the bird-life attracted to feeders.

Cooper's Hawk *Accipiter cooperii*

Finding code: 5
Fairly uncommon permanent resident

The revival of this shy woodland hawk in Washtenaw County is a remarkable success story. Recent research by Kielb shows that there are probably seven pairs nesting within the city limits of Ann Arbor alone. One factor that may have influenced the return of the Cooper's Hawk to its current status as a relatively common permanent resident is its apparent tolerance for humans. In recent years a number of successful nests have been built high above traveled woodland paths. Another factor may be the maturing of the remaining small woodlots in the area. The Cooper's Hawk is the benchmark accipiter against which the preceding and following species always need to be compared.

Northern Goshawk *Accipiter gentilis*

Finding code: 7
Fairly rare winter visitor
Early fall: 9 September (1985)
Late spring: 24 April (1977)
Maximum: only single individuals

Apart from invasion years, the powerful Northern Goshawk is a rare winter visitor to Washtenaw County from its resident territory in the northern forests. These irruptions occur about every ten years, the latest being during the winter of 1982-1983. Several goshawks were found regularly that year in the University of Michigan's north campus area and on the northeast side of Ann Arbor. Four were located on the CBC. Otherwise, goshawks are reported most years, but they are not quite of annual occurrence. Since 1983 most sightings have been of immatures. Survey period sightings include:

1. 24 April 1977 on Central Campus, University of Michigan (RO)
2. 3 February 1980 on Carpenter Road (TW)
3. 27 November 1980 in Dexter (CS)
4. 20 December 1980 two on the Ann Arbor CBC
5. 21 February 1982 on North Campus, University of Michigan (BWy)
6. 18 December 1982 in Superior Twp. (MK, DB, MP)
7. 27 December 1982 in Ypsilanti Twp. (MK)
8. 2 January - 24 March 1983 an adult in northeast Ann Arbor (MK)
9. 7-21 January 1983 an adult in Superior Twp. (MK)
10. 18 February 1983 an immature in Superior Twp. (MK)
11. 28 March 1984 at Platt and Willis Rds. (MK)
12. Week of 23 December 1984 (count week of Ann Arbor CBC)
13. 9 September 1985 an immature in northwest Ann Arbor (MK)
14. 7 November 1985 on Nixon Rd., Ann Arbor (MK)
15. 5 January 1986 five on the Ann Arbor CBC
16. 21 September 1986 an immature on North Campus, University of Michigan (MK)
17. 6 February 1987 along Huron Parkway, Ann Arbor (MK)
18. 2 January 1988 two on the Ann Arbor CBC
19. 4 March 1989 an adult at Noggles Rd. (MB)
20. 3 November 1990 an immature at Trinkle Road Marsh (VB, JS)

Red-shouldered Hawk *Buteo lineatus*

Finding code: 7
Fairly rare migrant, rare winter visitor
Spring dates: 5 March (1987) - 23 May (1982)
Fall dates: 6 August (1981) - 10 October (1984)

The Red-shouldered Hawk was once the most common nesting raptor in Washtenaw County, but there are now probably none nesting in the county. However, two birds seen in Lyndon Twp. in June 1986 (ABBM) and again in 1988 (DBr) suggest the possibility that a pair may still exist in this heavily wooded area. A thorough search for this species in 1989 (MK) turned up none in an area that had 19 pairs in 1942 (Craighead and Craighead 1956). Currently, Cooper's Hawks and Broad-winged Hawks are moving into woods that were previously used by Red-shouldered Hawks. There are occasional winter sightings of birds in the Ann Arbor area. They have been recorded on four of the last 15 Ann Arbor CBCs, and in 1991 one lingered into February at County Farm Park (JB, BP, VB).

Broad-winged Hawk *Buteo platypterus*

Finding code: 4 (in April)
Fairly common migrant and rare summer resident
Spring arrival: 3 April (1981)
Spring maximum: 30 on 28 April 1982 over Nichols Arboretum
Fall departure: 27 October (1977)
Fall maximum: 12 on 9 September 1979 at the Ann Arbor Landfill

The Broad-winged Hawk is a fairly common migrant in the county. The greatest numbers of migrants are seen from the middle of April until the end of the month, especially on days with light southerly winds. Broad-winged Hawks nested in or near Nichols Arboretum in 1988, 1989 and 1991. Currently this is the only semi-regular nesting location known in the county, although an additional nesting occurred in Lima Twp. in 1991. The secretive and quiet nature of the Broad-winged Hawk, in combination with its preference for larger, more mature tracts of woods, makes this a difficult species to locate in the summer. In the fall most migrants have departed by mid-September. There is an anecdotal reference to substantial fall migration in the southeastern corner of the county. This seems plausible since observations at Erie Metropark in Wayne County show that the migrating broad-wings head west, not south, after crossing the Detroit River.

Red-tailed Hawk *Buteo jamaicensis*

Finding code: 2
Common permanent resident

The Red-tailed Hawk is the common large hawk seen along roadways and fields throughout Washtenaw County. Historically, the red-tail was never as common as it is today. Currently many moderately sized woodlots in the county have single pairs of Red-tailed Hawks, with at least 10-12 pairs around the periphery of Ann Arbor. The population of Red-tailed Hawks in Superior Twp. had grown to 20 nesting pairs by 1990 (SP). The resident population is nearly doubled during migration and in the winter. Small numbers of migrants are seen soaring together from mid-March through April, and again in October and November. In the winter (December-February) numbers of Red-tailed Hawks can be seen along the main highways in the county, with the greatest concentrations along I-94. The annual CBC average during the survey period is 49 birds.

Rough-legged Hawk *Buteo lagopus*

Finding code: 6 (4 in peak years)
Uncommon winter visitor
Early fall: 27 September (1981)
Late spring: 1 April (1983)
Maximum: two on several occasions

This long-winged buteo is a winter visitor to Washtenaw County. The plumage of the rough-leg is the most highly varied of the buteos occuring in the county. There are two *color-morphs*, light and dark. In Washtenaw County the light morph dominates, with most individuals in the immature plumage. Typically, the first birds begin to appear in early November and are present until late March. Rough-legged Hawks are somewhat irregular in their appearance in Washtenaw County; there are some years when very few are present and other years when they are fairly common. Winters like 1989-1990, during which Rough-legged Hawks were quite plentiful, occur about every 4-5 years when their prey species (mainly meadow voles in the Arctic) experience a population crash. They have been seen on six of the last 15 CBCs. The best places to seek out this striking species are over large open fields and marshes.

Golden Eagle *Aquila chrysaetos*

Finding code: 9
Very rare winter visitor

The Golden Eagle is an inhabitant of vast expanses of wilderness. It does not nest in Michigan and is regularly seen only in the spring in eastern Chippewa County in the UP and in the fall in Monroe County. Occasionally in the winter there have been records from areas with large winter populations of Canada Geese, such as the Allegan SGA in the western LP and Thorn Lake in southeastern Jackson County. Prior to the survey period there is one record from over the central campus of the University of Michigan (17 October 1969, WR). There are only four records for the survey period, three, interestingly enough, from the western edge of the county close to Thorn Lake.

1. January 1985 a subadult at Thorn Lake in Jackson Co., occasionally straying into Manchester Twp. (MObs.)
2. 29 October 1990 on Noggles Rd. (MB)
3. 2 November 1991 three immatures east of Thorn Lake (DBr)
4. 14 November 1991 one at Rolling Hills County Park (MB)

Family Falconidae (falcons)

American Kestrel *Falco sparverius*

Finding code: 3 (in winter)
Fairly uncommon permanent resident, common in winter

This small brightly-colored falcon nests throughout the state, with the more northerly birds withdrawing to the southern Lower Peninsula or further south during the winter. As a result the relatively small permanent county population is much augmented at this time. The average total found on the Ann Arbor CBC during the survey period was 31 birds per year. The permanent population is patchily distributed and is largely concentrated in the open agricultural areas of the south-central and southeastern townships.

For example, kestrels can be seen hovering or sitting on utility wires in the shorebirding area of eastern Freedom Twp. Some of the birds nesting in the county use tree cavities, while others use crevices in farm or abandoned buildings.

Merlin *Falco columbarius*

Finding code: 8
Rare fall migrant

The Merlin is the rarest of the falcons to occur in Washtenaw County, with only seven records in 15 years. This small falcon, once called the Pigeon Hawk, is easily confused with both other falcon species and with Rock Doves (the common pigeon). Most people do not realize that this species is virtually the same size as an American Kestrel and is much smaller than a Peregrine Falcon. Unlike the other falcons it gives the impression of being a dark bird, even at a distance. Most of the county records are from the fall or early winter, presumably southbound migrants. Recent sightings are:

1. 12 October 1977 at Waterloo Rec Area (SH, JR)
2. 19 September 1981 at Nichols Arboretum (CH)
3. 10 October 1983 in northeast Ann Arbor (MK)
4. 5 January 1986 at Huron River and Zeeb Rd.(DBr, MBr)
5. 9 September 1988 at Saginaw Forest (RC)
6. 12 March 1990 at Independence Lake (MB)
7. 15 May 1990 in Freedom Twp. (RWy)

Peregrine Falcon *Falco peregrinus*

Finding code: 7
Fairly rare visitor in any season

Once called the Duck Hawk (with good reason!), the Peregrine Falcon is a national symbol of success in the reintroduction of a species into an area where it had been extirpated by human activities. Peregrines have been introduced — with varying success — into four areas of Michigan: downtown Detroit, downtown Grand Rapids, the eastern UP, and Isle Royale (ABBM). In 1992 a fifth site, Grand Island, in Lake Superior, was added to the list. As its name implies, the peregrine is a wanderer, and occasional birds pass through Washtenaw County. Nearly all recent sightings have occurred in the Ann Arbor area, either around city buildings or along the Huron River. Sightings are unpredictable but are most likely between January and April. Recent sightings include:

1. 10 May 1980 in Nichols Arboretum (RWy, BWy)
2. 5 November 1981 at the Ann Arbor Airport (MK)
3. 5 April 1983 in Superior Twp. (MK)
4. 1 March 1985 on the Medical Campus of the University of Michigan (ESa)
5. 12 February 1986 on the Central Campus of the University of Michigan (MK)
6. 11 August 1986 in downtown Ann Arbor (MK)
7. 27 September 1987 in downtown Ann Arbor (HM)
8. January-February 1988 on the Central Campus of the University of Michigan (MObs)
9. 9 March 1988 in downtown Ann Arbor (MK)
10. 2 November 1989 in Manchester (SSm)
11. 14 August 1990 on the Medical Campus of the University of Michigan (MK)
12. 1 March 1991 in northwest Ann Arbor (MK)

Order Galliformes (game birds)

Currently four species of this group may be encountered in Washtenaw County. Galliformes are chicken-like birds of various sizes, swift-running, ground-dwelling and unable to swim. They can fly rapidly but only for short distances. As these birds are of gastronomic interest, a number of species have been introduced — and reintroduced — in the county. Galliformes often form "coveys" of family groups in fall and winter.

Family Phasianidae (pheasants, grouse, turkeys, and quails)

Gray Partridge *Perdix perdix*

Not seen during the survey period; see chapter four

Ring-necked Pheasant *Phasianus colchicus*

Finding code: 3
Common permanent resident
Maximum: 19 on 5 January 1988 in Freedom Twp.

The ABBM survey indicates that the pheasant is common throughout the southern Lower Peninsula. The Ring-necked Pheasant is a bird of mixed habitats since fallow fields, fencerows, wooded edges, agricultural cropland and emergent wetlands all play a role in providing food and protective cover during the course of the year. However, pheasants seem to thrive best when they have access to well-cared-for agricultural land. The reduction of such land in the county may partly explain the fact that pheasants have generally declined in Washtenaw during the survey period. This species is easier to find early in the season (April-June) when males are crowing on territory. Individuals or groups are visible in the fall and winter foraging amongst corn stubble.

Ruffed Grouse *Bonasa umbellus*

Finding code: 5
Fairly uncommon permanent resident
Maximum: 4 on 17 October 1987 at Stinchfield Woods

The Ruffed Grouse is a secretive bird of forest regrowth for whom the aspen is a particularly important source of food (ABBM). It is largely absent from extreme southeast Michigan. In Washtenaw County there are occasional reports from Chelsea SGA, the Dexter area, Webster Twp. (where most Ann Arbor CBC records are from) and the Huron River metroparks, but its main areas today would seem to be Stinchfield Woods in the north and the four westernmost townships. Even at Stinchfield, birds are more difficult to find than as recently as five years ago. The county status of the Ruffed Grouse is understudied; it may in fact already be a code 6 species.

Northern Bobwhite *Colinus virginianus*

Finding code: 4
Fairly common permanent resident in agricultural areas
Maximum: 9 on 29 October 1990 on Noggles Rd.

The bobwhite reaches the northern limit of its range in lower Michigan and the population can be decimated in severe winters. At present this small game bird is fairly common, especially in the central and southern agricultural areas of the county. It is more often heard than seen since its loud clear *bob-white* call carries far in spring and early summer. During this time the bobwhite is a bird of rural fencerows, although it withdraws into deeper cover as winter approaches.

Greater Prairie-Chicken *Tympanuchus cupido*

No longer occurs in the county; see chapter four

Wild Turkey *Meleagris gallopavo*

Finding Code: 7
Fairly rare permanent resident
Maximum: 2 on several occasions since 1987

The indigenous Wild Turkey (or "gobbler") had been eradicated in Michigan by 1900 (Wood 1951). It was only reintroduced into the northern Lower Peninsula in 1954, where there are now estimated to be some 50,000 birds (ABBM). Subsequent DNR and private releases in or near Washtenaw County have recently established a small local population with sightings reported from 1983 (ABBM). The turkey, however, is a very wary bird and hard to find despite its considerable size. There are recent reports from Lyndon, Sylvan and Manchester Twps.

Order Gruiformes (cranes and rails)

Family Rallidae (rails)

Yellow Rail *Coturnicops novaboracensis*

No records during the survey period; see chapter four

King Rail *Rallus elegans*

No records during the survey period; see chapter four

Virginia Rail *Rallus limicola*

Finding code: 5
Fairly uncommon migrant and summer resident
Spring arrival: 23 April (1990)
Fall departure: 5 September (1988)
Maximum: 5 in June 1983 in Dexter Twp.

The Virginia Rail is a furtive denizen of cattail marshes. Consequently, unless it is called out by tape, it is much more likely to be heard than seen. One regular nesting site in the county is the marsh close to Mitchell-Scarlett Woods. Because of the secretive nature of this species, migration data are sparse. The Virginia Rail occasionally attempts to over-winter in the county, single birds having been found on three of the last 15 Ann Arbor CBCs.

Sora *Porzana carolina*

Finding code: 4
Fairly common summer resident and migrant
Spring arrival: 3 April (1988)
Fall departure: 29 September (1990)
Maximum: 5 on 14 May 1990 at Mitchell-Scarlett Woods

The Sora is the common rail of the county, and its pony-like "whinny" can be heard from many marshes. The Sora seems to accept a wider range of habitat than the Virginia Rail since it also summers in swampy meadows and waterlogged grassland. But, like the previous species, it is difficult to observe.

Common Moorhen *Gallinula chloropus*

Finding code: 6
Uncommon migrant and summer resident
Spring arrival: 5 May (1991)
Fall departure: 6 October (1990)
Maximum: 6 adults on 17 July 1991 at Trinkle Road Marsh

As the finding code indicates, this species is, in fact, not at all common in Washtenaw County, southern Michigan being towards the northern edge of its nesting range. Migrant birds are scarce, although several have been seen in recent years at Swift Run Pond in late September and early October. There are a number of breeding records: at Saline Nature Park in 1983; at Swift Run Pond in 1983 and 1985; at Winnewanna and at Sharon Hollow Marsh in 1987; and at M-14 and Gotfredson Road in 1991. However, the moorhen's current stronghold is Trinkle Road Marsh, where family groups have been observed during the last three summers. In 1991 there were probably three nesting pairs.

American Coot *Fulica americana*

Finding code: 2 (in migration)
Common migrant, uncommon in winter; rare nesting species
Spring dates: 12 March (1988) - 24 April (1988)
Spring maximum: 75 on 9 April 1991 at Independence Lake
Fall dates: 28 August (1988) - 14 November (1987)
Fall maximum: 10 on 15 October 1988 at Iron Creek Mill Pond

The coot typically nests to the north and west of southeast Michigan and winters further south. That said, there are recent records of the American Coot in the county for every month of the year. However, it only occurs in numbers during the spring and fall migration periods. In most years, one or two birds attempt to over-winter, particularly in the open channel between

Little Portage and Portage Lakes in the north of the county, or at Gallup Park on the Huron River in Ann Arbor. A pair of coots successfully nested at Trinkle Road Marsh in 1991. Seven young were seen on June 22 and five a week later.

Family Gruidae (cranes)

Sandhill Crane *Grus canadensis*

Finding Code: 4
Fairly common migrant and local summer resident
Spring arrival: 28 February (1983)
Fall departure: 22 November (1982)
Maximum: 60 on 22 November 1982 over Ann Arbor

Of the county's nesting species none is more majestic to watch or more thrilling to hear than the Sandhill Crane. This imposing species has rebounded in lower Michigan as a summer resident over the last 30 years (ABBM). One of its current strongholds is Jackson County. Many people visit the Phyllis Haehnle Sanctuary a few miles west of the county line to view the large numbers of cranes which gather there in fall prior to migration. It is therefore not surprising that the main nesting area in Washtenaw County lies along the western edge, even though nesting has also been reported in recent years from Chelsea SGA and Dexter Mill Pond. Sandhills arrive in March, at which time they are most vocal as they begin to establish territories. They often nest in cattail marshes often with extensive scrubby margins. Family groups begin to appear in the second half of May. Later in the season and on migration, groups of sandhills forage on newly planted fields, pasture and stubble. During these times they can occur in almost any of the agricultural areas of the county. Most birds leave by the end of October. The maximum count is of a late-migrating flock flying over Ann Arbor (RWy).

Order Charadriiformes (plovers and shorebirds)

Shorebirds or "waders" have been rapidly gaining in popularity among birdwatchers all over the world. This phenomenon is even detectable in Washtenaw County, despite its very restricted shorebird habitat (see Site Guide). In fact, regular shorebird routes have only been run in the county since the middle 1980s. While this development has skewed the records somewhat towards the later half of the survey period, regular observations do justify a modest amount of quantitative data. This section, therefore, includes histograms for five common migrant shorebirds. Twenty-seven species have been recorded during the survey period, although 12 of them are very rare (finding code 9 or 10).

Family Charadriidae (Plovers)

Black-bellied Plover *Pluvialis squatarola*

Finding Code: 9
Very rare migrant
Based on the available evidence, this species appears to be a rare and irregular migrant through the county. Only two sightings have been recorded during the survey period, one in spring and one in fall:

1. 28 April 1988 one at Schneider Road Pond (RW)
2. 18 August 1989 three in a recently-plowed field near the above (VB, JS)

Lesser Golden-Plover *Pluvialis dominica*

Finding code: 10
Extremely rare migrant

This plover is a rare spring and uncommon fall migrant in southeast Michigan. Wood found it in the Ann Arbor region "in late summer and fall only on rare occasions" (1951:167). According to Macklin Smith, Washtenaw County may be relatively unattractive to this migrant because of the shortage of large short-grass meadows and the absence of sod farms. If it does occur, it may be present in numbers; the largest flock recorded in the county is of 70 on 14 August 1970 (AMa). There is only one record during the survey period of eleven in a ploughed field off Sharon Valley Rd., Manchester Twp. on 18 August 1991 (WS).

Semipalmated Plover *Charadrius semipalmatus*

Finding Code: 5 (second half of May)
Fairly uncommon spring migrant, rare in fall
Spring dates: 12 May (1986) - 28 May (1988)
Spring maximum: 8 on 21 May 1988 in Freedom Twp.
Fall dates: 6 October 1981 (only sighting)

This strongly-patterned little plover, distinguished by its stubby, yellowish bill and its "single-strand necklace," has, in recent years, proved to be an irregular spring migrant in small numbers, most easily found in the Freedom Twp. shorebirding area. The finding code is something of an average, as sightings over the last six years have been variable, with extremes of no sightings (1990) to 40 birds (1988). The scarcity of fall records is consistent with expert opinion that the Semipalmated Plover is more common in the interior of the U.S. on spring passage (Hayman, Marchant, and Prater 1986). Even though Wood (1951:162) commented that "about Ann Arbor occasional individuals are seen to mid-September," during the 1977-1991 survey period we have only traced one fall record: a single bird on 6 October 1981 at Gallup Park, Ann Arbor (MK).

Piping Plover *Charadrius melodus*

Not seen during the survey period; see chapter four

Killdeer *Charadrius vociferus*

Finding Code: 2
Common migrant and summer resident
Spring arrival: 8 March (1988)
Fall departure: 15 November (1989)
Maximum: 135 on 18 August 1989 in Freedom Twp.

The widespread and aptly named Killdeer is well known to many people in Washtenaw County, who recognize its noisy call, its unique double breastband and its strategies for luring intruders away from its territory. The Killdeer is likely to be found wherever other shorebirds congregate. In addition, it is common in drier open spaces, including those in industrial and suburban areas, where it often nests — even on the graveled roofs of lowish flat buildings (as at Swift Run Pond). Downy young have been seen on numerous occasions between mid-May and early July. In August and September, Killdeer sometimes gather on the ground in quite large groups of 40 or more birds; at this time it can become a code 1 bird. Killdeer mostly winter in the southern half of the U.S. and further south, but there are occasional reports of wintering birds from southern Michigan counties, particularly from the Lake Michigan shore in Berrien County and the Lake Erie shore in Monroe County. Single Killdeer have been found on two of the last 15 Ann Arbor CBCs. There is one February record, 4 February 1981 (TC), which may represent an over-wintering bird or an exceptionally early migrant.

Family Scolopacidae (shorebirds)

Greater Yellowlegs *Tringa melanoleuca*

Finding Code: 4 (in April)
Fairly common migrant
Spring dates: 6 April (1987) - 12 May (1986)
Spring maximum: 13 on 14 April 1988 on Steinbach Rd.
Fall dates: 16 July (1988) - 11 November (1990)
Fall maximum: 5 on 6 October 1991 at Schneider Road Pond

The Greater Yellowlegs is the largest of the regularly occurring shorebirds in the county. In spring the species is primarily an April migrant with few remaining into May. During April, groups may be found, but in fall solitary birds, or loosely associating twos or threes, are the norm. Washtenaw County records corroborate other reports from Michigan that this species is consistently less common on passage than the Lesser Yellowlegs (see histogram).

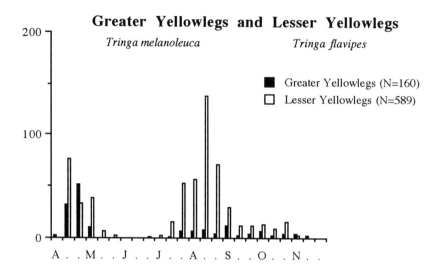

Greater Yellowlegs and Lesser Yellowlegs

Tringa melanoleuca   *Tringa flavipes*

■ Greater Yellowlegs (N=160)
□ Lesser Yellowlegs (N=589)

Lesser Yellowlegs *Tringa flavipes*

Finding Code: 3 (in second half of April and in August)
Common migrant
Spring dates: 11 April (1986) - 21 May (1988)
Spring maximum: 45 on 14 April 1988 on Steinbach Rd.
Fall dates: 29 June (1991) - 11 November (1989)
Fall maximum: 65 on 18 August 1988 at Steinbach and Bethel Church Rds.

This dainty species is one of the most common passage shorebirds in the county, distributed quite widely in suitable habitat. It arrives and departs in spring about 7-10 days later than the Greater Yellowlegs. The coincidence of earliest spring arrival and maximum number indicates the tendency — which it shares with the Pectoral Sandpiper — for larger groups to arrive suddenly and then slowly diminish. The histogram indicates the peak periods of the migration. Single and isolated examples of the two yellowlegs species can be hard to identify because they differ essentially in size. However, the Greater Yellowlegs can be seen to have a proportionally thicker and often slightly upturned bill. In the fall adult migrants precede the juveniles.

Solitary Sandpiper *Tringa solitaria*

Finding Code: 3 (early May and August)
Common migrant
Spring dates: 22 April (1987) - 4 June (1987)
Spring maximum: 14 on 5 May 1991 at Steinbach and Bethel Church Rds.
Fall dates: 4 July (1991) - 10 October (1989)
Fall maximum: 21 on 3 August 1991 at Swift Run Pond

The Solitary Sandpiper arrives towards the end of April and some years may stay until early June. The first southbound birds return in the first half of July but are most common in August (see histogram). In many ways, this graceful bird is the classic shorebird of the county since it is one of the only species (along with the Upland Sandpiper) more likely to occur inland than on the more extensive shorebird habitat along the Lake Erie coastline. The solitary prefers small ponds, mud pools and patches of waterlogged grass to more extensive wetlands. As its name implies, this species tends not to congregate in flocks; on the other hand, it is not exactly solitary either, as suggested by the relatively high maximum counts. The Solitary Sandpiper is the only Washtenaw County shorebird with a prominent white eye-ring. Like some other waders, it has the habit of raising its wings high when alighting on the ground.

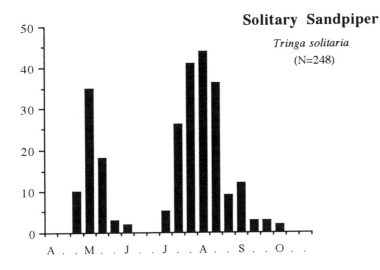

Solitary Sandpiper

Tringa solitaria

(N=248)

Willet   *Catoptrophorus semipalmatus*

Finding Code: 10
Vagrant

This species has a decided preference for the Atlantic and Pacific coasts and is always uncommon in the Great Lakes region, particularly away from the lakeshore. There is only one county sighting during the survey period. A single bird was observed towards dusk on 15 June 1989 at Swift Run Pond, feeding in shallow water and flying to roost on a snag in deeper water, showing in the process its diagnostic black and white wing pattern (VB, JS). The bird could not be located the next day. Given the date, this bird was presumably a summer straggler, especially since at least one Willet summered at Pte. Mouillee that year. The only other record this century is of three birds at Whitmore Lake on 20 August 1935 (Wood 1951).

Spotted Sandpiper   *Actitis macularia*

Finding Code: 3
Common summer resident
Spring arrival : 29 March (1980)
Fall departure: 13 October (1991)
Maximum: 6 on 18 June 1988 at Schneider Road Pond

The Spotted Sandpiper is a common but local nesting species in the county, frequenting lakes, ponds and river edges which have limited vegetation at the waterline. There are probably several breeding pairs in each township. The "spottie," with its characteristic teetering rump, usually arrives towards the end of April, and the nesting population is largely gone by the beginning of September. The female is dominant in courtship, and in May she can sometimes be seen displaying (flying up and gliding back to land near the male, then drooping her wings and holding her head high). In July and August, juveniles (without spotted breasts) scurry about in the vicinity of their parents. The position of migrating Spotted Sandpipers in Washtenaw County remains unclear, since the number of birds observed does not seem to be greatly inflated during the expected migration peaks (in contrast to the situation described by Brock for the Indiana Dunes). However, it is likely that the few birds found in the county after mid-September are southbound migrants from further north. There are only two October records during the survey period: 10 October 1981 at Gallup Park (MK) and 13 October 1991 at North Bay Park, Ford Lake (VB, JS).

Upland Sandpiper *Bartramia longicauda*

Finding code: 7
Rare and local migrant, fairly rare and local summer resident
Spring arrival: 7 May (1982)
Fall departure: 5 August (1987)
Maximum: 4 on 30 July 1982 in Dexter Twp.

The Upland Sandpiper is rarely found with other shorebirds, and its status in Washtenaw County is under-researched. Easily identifiable by its distinctly rounded head and large, liquid, "shoe-button" eyes, the upland is a bird of open prairies and grasslands. The only known semi-regular nesting habitat in the county is the Ann Arbor Airport, where successful nesting was last recorded in 1989 (MObs). However, it is regularly observed at nearby Willow Run Airport in Wayne County. The Upland Sandpiper is known as a very early fall migrant, and a flock of four on 30 July 1982 near Dexter (RW) may represent migrating birds.

Whimbrel *Numenius phaeopus*

No verified sightings during the survey period; see chapter four

---

Hudsonian Godwit *Limosa haemastica*

Finding Code: 9
Very rare migrant

This large and imposing shorebird is uncommon anywhere in Michigan and very rare inland. Immediately prior to the survey period there was one sighting of a Hudsonian Godwit in October 1976 at Dolph Park (MObs). Since that time there have been two additional sightings:

1. 23 October 1982 one near Ann Arbor (RWy)
2. 19 October 1987 one at the M-14 Water Treatment Ponds (MK)

Ruddy Turnstone *Arenaria interpres*

Finding Code: 10
Extremely rare spring migrant

Although the turnstone can be a fairly common migrant along the shores of Lake Michigan and Lake Erie, it is seldom reported inland. The only sighting for the survey period is of a female in breeding plumage at Schneider Road Pond on 22 May 1988 (VB, JS). Wood (1951), for an earlier period, notes occasional sightings in Washtenaw County, predominantly in the last ten days of May.

Red Knot *Calidris canutus*

Finding Code: 10
Extremely rare fall migrant

The Red Knot is primarily a coastal migrant since it tends to congregate on extensive tidal mudflats. As a consequence, it is uncommon on passage in Michigan and rare away from the Great Lakes shorelines. There is only one recent county record — of a fall migrant on a sandbar in the Huron River on 6 September 1979 (MK).

Sanderling *Calidris alba*

Finding Code: 9
Very rare migrant

The Sanderling is the most sprightly of the small sandpipers that migrate through the county to and from their arctic nesting grounds. It is the Sanderling that beach vacationers notice as it scurries back and forth, always just out of the reach of the waves. Inland it is something of a vagrant with only two recent county records:

1. 21 May 1988 two birds approaching full breeding plumage at a temporary pond on South Fletcher Rd. near Jackson Rd. (VB, SH, JS)
2. 27 July 1991 at the Pleasant Lake farm pond (JS)

"Peeps" (Semipalmated, Western, Least, White-rumped, and Baird's Sandpipers)

The group of five closely related *Calidris* sandpipers occurring in the Great Lakes Region are referred to as "peeps." These birds require careful study and knowledge of their complex plumages in order to identify them properly (Veit and Jonsson 1984). Unfortunately, as a group few are seen in the county each year, and never in large mixed groups allowing comparisons. In general, these birds are best studied in nearby Monroe County, although the adventurous birdwatcher can enjoy searching for them along the Shorebird Routes (see Site Guide).

Semipalmated Sandpiper *Calidris pusilla*

Finding code: 5
Fairly uncommon migrant
Spring dates: 5 May (1990) - 28 May (1990)
Spring maximum: 6 on 28 May 1990 at Schneider Road Pond
Fall dates: 16 July (1988) - 6 October (1981)
Fall maximum: 7 on 12 August 1989 at Schneider Road Pond

This diminutive, black-legged "peep" is not as common in the county as its straw-legged counterpart, the Least Sandpiper. Nevertheless, modest numbers pass through the county in both spring and fall, usually singly or in small groups. In recent times, there have been about a dozen records of Semipalmated Sandpipers per year, which have been fairly evenly distributed between spring and fall.

Western Sandpiper *Calidris mauri*

Finding code: 9
Very rare migrant

The problems in distinguishing this uncommon Great Lakes migrant from the much more common Semipalmated Sandpiper are notorious. Nor are the difficulties lessened by the fact that migrating "peeps" in the county are normally silent unless alarmed into flight. There are two acceptable recent records:

1. 12 May 1986 one at a temporary pond in Saline Twp. (RW)
2. 12 August 1988 at a temporary pond on N. Zeeb Rd. near Daly Rd. (JS, VB)

Least Sandpiper *Calidris minutilla*

Finding code: 4
Fairly common migrant
Spring dates: 28 April (1988) - 28 May (1988)
Spring maximum: 9 on 22 May 1988 at Schneider Road
Fall dates: 30 June (1988) - 2 September (1987)
Fall maximum: 14 on 26 August 1989 at Pleasant Lake farm pond

This tiny, hunched sandpiper is the common "peep" of the county. In recent years, for example, it has proved 3-4 times as common as the Semipalmated Sandpiper. It is typically found as singles or in busy groups of 3-7 birds, the latter especially at the Scio Church farm pond or in the major shorebirding area. Given the reports by Wood (1951) and Walkinshaw (1978), it is surprising that the Least Sandpiper has not been noted through much of September.

White-rumped Sandpiper *Calidris fuscicollis*

Finding code: 9
Very rare migrant

This species and the following are similar in size, and in having long wings. Both are uncommon in Michigan. Typically the white-rump is a spring migrant, while the Baird's is more common in the fall. County sightings corroborate this. There are only two recent records of this scarce county migrant:

1. 3 September 1986 a flock of seven at the M-14 Water Treatment Pond (MK)
2. 13 May 1989 one at Dexter Mill Pond (KH, GJ, KJ)

Baird's Sandpiper *Calidris bairdii*

Finding code: 7
Fairly rare fall migrant

In the last five years, there have been five records in the county of this small, long-winged sandpiper. All of the records have been of juveniles in their distinctive "scaly" plumage. Details of the sightings are as follows:

1. 2 September 1987 three birds at Schneider Road Pond (RW)
2. 29 September 1989 one in a flooded depression in a field off N. Zeeb Rd. (VB, JS, RW)
3. 11 October 1989 one at the same location as previous (VB, JS)
4. 11 August 1991 five at the M-14 Water Treatment Pond (MK)
5. 13 August 1991 three at the Bemis Rd. prison facility pond (MSm)

As the above list indicates, the Baird's Sandpiper in Washtenaw County, as elsewhere in the state, is primarily a fall migrant. There is a single historical spring record: 26 May 1935 at Whitmore Lake (Wood 1951).

Pectoral Sandpiper *Calidris melanotos*

Finding Code: 2
Common migrant
Spring dates: 10 April (1988) - 22 May (1988)
Spring maximum: 358 on 15 April 1988 on Steinbach Rd.
Fall dates: 13 July (1991) - 11 November (1989)
Fall maximum: 35 on 18 August 1989 at Steinbach and Bethel Church Rds.

The chunky Pectoral Sandpiper is, in terms of total numbers, probably the most common of the migrating shorebirds in the county. The phenomenon of an explosive spring arrival followed by a steady diminution was well illustrated during the "invasion" year of 1988. Numbers in a flooded meadow on Steinbach Rd. south of Pleasant Lake Rd. were 358 on 15

April, 130 on 21 April, and 63 on 22 April (RW). The fall migration period can, in any one year, extend for more than three months, but it usually peaks in the middle of August (see histogram).

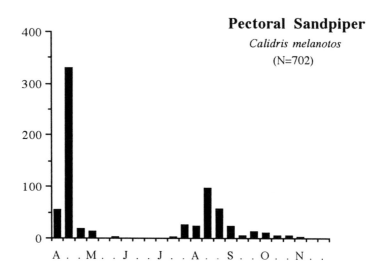

Pectoral Sandpiper
Calidris melanotos
(N=702)

Dunlin *Calidris alpina*

Finding code: 5 (second half of May)
Fairly uncommon spring migrant, fairly rare in fall
Spring dates: 15 April (1986) - 28 May (1990)
Spring maximum: 19 on 21 May 1989 on S. Fletcher Rd.
Fall dates: 6 October (1989) - 27 October (1991)
Fall maximum: 21 on 27 October 1991 at Schneider Road Pond

The Dunlin is primarily a late spring migrant in Washtenaw County, observable most years in the Freedom Twp. shorebirding area during the last ten days of May. At this time the birds are in full breeding plumage and easily recognizable by their reddish backs and black patches on the lower belly. Outside this period the Dunlin is a scarce visitor. The earliest reported arrival date (15 April) is very unusual since the next earliest sighting is for 12 May. There have been only six fall records of Dunlin in the last six years, three at the Scio Church farm pond and three from Schneider Road. In fall, the Dunlin is therefore a code 7 bird. The arrival and departure dates suggest that the Dunlin is a narrow-window visitor to Washtenaw County on both northbound and southbound passage.

Stilt Sandpiper *Calidris himanotopus*

Finding Code: 9
Very rare fall migrant

Although there are county records of Stilt Sandpipers from earlier periods in July and September, we have traced no spring records. The Stilt Sandpiper is similar in size and shape to the common Lesser Yellowlegs, but it has a much heavier bill. There are three fall records for this mid-sized shorebird during the survey period, all in August:

1. 11 August 1982 one at Schneider Road Pond (RW)
2. 8 August 1989 one partly retaining breeding plumage seen at Schneider Road Pond (VB, JS)
3. 17 August 1991 a juvenile at a pond on N. Zeeb Rd.(VB, JS)

Buff-breasted Sandpiper *Tryngites subruficollis*

Not recorded during the survey period; see chapter four

Short-billed Dowitcher *Limnodromus griseus*

Finding Code: 7
Fairly rare migrant
Spring dates: 12 May (1986) - 28 May (1990)
Spring maximum: only single individuals
Fall dates: 8 July (1991) - 16 September (1989)
Fall maximum: 4 on 14 September 1987 at the prison pond on Bemis Rd.

There are only eleven records of the Short-billed Dowitcher during the 1986-1991 period: three in May, three in July, two in August, and three in

September. Nine of these sightings have been of single birds. The July records are of birds still retaining breeding plumage.

Long-billed Dowitcher *Limnodromus scolopaceus*

No acceptable records during the survey period; see chapter four

---

Common Snipe *Gallinago gallinago*

Finding Code: 4 (in April and October)
Fairly common migrant, rare summer resident
Spring dates: 4 April (1978) - 14 May (1989)
Spring maximum: 12 on 14 April 1990 at Bethel Church and Lima Center Rds.
Fall dates: 10 August (1989) - 17 November (1990)
Fall maximum: 14 on 10 October 1987 at Schneider Road Pond

The snipe is a fairly common migrant through Washtenaw County, although its camouflage plumage, preference for fairly tall grass and typical stillness can make it hard to spot. In spring, birds can sometimes be heard and seen performing their "winnowing" display flight. When disturbed, snipe tend to "tower" into the sky, but then fall towards the ground like a stone. During the last five years, there have been at least three summer sightings of single Common Snipe in the county (VB, BP, ESh, JS). However, although this species might be expected to nest in one or two secluded corners of the county, there are no recent records. There are also a few records of snipe being seen during the winter period (MB), suggesting that occasional birds may attempt to over-winter in the county. Common Snipe have been recorded on three of the last 15 Ann Arbor CBCs. The migration peaks can be seen from the histogram.

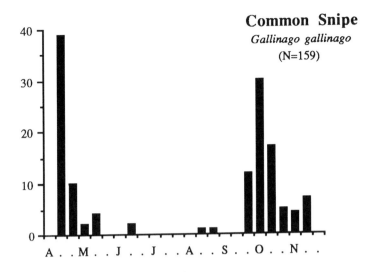

Common Snipe
Gallinago gallinago
(N=159)

American Woodcock *Scolopax minor*

Finding Code: 6
Uncommon migrant and summer resident
Spring arrival: 22 March (1980)
Fall departure: 28 October (1988)
Maximum: 8 on 28 October 1988 at Iron Creek Mill Pond

During most of the year, the American Woodcock is an elusive woodland bird of largely nocturnal habits. As such, it is almost never found on shorebirding expeditions. These characteristics make it a code 6 bird. Fortunately, the woodcock have traditional display grounds on spring migration, where at dusk the males perform their spectacular spiraling, plummeting flight displays. In Washtenaw County, this occurs most reliably at the end of March. One site is in the conservation area behind Pioneer High School in Ann Arbor. There are several nesting records during the survey period (TSc), most from Sharon Twp (MB), and fledglings have been seen as early as 28 April (1984) north of Ypsilanti (ABBM). Woodcock have also been flushed on several occasions in summer at the Matthaei Botanical Gardens (TW). The few records after late August indicate that the woodcock is hard to detect on fall migration.

Wilson's Phalarope *Phalaropus tricolor*

Finding code: 9
Very rare migrant

The Wilson's Phalarope is a rare bird in Michigan with its main nesting range well to the west of the state. No confirmed nesting was established during the Atlas period (ABBM), although there were several "probables" for the Saginaw Bay area. In August, if extensive shorebird habitat is available at Pte. Mouillee, surprisingly large numbers of this species (10-20) can be found in migration. In Washtenaw County during the survey period, there were two sightings:

1. 24 August 1984 two at a seasonal pond in northeast Ann Arbor (MK)
2. 18 May 1991 a pair in breeding plumage at the Schneider Road Pond (VB, JS)

Red-necked Phalarope *Phalaropus lobatus*

Finding Code: 9
Very rare fall migrant

This species used to be called the Northern Phalarope because of its breeding territory in the low arctic. It winters at sea in the southern hemisphere (Godfrey 1986). Red-necked Phalaropes are rare spring migrants anywhere in Michigan and only slightly more common in fall. From 1977-1991 there are two fall records of this species in the county:

1. 24 August 1984 one on a seasonal pond in northeast Ann Arbor (MK)
2. 21 September 1989 a juvenile at the horse pond on Scio Church Rd. (VB, JS, RW)

Red Phalarope *Phalaropus fulicaria*

No records during the Survey Period; see chapter four

Family Laridae (gulls and terns)

These two groups of birds appear similar on visual impression. Both are largely white in adult plumage and both are associated with water, above which they often search for food. Gulls, however, have profited from human activity, while the more sensitive terns have failed to adjust to human intrusion and harassment by gulls. As a result, gulls proliferate and terns decline. In Washtenaw County three species of gulls can be assigned Finding codes below 5, but no tern species currently has a Finding code of less than 6.

Subfamily Larinae (gulls)

Bonaparte's Gull *Larus philadelphia*

Finding code: 5
Fairly uncommon migrant
Spring dates: 24 March (1990) - 4 May (1982)
Spring maximum: 40 on 19 April 1982 at Montibeller Twp. Park
Fall dates: 13 October (1990) - 7 December (1991)
Fall maximum: 20 on 15 November 1987 on the Huron River near Dixboro Rd.

The Bonaparte's Gull is the only small gull likely to be seen in Washtenaw County. It migrates through in April on its way to its breeding grounds in western Canada and returns in late fall (mid-October to early December) en route to its wintering areas on Lake Erie and further south. Fall birds do not have black heads but can be identified by their red legs and "white wedges" in the upper wings. Birds may occur as lone individuals or in traveling flocks of up to 20 or so. The Bonaparte's Gull is something of a narrow-window migrant, since in any one migration period all the birds may pass through within ten days.

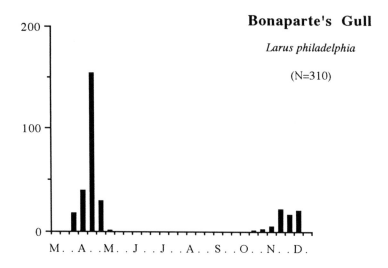

Bonaparte's Gull

Larus philadelphia

(N=310)

Ring-billed Gull   *Larus delawarensis*

Finding code: 1
Common to abundant visitor
Fall maximum: 296 on 4 November 1989 on Trinkle Rd.

The mid-sized ring-bill is the most common gull of the county. They can be found throughout the year, although they do not nest here. Typically, these are the gulls that follow the plow, loaf on playing fields and hang out at shopping malls. Dusky juveniles can be common in summer.

Herring Gull *Larus argentatus*

Finding Code: 2 (in winter)
Common visitor except in summer

The rather ominous-looking Herring Gull is the only large gull to occur regularly in the county. It is present in variable numbers throughout the year except for the summer months when it is gone to the Great Lakes beaches. It is most common in winter. On the 1984 Ann Arbor CBC 679 Herring Gulls were recorded, but numbers have tended to decline in more recent years due to changes in landfill operations. Herring Gulls can be found among the more common Ring-bills on the Huron River in winter, especially along the ice edge.

Iceland Gull *Larus glaucoides*

None seen during the survey period; see chapter four

Lesser Black-backed Gull *Larus fuscus*

Finding code: 10
Vagrant

This species is uncommon anywhere in the Great Lakes, even at the gull mecca of Niagara Falls. There is a single county record during the reporting period: an adult in winter plumage at Ford Lake on 7 December 1985 (MK).

Glaucous Gull *Larus hyperboreus*

Finding code: 9
Very rare winter visitor

The Glaucous Gull is a large "white-winged" arctic species never common in the Great Lakes Region. In the last 15 years there have been two reports of single birds from the Ann Arbor landfill, both on CBC, one on 30 December 1979, the other on 15 December 1990 (RF, NF). Historically, the maximum seen was three on 20 January 1967 on Ford Lake (HT).

Great Black-backed Gull *Larus marinus*

Finding code: 9
Very rare winter visitor

This enormous dominant species has been increasing in numbers in western Lake Erie. The second Washtenaw County report was of two adults on the 1990 CBC, and the third of three on the 1991 CBC, all at the Ann Arbor landfill (RF, NF). It is possible that further winter occurrences of this species in the county may be noted and in consequence the finding code will fall. There is a remarkable record of 15 on 20 January 1967 on Ford Lake (HT). The 1967 record for this and the preceding species may represent storm-driven birds.

Subfamily Sterninae (terns)

Caspian Tern *Sterna caspia*

Finding code: 6
Uncommon migrant and summer visitor
Spring arrival: 13 May (1989)
Fall departure: 13 October (1991)
Fall maximum: 6 on 4 August 1991 at Ford Lake

The adult Caspian Tern is an impressive bird. It is almost as large as a Herring Gull, has brilliant white wings and a vivid reddish-orange bill, and plunge-dives for fish. Throughout the survey period, occasional birds have been seen along the Huron River downstream of Ann Arbor (MS). During the last five years there have been eight records for this visitor:

1. 18 August 1988 one at US-23 and Washtenaw (MK, RP, PC, GH)
2. 13 May 1989 two at Independence Lake (JC, ES)
3. 22 May 1990 three at Independence Lake (MB)
4. 31 July 1990 four at Independence Lake (MB)
5. 12 August 1990 one at Swift Run Pond (RW)
6. 27 July 1991 one at South Lake (RW, JW)
7. 3-4 August 1991 maximum of six at Ford Lake (VB, JS)
8. 13 October 1991 one at Ford Lake (VB, JS)

Common Tern   *Sterna hirundo*

No confirmed records during the survey period; see chapter four

Forster's Tern   *Sterna forsteri*

Finding code: 6 (in April)
Uncommon spring migrant
Spring dates: 4 April (1991) - 14 May (1989)
Spring maximum: 35 on 16 April 1990 at Iron Creek Mill Pond

In recent years the Forster's Tern has been entirely a spring migrant in Washtenaw County, usually flying east-west. Curiously, for such an uncommon species, all recent reports have been of at least two birds.

Least Tern *Sterna antillarum*

Not seen during the survey period; see chapter four

Black Tern *Chlidonias niger*

Finding code: 7
Fairly rare spring migrant and summer visitor
Spring-Summer Dates: 4 May (1989) - 22 June (1988)
Spring maximum: 6 on 1 June 1983 at Iron Creek Mill Pond

The last known nesting colony of Black Terns in the county was abandoned at Iron Creek Mill Pond after the mid-1960s (MB). Unfortunately, the Black Tern is very sensitive to human disturbance and has disappeared from traditional nesting sites in Washtenaw County as well as much of its Great Lakes Region range. Today, the Black Tern is but a passage visitor to the county, and an infrequent one at that. There have been hopes that it might attempt to nest at Winnewanna lake in the northwest corner of the county, but a survey by RW in the spring and summer of 1991 failed to produce any sign of them.

Family Columbidae (pigeons and doves)

Rock Dove *Columba livia*

Finding code: 1
Abundant permanent resident

The Rock Dove or common pigeon is usually regarded as a bird of urban settings, yet these birds are familiar to everyone, for they are widely distributed throughout the county. Silos, barns and grain-storage facilities are common country habitats. The Rock Dove roosts and nests in cavities or sheltered ledges on buildings as well as under highway bridges. Its irruptive group flights from the tops of large buildings are well known. For the past 15 Ann Arbor CBCs there has been an annual average of over 1,000 Rock Doves.

Mourning Dove *Zenaida macroura*

Finding code: 1
Common permanent resident

The soft cooing of this dove can be heard during the early morning hours in the warmer months of the year. A common species that can be found in almost any city, town, suburb or rural setting, the Mourning Dove is among the first birds to nest in the spring and the last to have young leave the nest in the late summer. Individual birds and small groups will visit elevated bird feeders or feed on grain scattered on the ground at feeding stations. In agricultural areas with wheat or corn stubble, foraging flocks of more than one hundred birds can be seen. During the winter groups of birds commonly sit low in brushy tangles along fencerows or along borders of wooded areas seeking shelter from the wind while roosting during the day.

Family Cuculidae (cuckoos)

Black-billed Cuckoo *Coccyzus erythrophthalmus*

Finding code: 5
Fairly uncommon migrant and summer resident
Spring arrival: 9 May (1991)
Fall departure: 17 October (1987)
Maximum: 2 on several occasions

This and the following species are retiring birds of the forest and forest edge, where they tend to nest in dense tangles and shrubs. Both species are well known for congregating to feed on outbreaks of hairy caterpillars. Some years cuckoos are fairly common in the county (as in 1988); in others they can be uncommon. The finding codes are therefore something of an average. The Black-billed Cuckoo is a fairly late spring migrant, not usually arriving until the middle of May. Although it nests in fairly small numbers throughout the state (ABBM), there is little evidence of fall migration through the county.

Yellow-billed Cuckoo *Coccyzus americanus*

Finding code: 5
Fairly uncommon migrant and summer resident
Spring arrival: 30 April (1990)
Fall departure: 6 October (1986)
Maximum: 2 on several occasions

While the main breeding range of the Yellow-billed Cuckoo is more southerly than that of the Black-billed Cuckoo, their ranges overlap in
Washtenaw County. Most years Washtenaw County seems to host slightly
more Yellow-billed than Black-billed Cuckoos. One fairly regular location
is Searles Nature Reserve. This species is typically a late spring migrant,
arriving in the second half of May.

Order Strigiformes (owls)

Seven species of owls occur in Washtenaw County. An eighth species, the
Barn Owl, is no longer found here. Owls normally require special efforts
on the part of the observer, or listener, in order to locate even the more
common species (see Owling in the Site Guide). The two common county
residents, the Eastern Screech Owl and Great Horned Owl, can fairly
readily be found in woodland habitats countywide. The remaining species
require a much greater effort to locate. The Barred Owl is a rare resident
along the western edge of the county. Listening for their nocturnal calling
in April and May offers the best chance of locating this scarce resident.
The *Asio* owls, long- and short-eared, usually require extensive winter
searches of appropriate habitat. Finding the Northern Saw-whet Owl is
serendipity. Finally, the exception is the rare Snowy Owl, which will
typically be highly visible as it sits on the top of a city building or county
barn.

Family Tytonidae (barn owls)

Barn Owl *Tyto alba*

Not seen during survey period; see chapter four

Family Strigidae (typical owls)

Eastern Screech-Owl *Otus asio*

Finding code: 3
Common permanent resident

The small Eastern Screech-Owl is a common resident throughout the county, nesting in tree cavities in many woodlots. Surveys in 1990 and 1991 showed that this species has a nesting density of 5-10 pairs per township. The best way to find screech owls is to listen for them at woodlot fringes just before dawn or after dusk when it is clear and calm. Both calls, the whinny and the tremolo, can be heard, sometimes from the same bird. Gray and brown color-morphs dominate throughout the county with very few red morphs reported. One red-morph has been resident for several years along the Huron River near St. Joseph Hospital and another, an injured bird rescued in Freedom Twp. (17 September 1989, VB, JS), was later rehabilitated and released (SS). Good spots to find screech owls are Nichols Arboretum, Matthaei Botanical Gardens, Eberwhite Woods, Embury Road, and many woodlots along the Huron River. While screech owls are permanent residents and may call at any time of year, they are most frequently heard in March and April, when they are reestablishing pair bonds and territories.

Great Horned Owl *Bubo virginianus*

Finding code: 3
Common permanent resident

This large nocturnal predator is common throughout the county. Surveys in 1990 and 1991 showed that this species has a nesting density of 3-5 pairs per township. This large owl does not build a nest but primarily uses old Red-tailed Hawk nests, and to a lesser extent old crow and squirrel nests. Not surprisingly the number of pairs of Great Horned Owls is close to (but less than) the number of pairs of Red-tailed Hawks. Roosting Great Horned Owls are sometimes seen during the day sitting quietly at the fringe of woodlots. These roosting owls are sometimes discovered by groups of crows who incessantly "mob" the owl until it is forced to seek shelter.

Hearing a group of crows, with Blue Jay attendants, screaming loudly, or seeing them diving repeatedly at something in a tree or snag, should alert the birdwatcher to the possibility of a Great Horned Owl.

Snowy Owl *Nyctea scandiaca*

Finding code: 8
Rare winter visitor

The arctic-nesting Snowy Owl is a rare visitor to Washtenaw County, but even the novice can recognize the stunning all white adult male, or nearly white adult female. Most people, however, are surprised to see the mottled black and white or dusky-looking juveniles that more frequently winter in southern Michigan. Most years no Snowy Owls venture into Washtenaw County; however, every few years a small number do appear, and these always cause a stir among birdwatchers, photographers, and local newspapers. There is no predictable pattern to the appearance of Snowy Owls in the county, or for how long they will stay. Recent sightings include:

1. 26 November 1980 at the Ann Arbor Airport (SH)
2. March-April 1987 downtown Ann Arbor and UM (MObs)
3. 1 March 1988 North Campus, University of Michigan (MK, SK, AK, DC)
4. January 1991 Central Campus, University of Michigan (MObs)
5. 20-27 March 1991 Central Campus, University of Michigan (MObs)
6. November - 9 December 1991 downtown Ann Arbor (MObs)

Barred Owl *Strix varia*

Finding code: 7
Fairly rare permanent resident
Maximum: 5 calling 6 September 1991 off Noggles Rd.

The booming *who-cooks-for-you* calls of the Barred Owl are no longer commonly heard in the county. Once a more common resident, the Barred Owl is now reduced to a few pairs in the western part of the county. Unlike the Great Horned Owl, which is resident in areas with scattered woodlots, the Barred Owl prefers larger tracts of woods. Typically this species is associated with the Red-shouldered Hawk in closed-canopy woods or densely wooded river bottoms. Places where there is still a chance of locating this rare resident are in the northwest part of the county in the Waterloo Rec Area and Cedar Lake (TSc), south to Manchester (MB).

Long-eared Owl *Asio otus*

Finding code: 8
Rare winter visitor

The Long-eared Owl is a species associated with large conifer stands, which are few and far between in the county. During the years prior to the survey period, there were occasional reports of nesting long-ears, but none has been reported since 1977. Because of their secretive and nocturnal nature there remains the possibility that a pair or two may still exist. Most recent records of the Long-eared Owl are from the Ann Arbor CBC :

1. 12 December 1977 on Cherry Hill Road (M)
2. 27 February 1980 near Saline (EB, RWy)
3. 23 April 1985 near Ann Arbor (JM)
4. 31 December 1986 roadkilled bird at M-52 and Bethel Church Rd. (UMMZ, MB)
5. 3 January 1987 on the Ann Arbor CBC
6. 2 January 1988 on the Ann Arbor CBC
7. 16 December 1989 on the Ann Arbor CBC

Short-eared Owl *Asio flammeus*

Finding code: 8
Rare winter visitor

The Short-eared Owl is a rare winter visitor in the county. This owl is a species of open fallow fields, grassland, and marshes and is commonly regarded as the night-shift counterpart of the Northern Harrier. Both species are highly crepuscular, thus at dawn and dusk either may be seen hunting over appropriate habitat. With dropping light levels the Short-eared Owl takes over the hunt. Short-eared Owls look like giant moths as they hunt for meadow voles, slowly gliding and flapping over the open fields. Most recent records have come from the Ann Arbor CBC:

1. 30 December 1979 on the Ann Arbor CBC
2. 26 January 1980 one in Pittsfield Twp. (MK)
3. 26 November - 20 December 1980 three in the Ann Arbor area (MObs)
4. 20 March 1981 one in Pittsfield Twp. (MK)
5. 17 December 1988 two on the Ann Arbor CBC (JJ)

Northern Saw-whet Owl *Aegolius acadicus*

Finding code: 8
Rare visitor

The Northern Saw-whet Owl is the smallest of Michigan's owls. As it mainly occurs as a nesting species in the northern parts of the state, the May occurence listed below is intriguing. The saw-whet is typically extremely nocturnal in its activities; thus it is rarely encountered without extensive searching. However, the soft *toot-toot-toot* calls of the saw-whet (suggesting the beeping noise of a garbage truck backing up) readily identify this species when heard. Unfortunately for birdwatchers in the southern counties of Michigan, wintering saw-whets rarely call, making them difficult to find. Recent records include:

1. 20 December 1981 on the Ann Arbor CBC (AM)
2. 18 December 1982 roadkilled bird outside of Parker Mill (MK)
3. 25 August 1983 at Iron Creek Mill Pond (MB)
4. 15 May 1987 in the Waterloo Rec Area, Lyndon Twp. (MK, TWi)
5. mid-October 1990 an injured bird collected in Lodi Twp. and later released (SS)
6. 17 January 1991 off Maple Rd. just north of Ann Arbor (MK, RWy)
7. 14 October 1991 an injured bird collected in Pittsfield Twp. and later released (SS)

Order Caprimulgiformes

Family Caprimulgidae (nighthawks and Whip-poor-will)

Common Nighthawk *Chordeiles minor*

Finding code: 3
Common migrant and local summer resident
Spring arrival: 14 May (1988)
Fall departure: 2 October (1988)
Fall maximum: 114 on 5 September 1991 over western Ann Arbor

The *peent* call of the Common Nighthawk starts to become evident around the middle of May, though it is more commonly heard in late May and June. This crepuscular species is now an urban county resident since it has taken to nesting on the flat gravel roofs of commercial buildings. Before many of the campus roofs were "silvered," nighthawks were more common in Ann Arbor (RBP). These birds can be seen swooping for moths and other large insects in downtown Ann Arbor, on the Central Campus of the University of Michigan, on the campus of Eastern Michigan University, and in downtown Ypsilanti. In the fall nighthawks congregate in larger flocks as they begin their southern migration. This fall build-up of feeding and migrating nighthawks is well captured by the histogram, most of the large counts coming from western Ann Arbor in early evening around the end of August. Survey records suggest that the main nighthawk passage is through the eastern half of the county.

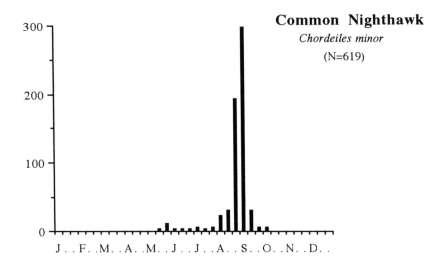

Common Nighthawk

Chordeiles minor

(N=619)

Whip-poor-will *Caprimulgus vociferus*

Finding code: 7
Fairly rare spring migrant and possible summer resident
Spring and summer dates: 28 April (1981) - 30 June (1988)
Spring maximum: 10 on 20 May 1990 in Lyndon Twp.
Fall record: 18 August 1989 at Saginaw Forest

The incessant nightly calling of a Whip-poor-will is now a rare sound in Washtenaw County. Nearly all the recent spring records come from the westernmost tier of townships around the middle of May, particularly from Manchester and Lyndon (SH, MB). There are two records from the summer, June 1978 along Grass Lake Rd. (TSc) and 30 June 1988 along Embury Rd. in Lyndon Twp. (DBr), and one from mid-August at Saginaw Forest (RC). It is possible that Whip-poor-wills may be a little more common than the Finding code indicates because few observers drive the back roads in the evening hoping to hear their remarkable calls.

Order Apodiformes (swifts and hummingbirds)

Family Apodidae (swifts)

Chimney Swift *Chaetura pelagica*

Finding code: 2
Common migrant and locally common summer resident
Spring arrival: 22 April (1989)
Fall departure: 2 November (1987)
Maximum: *c.* 180 on 4 October 1990 over downtown Ann Arbor

Chimney Swifts are a common sight and sound in all the cities and towns of Washtenaw County from late April through late September with few remaining into October. As their name implies, these little cigar-shaped aerial acrobats nest in larger chimneys and have profited from human development. In late August and September the county population is augmented by migrants from further north.

Family Trochilidae (hummingbirds)

Ruby-throated Hummingbird *Archilochus colubris*

Finding code: 5
Fairly uncommon migrant and summer resident
Spring arrival: 17 April (1977)
Fall departure: 28 September (1987)
Maximum: 3 on 12 September 1988 at Winnewanna

This tiny gem of the bird world is not easy to find in Washtenaw County. Its size and zipping flight make it elusive unless it comes to a nectar feeder or brightly colored tubular flowers, although attempts to attract hummingbirds by these means are not always successful. County hummingbirds seem to nest in certain residential areas or in swampy woods. Of the latter type of habitat Sharon Hollow is a fairly reliable location. The Ruby-throated Hummingbird nests widely throughout Michigan, but fall migration records in the county are rather thin. The fact that up to 500 birds a day have been seen passing through Holiday Beach on Lake Erie in mid-September (Kielb 1989) might indicate that the hummingbird fall migration pattern is similar to that of the Broad-winged Hawk.

Order Coraciiformes (kingfishers and allies)

Family Alcedinidae (kingfishers)

Belted Kingfisher *Ceryle alcyon*

Finding code: 4
Fairly common permanent resident

The loud rattling call of the kingfisher is often the first indication of its presence. In the summer and fall it can be found in a variety of habitats — along rivers and streams, in gravel pits (where it can excavate its nesting burrow) and around ponds and lakes of various sizes. In winter it requires open water and so settles around the faster-flowing sections of rivers and streams. There is usually a pair in winter along Fleming Creek in the Matthaei Botanical Gardens. The CBC average of 14 birds a year would suggest that only a minority of the county kingfishers withdraw south for the winter.

Order Piciformes

Family Picidae (woodpeckers)

Woodpeckers are a visible and highly audible part of the avifauna in the county's wooded areas. Most are boldly-patterned black and white birds with some red around the head. They often first announce their presence through their sharp ringing calls or by their drumming on trees. Three species are common in Washtenaw County: the Downy Woodpecker, the Red-bellied Woodpecker and the Northern Flicker, although this last normally withdraws in winter. Less common are the Hairy and Red-headed Woodpeckers, while the Yellow-bellied Sapsucker is a fairly uncommon migrant. Finally, the Black-backed and Pileated Woodpeckers are rare wanderers from further north. In general, woodpeckers in the county seem to be holding their own, aided by maturing woodlots and suet at winter feeders. One threat they face is from the European Starling. The starling is a cavity-nesting bird which does not excavate its own nest. Unfortunately, this aggressive bird is quite successful at evicting woodpeckers from their nest-holes.

Red-headed Woodpecker *Melanerpes erythrocephalus*

Finding code: 5
Fairly uncommon permanent resident, reduced in winter
Maximum: 5 on 21 February 1983 at Iron Creek Mill Pond

The Red-headed Woodpecker is one of the most handsome birds in all North America — indeed, according to Alexander Wilson, "the father of American ornithology," it was the most beautiful of all (Terres 1980). A mid-sized bird flying away showing a stunning white and black contrast is a Red-headed Woodpecker. Although red-heads have been observed every month of the year during the last few years, most appear to withdraw southward in September and return in April. A few may remain during the winter but in fluctuating numbers, perhaps depending on the available supply of acorns. In 1977 a remarkable total of 35 were recorded on the CBC, but since then numbers have sharply declined, only one individual being found (1989) in the last five years. In contrast to the winter picture, the Red-headed Woodpecker seems to be on the increase as a summer resident. Then it tends to occur in more open areas where it frequents the woodland edge, especially around dead, barkless trees, which it uses for nest-holes. Currently the most reliable location is Arkona Road Swamp with up to two nesting pairs.

Red-bellied Woodpecker *Melanerpes carolinus*

Finding code: 2
Common permanent resident
Maximum: 5 on 21 November 1987 at Little Portage Lake

The zebra-backed red-belly is a regular inhabitant of deciduous county woodlots and a common visitor to parks and suburban areas. It will visit suet feeders in cold weather. Its loud *churr* call can be heard at most times of the year, but is most frequent during the nesting period in April and May. In early spring, pairs of Red-bellied Woodpeckers will sometimes pair-bond by tapping gently in rhythm on different trees (Kilham 1983).

Yellow-bellied Sapsucker *Sphyrapicus varius*

Finding code: 5
Fairly uncommon migrant, fairly rare winter visitor
Spring dates: 6 April (1991) - 11 May (1979)
Spring maximum: 6 on 18 April 1989 in Eberwhite Woods
Fall dates: 27 August (1980) - 21 November (1987)
Fall maximum: 3 on 6 October 1991 at Dolph Park

This woodpecker passes through Washtenaw County to and from its nesting areas in the northern Lower Peninsula and further north. The migration peaks most years are the second half of April and late September/early October. In spring migration especially, passage birds tend to move through within a narrow window of about ten days. Spring birds sometimes drill rows of small holes which then exude sap (hence the name). Insects that come to the sap are fed on by the sapsucker. Apparently some individual trees are quite attractive to sapsuckers and are used year after year during migration. There is evidence that this sap is an important food source for the early-arriving Ruby-throated Hummingbirds (Dennis 1981). Occasionally a sapsucker or two attempts to overwinter in the county (recorded on nine of the last 15 CBCs); as often as not, these overwintering birds are odd-looking subadults.

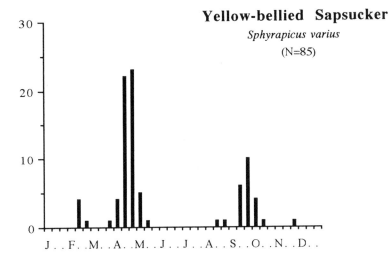

Yellow-bellied Sapsucker
Sphyrapicus varius
(N=85)

Downy Woodpecker *Picoides pubescens*

Finding code: 2
Common permanent resident
Maximum: 6 on 2 July 1988 at Park Lyndon North

The small Downy Woodpecker is a common and widespread county resident, nesting and foraging in a large range of wooded and semi-wooded habitats. This is a tame bird which comes commonly and easily to feeders. Its abundance can be gauged from the fact that the annual average of downies found on the last 15 CBCs exceeds 100 birds.

Hairy Woodpecker *Picoides villosus*

Finding code: 4
Fairly common permanent resident
Maximum: 3 on 17 October 1987 at Saginaw Forest

The Hairy Woodpecker is a larger version of the downy and is best identified by its proportionally much larger bill. As the finding code suggests, the Hairy Woodpecker is much less common than its smaller counterpart. Although it will come to feeders, the hairy is restricted as a nesting species to the larger and more mature woodlots in the county. The CBC average of 16 birds underscores the contrast in numbers with the previous species.

Black-backed Woodpecker *Picoides arcticus*

Finding code: 10
Vagrant

There is a record of a single female of this boreal woodpecker on 24 October 1977 near Delhi Metropark along the Huron River (MK).   It is apparent that in some years a small number of these northern woodpeckers either disperse or migrate south very early in the fall migration.   There are September records for this species from nearby Belle Isle (18 September 1977 MK) and southern Ontario (15 September 1985 AC). Just prior to the survey period there was one spring record from Nichols Arboretum (9-23 April 1975 MObs). Additionally, there are two specimens from the 1880s (Wood 1951) and a sighting of a female on 12 November 1942 in Ypsilanti (Sturgeon 1946). These are the only documented records for the county.

Northern Flicker *Colaptes auratus*

Finding code: 2
Common permanent resident, reduced in winter
Maximum: 15 on several April dates in Nichols Arboretum

The Northern Flicker is a conspicuous bird. It is the largest of the common county woodpeckers, has a ringing call and often forages on open ground near woods. It nests in a wide variety of habitats including large sentinel trees. Most of the county flickers withdraw south in the winter, leaving behind a much diminished population, with an average of 16 on the last 15 Ann Arbor CBCs. However, as the Northern Flicker is a common breeding species throughout the state, county numbers are augmented by migrants in both spring and fall.

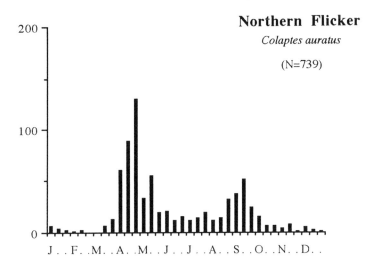

Northern Flicker

Colaptes auratus

(N=739)

Pileated Woodpecker *Dryocopus pileatus*

Finding code: 9
Very rare visitor

The impressive Pileated Woodpecker was a regular part of the county avi-fauna 150 years ago, before the forest clearance. There are four county records prior to the survey period: 15 October 1875 in Lodi Twp., 5 May 1939 at Silver Lake (Wood 1951), 13 February 1949 in the Ann Arbor area (HHa), and October 1976 at Zeeb and Liberty Rds. (RBP). Today, it is restricted to the more extensive woodlands to the north and west of Washtenaw County. However, it seems that occasional fall dispersals of young woodpeckers occur. There are three county sightings during the survey period, all of single birds:

1. 13 November 1977-15 January 1978 around Leslie Golf Course (MK)
2. 25 August 1986 along Huron Parkway (MK)
3. 8 May 1987 at Silver Lake (TWi)

A Pileated Woodpecker has been observed on several occasions in recent years at Kensington Metropark in Oakland County. It is therefore possible that North America's largest woodpecker will one day return to the wooded habitat in the county's northwest corner.

Order Passeriformes (perching birds)

Family Tyrannidae (flycatchers)

Eleven species of flycatchers have been regularly recorded in the county during the survey period. Three of these species breed in the more northerly part of the state and are only seen on migration. The remaining eight all nest in Washtenaw County, although mostly in quite small numbers and in restricted habitats. Flycatchers tend to perch in upright positions on branches from which they sally forth to hawk passing insects. Since they are largely restricted to this source of food, none but the phoebe, which will eat fruits and sometimes stays until November, remain in the county during the colder months. The five small *Empidonax* flycatchers have been given a separate introduction because they present special identification problems.

Olive-sided Flycatcher *Contopus borealis*

Finding code: 6
Uncommon migrant
Spring dates: 7 May (1991) - 26 May (1990)
Spring maximum: only single individuals
Fall dates: 27 July (1988) - 27 September (1990)
Fall maximum: only single individuals

Only small numbers of this uncommon species are seen each year during its passage from Central America to the northern boreal forests of Michigan and Ontario and on its return. As the dates suggest, the olive-sided is a late spring and early fall migrant. Most often it is found perched at the top of a dead snag showing its gray-green vest and (sometimes) its fluffy white tufts on either side of the rump. The *quick, three-beers* call common to the northern bogs is rarely heard in migration. Nichols Arboretum and Dolph Park are two of the more likely locations for finding this species.

Eastern Wood-Pewee *Contopus virens*

Finding code: 2
Common migrant and summer resident
Spring arrival: 3 May (1989)
Fall departure: 28 September (1989)
Fall maximum: 6 on several occasions

Aptly named for its plaintive *pee-a-wee* call, the pewee is the most common flycatcher in both the state and the county. It arrives in early May and departs for Central America in September. In Washtenaw County, pewees spend their summers in relatively open and mature woodlots composed principally of deciduous trees, where they can be heard calling right up to departure. Pewees seem little disturbed by human activity at ground level and so are as common in public woodlots and parks as in more secluded areas. Adults feeding fledged young have been seen as early as mid-June.

Empidonax Flycatchers (Yellow-bellied, Acadian, Alder, Willow, and Least Flycatchers)

As a group the *Empidonax* flycatchers are the most difficult of the flycatchers to identify with certainty on every occasion. Frequently in migration these birds (whose similar appearance strengthens the belief in their close kinship) remain silent, thus leaving them as the frustrating journal entry birdwatchers are all familiar with: Empidonax sp. One local birder (BP) refers to these silent types as the "trappist flycatchers," an appropriate name under the circumstances. With much practice these birds when silent can sometimes be identified with a moderate degree of certainty. An excellent five-part series on the identification of *Empidonax* flycatchers appeared in *Birding* during 1985-1987 (Whitney and Kaufman). When they do vocalize, each species has a distinct call that will quickly separate it from the others, although distinguishing the calls of the willow and alder still remains a problem for some people. Roger Tory Peterson provides some wonderful historic perspective on problems with their identification (Peterson 1987). Birdwatchers should learn the calls and habitat requirements of these species if they intend to locate and differentiate them in the field.

Yellow-bellied Flycatcher *Empidonax flaviventris*

Finding code: 6
Uncommon migrant
Spring dates: 7 May (1982) - 4 June (1988)
Spring maximum: 2 on 16 May 1989 in the Nichols Arboretum
Fall dates: 30 August (1989) - 16 September (1990)
Fall maximum: only individuals

This neotropical migrant is an uncommon summer resident in the swamps and spruce bogs of the Upper Peninsula. On spring migration it is indeed the most yellow of the Empidonax flycatchers, but it tends to stay hidden in the undergrowth or in the shadows of denser woods, as does the greenish Acadian Flycatcher. Its song is comparatively soft and plaintive. The Yellow-bellied Flycatcher is a late migrant and can be most likely found in places like Nichols Arboretum and Park Lyndon during the second half of May.

Acadian Flycatcher *Empidonax virescens*

Finding code: 5
Uncommon migrant and local summer resident
Spring arrival: 11 May (1988)
Fall departure: 28 August (1991)
Maximum: 5 on 19 June 1988 at Sharon Hollow Nature Preserve

The Acadian Flycatcher is a southern species, and Washtenaw County is close to the northern edge of its nesting area. The Acadian is best recognized by its explosive *pit-see* or *wake-up!* (RBP) song. Relatively few migrants are heard, even in Nichols Arboretum or Matthaei Botanical Gardens. As a summer resident, the Acadian Flycatcher requires tall, moist, extensive woodlands and so is largely confined to the westernmost townships. During the summer there are usually a few nesting pairs in the McClure and Loveland Rds area and along Embury Rd. However, in recent years another reliable location for the Acadian Flycatcher has been Sharon Hollow Nature Preserve.

Alder Flycatcher *Empidonax alnorum*

Finding code: 6
Uncommon migrant
Spring dates: 24 April (several years) - 4 June (1988)
Spring maximum: 4 on 18 May 1991 in the Waterloo Rec Area
Fall date: 9 September (1988)

The guidebooks typically describe the song of the Alder as *fee-bee-o,* although the last brief syllable can be difficult to hear, leaving something resembling *free-beer*; an alternate description may be *knee-deep*, as suggested by Payne (ABBM). Even to the ear of experienced listeners the call of the alder is difficult to describe. Small numbers of Alder Flycatchers are heard in migration as they journey north to their swampy nesting grounds in the upper part of the state. Most county records for this flycatcher either come from mature wooded areas like Nichols Arboretum or from swampy areas like the northern end of Loveland Rd. As fall birds are generally silent, useful fall records are sporadic. Although there is confirmed ABBM nesting from Livingston County, the Atlas record for Washtenaw (30 May 1988, Lyndon Twp.), and even the latest spring date recorded (4 June 1988, SH), are not sufficiently late to exclude the possibility that these birds were late migrants. Further study is needed regarding the summer status of this species.

Willow Flycatcher *Empidonax traillii*

Finding code: 4
Fairly common migrant and summer resident
Spring arrival: 5 May (1981)
Fall departure: 16 September (1990)
Maximum: 4 on 23 July 1988 in Chelsea SGA

The Willow Flycatcher has a more southerly nesting area than its look-alike cousin, the Alder Flycatcher. The Willow is a common summer resident in the bottom half of the Lower Peninsula, but rare further north. The *fitz-bew* call of the Willow Flycatcher can be heard through late spring and summer in its preferred habitat of damp areas containing low scrubby willows and bushes.

Least Flycatcher *Empidonax minimus*

Finding code: 2
Common migrant and fairly uncommon summer resident
Spring arrival : 30 April (1981)
Fall departure: 17 September (1989)
Maximum: 7 on 19 May 1980 at the Nichols Arboretum

The Least Flycatcher, called the *che-bec* (or *que-bec* if you are Canadian) for its compressed call, is the most commonly encountered *Empidonax* during the spring and fall migration. As both migrant and summer resident, it favors the same mature woodlots as the Eastern Wood-Pewee. However, the Least Flycatcher is much less common as a summer resident. The ABBM comments, "A reduced status, as first noted by Zimmerman and Van Tyne (1959), is now evident over large areas in southern Michigan." Summering birds have recently been reported from Chelsea SGA and from various locations in the western townships.

Eastern Phoebe *Sayornis phoebe*

Finding code: 5
Fairly uncommon migrant and uncommon summer resident
Spring arrival: 13 March (1989)
Late fall date : 25 October (1989)
Maximum: 6 on 3 October 1987 at Eberwhite Woods

The Eastern Phoebe is the earliest of the flycatchers to return to Washtenaw County and the last to depart. As a migrant the dark-headed, tail-pumping phoebe can be seen in a wide variety of habitats, but as a summer resident it is most likely found near bridges over streams and creeks, since it has the habit of nesting under these man-made structures.

Great Crested Flycatcher *Myiarchus crinitus*

Finding code: 4
Fairly common migrant and summer resident
Spring arrival: 29 April (1989)
Fall departure: 17 September (1980)
Maximum: 10 on 11 May 1985 in the Waterloo Rec Area

This large flycatcher is a woodland bird often first detected by its grating *reep* call and then glimpsed as a flash of yellow and rufous as it snatches a passing insect. Unlike other county flycatchers, it nests in tree cavities and so requires woodlots with large old trees. Within the Ann Arbor area, summering Great Crested Flycatchers can be usually found at Mitchell-Scarlett Woods, Nichols Arboretum, and Eberwhite Woods.

Eastern Kingbird *Tyrannus tyrannus*

Finding code: 3
Common migrant and summer resident
Spring arrival: 28 April (1990)
Fall departure: 26 September (1980)
Maximum: 11 on 24 July 1988 at Saline Wilderness Park

This large flycatcher is the open habitat equivalent of the preceding species. Because of its snappy black-backed and white-bellied appearance and because of its habit of perching in the open (as on utility wires), the kingbird is the most easily encounterable of the county's flycatchers. It gets its name from its "lordly and dominating character" (Gruson 1972:171) including its fearless habit of flying up and harrassing any passing raptor or crow. Its summer territory can include agricultural areas, old fields, roadside edges, and river, lake and pond edges.

Western Kingbird *Tyrannus verticalis*

No accepted records during the survey period; see chapter four

---

Scissor-tailed Flycatcher *Muscivora forficata*

Finding code: 10
Vagrant

There is one record for this spectacular vagrant from the south-central U.S.:
(17 July 1982) for Superior Twp. in the vicinity of M-14 and Gotfredson
Road (MK). The long, streaming tail, unique among nesting avifauna,
makes this one of the easiest to identify of all North American flycatchers.

Family Alaudidae (larks)

Horned Lark *Eremophila alpestris*

Finding code: 4
Fairly common migrant, fairly uncommon resident
Maximum: 63 on 26 January 1988 in Manchester Twp.

In the county, the Horned Lark is a prototypical bird of sparsely vegetated
fields, although it can also be found along roadsides or on short-grass areas.
Ann Arbor Airport is one of the more reliable sites for this interesting
species. Horned Larks occur in small numbers throughout the county all
year, but somewhat larger flocks can be seen during migration. The Horned
Lark is the first spring migrant to return, northward-moving groups being
seen from as early as the second half of January to mid-March. The fall
migration runs from mid-September to mid-November. Young birds have
been seen in the agricultural areas from May to August.

Family Hirundinidae (swallows)

The swallows represent a small group of birds which are constantly on the
wing capturing flying insects. During the summer months all six of the
eastern North American swallow species are scattered across the county,
each to its own rather specialized nesting habitat. The Barn Swallow is the
most uniformly distributed, followed by the Tree Swallow. The remaining
species are more local in their distribution during the nesting season and
require more effort to find. During migration mixed flocks of swallows are
typically encountered over many bodies of water. Cool mornings in May

will produce exciting views of these often difficult-to-observe birds, as they dart close to the water surface in pursuit of low-flying insects. Identifying and counting swallows in mixed flocks can be a challenging, though frustrating experience, as individual birds weave in and out of others.

Purple Martin *Progne subis*

Finding code: 4
Fairly common migrant and local summer resident
Spring arrival: 5 April (1991)
Late fall: 7 September (1985)
Maximum: *c.* 4,500 on 6 August 1980 at a roost in Ann Arbor

The well-known Purple Martin is a common summer resident only in those scattered county locations where martin houses are occupied. Small numbers of migrant martins begin to show up in the county in mid-April. Starting in early July wandering martins can be seen across the county, with migratory roosts starting to form around this time. In late July numbers of martins can be seen migrating south in the early evening, peaking in the second half of August and continuing into early September.

Tree Swallow Tachycineta bicolor

Finding code: 1 (in migration)
Abundant migrant and common summer resident
Spring arrival: 13 March (1986)
Fall departure: 11 October (several years)
Maximum: *c.* 300 on 20 March 1988 at M-14 and Maple Road

The iridescent blue-green of the Tree Swallow is one of the early signs that spring migration is underway. Starting sometimes as early as late March, small numbers of Tree Swallows begin to appear over ponds, lakes and rivers throughout the county. By mid-April migrants are everywhere. A small proportion of this large population remains in the county. In early May Tree Swallows begin setting up territories around hollow stumps, old woodpecker cavities near water and nest boxes. By early June there are young swallows present, sometimes in the same fields with young bluebirds. Tree Swallows are frequently the last of the swallows to depart for the winter with small numbers remaining into October.

Northern Rough-winged Swallow   *Stelgidopteryx serripennis*

Finding code: 4
Fairly common migrant and summer resident
Spring arrival: 14 April (1988)
Fall departure: 15 September (1987)
Maximum: 11 on 9 July 1988 in Sylvan Twp

The rough-wing is the most solitary of the swallows in terms of nesting behavior, although small groups can occasionally be found. This species frequently nests under bridges, but the most effective way to find rough-wings is to search for small gravel pits where they associate with nesting Bank Swallows. Learning the call of this species and that of the Bank Swallow will aid considerably in locating and identifying this less common summer resident.

Bank Swallow   *Riparia riparia*

Finding code: 2
Common migrant and locally abundant summer resident
Spring arrival: 24 April (1987)
Fall departure: 23 September (1988)
Maximum: *c.* 1,600 on 10 August 1990 at Noggles and Kuhl Rds.

The smallest of the county swallows also tends to be among the most social of birds during the nesting season. Bank Swallows are most often observed in numbers at colonies located in sand and gravel pits where they nest colonially in the steep banks. The birds also forage in loose flocks away from the colony over open fields or bodies of water during June and July.

Cliff Swallow   *Hirundo pyrrhonota*

Finding code: 6
Uncommon migrant and summer resident
Spring arrival: 27 April (1988)
Fall departure: 18 August (1991)
Maximum: 18 on 20 July 1991 at the M-14 - Huron River Bridge

The Cliff Swallow, the least common of the swallows to occur in Washtenaw County, is most easily identified by its creamy-colored rump patch. There is no doubt that the Cliff Swallow has suffered from nest disruptions caused by House Sparrows. During the last ten years a small number have nested erratically under the eaves of several barns on farms in Freedom Twp. and elsewhere. In the spring of 1991 small colonies were located under the Huron Parkway and M-14 bridges over the Huron River in Ann Arbor.

Barn Swallow *Hirundo rustica*

Finding code: 1
Abundant migrant and common summer resident
Spring arrival: 7 April (1989)
Fall departure: 8 October (1988)

The brightly-colored, "swallow-tailed" Barn Swallow is second only to the Tree Swallow in numbers on migration. Barn Swallows are also very common summer residents, when they can be seen darting over fields, streams and rivers. They nest under bridges and in barns throughout the county.

Family Corvidae (crows, ravens, and jays)

Gray Jay *Perisoreus canadensis*

Not seen during the survey period; see chapter four

Blue Jay *Cyanocitta cristata*

Finding code: 1
Common permanent resident

The raucous Blue Jay is a common resident and migrant in Washtenaw County, found in almost any habitat from the most urban, such as downtown Ann Arbor, to the most wooded, such as the Waterloo Rec Area.

There is also a large influx of jays in mid-September when northern birds pass through the county. Blue Jays are known for their mobbing of hawks and owls, at which times 10-20 birds may congregate. The Ann Arbor CBC annually tallies over 300 jays.

Black-billed Magpie *Pica pica*

Not seen during the survey period; see chapter four

American Crow *Corvus brachyrhynchos*

Finding code: 1
Common permanent resident

The American Crow is one of the most abundant species in North America, Washtenaw County included. This large black noisy permanent resident can often be seen in large numbers outside of the nesting season (late May - early August) of the year. Their ubiquitous nature extends to their nesting, where they use a multitude of habitats, from the large pines on the University of Michigan campus in Ann Arbor and residential areas within Ann Arbor to the most wooded areas of the county. American Crows form large fall and winter roosts, sometimes composed of hundreds of individuals. For many years a large roost has been located annually in the Forest Hill Cemetery at Observatory and Geddes, adjacent to the Nichols Arboretum in Ann Arbor, with another roost located near the Ann Arbor landfill. These large flocks pass over downtown Ann Arbor at dawn and dusk in the fall and winter.

Common Raven *Corvus corax*

Not seen during the survey period; see chapter four

Family Paridae (titmice and chickadees)

Black-capped Chickadee *Parus atricapillus*

Finding code: 1
Common permanent resident

Because of its habit of nesting close to human habitation and visiting feeders readily, the Black-capped Chickadee is one of the best known and best liked of the common year-round residents. Chickadees are also common in mixed species flocks, where other species follow them through the woods. Therefore, flocks of chickadees should be examined to see if less common species are accompanying them.

Boreal Chickadee *Parus hudsonicus*

Finding code: 9
Very rare visitor

Boreal Chickadees are rare visitors in Michigan's Lower Peninsula from their permanent range in the north. Prior to the survey period there are records of a single bird on 9 December 1951 from Ann Arbor (JV) (Burrows 1954), two at a feeder on 2 December 1951 and at least five at a feeder on 5 December 1951 (O'Reilly 1954). From November 1972 through February 1973 there were numerous sightings in the Ann Arbor area. A maximum of six were at a feeder in Dexter (6 November 72 WAS), three at a feeder in Ann Arbor (11 November 72 PR), and seven on 30 December 72 (Ann Arbor CBC). There are only two county records during the survey period:

1. 22 November 1977 at Matthaei Botanical Gardens (MK)
2. 2 April 1982 on Central Campus, University of Michigan (MK)

Tufted Titmouse *Parus bicolor*

Finding code: 2
Common permanent resident

The Tufted Titmouse is a common woodland resident in Washtenaw County, readily identifiable by its soft gray plumage, crested head, and large dark eyes. Though they are much more visible in the winter, when large numbers are seen at feeders, the titmouse is a widespread permanent resident. Among its great variety of calls the best known is the frequently heard *peter, peter, peter.* Many large woods have titmice present throughout the year.

Family Sittidae (nuthatches)

Red-breasted Nuthatch *Sitta canadensis*

Finding code: 4
Fairly common migrant and winter resident
Fall arrival: 1 September (1977)
Spring departure: 20 May (1990)
Maximum: 18 on 14 November 1987 at Stinchfield Woods

The movements of this small nuthatch are somewhat erratic, but in most years it can be found in the county from October to early April. It has been recorded in fairly small numbers, an average of 13, on all of the last 15 Ann Arbor CBCs. Although the Red-breasted Nuthatch can occur in many of the county's wooded habitats, the most reliable location is the extensive pine plantations of Stinchfield Woods. The status of this bird in summer is uncertain. Small parties have been heard during July-August at the above site, adults with young have been seen at Saginaw Forest (RC), and there was a nesting attempt in the Matthaei Botanical Gardens (NF, RF). The soft *toot toot* of the red-breast quickly alerts the birdwatcher to its presence.

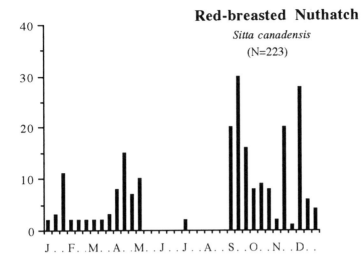

Red-breasted Nuthatch

Sitta canadensis

(N=223)

White-breasted Nuthatch *Sitta carolinensis*

Finding code: 2
Common permanent resident

The White-breasted Nuthatch is a common woodland species in the county and tends to be found in association with those other common residents, the Tufted Titmouse and the Black-capped Chickadee. Like the other two species, the White-breasted Nuthatch also inhabits residential areas and visits feeders in winter. This is the common gray and white bird that calls *yank, yank* and works its way *up or down* the tree trunk for food. Like the woodpeckers, it nests in tree cavities.

Family Certhiidae (creepers)

Brown Creeper   *Certhia americana*

Finding code: 3 (in migration)
Common migrant, uncommon in winter
Fall arrival: 14 September (1991)
Spring departure: 3 May (1988)
Maximum: 16 on 25 April 1984 in Nichols Arboretum

The Brown Creeper is more a migrant and less a winter visitor than the Red-breasted Nuthatch; indeed the histogram shows a clear migration peak in April and a less obvious one in October. The Creeper, often first detected by its thin wispy call, can be seen spiraling up a tree trunk then flitting to the base of a nearby tree to repeat this foraging behavior. The Creeper's cryptic coloring and soft vocalizations result in its being overlooked by inexperienced birdwatchers. According to the ABBM, the Brown Creeper is an uncommon nesting species throughout the state except in the south-ernmost counties. There is one ABBM record of a summering creeper in Augusta Township in 1983 and a presurvey record from 26 June 1969 at Morgan's Woods (NS, MS). Further examination of suitable habitat such as Stinchfield Woods may turn up other summer records.

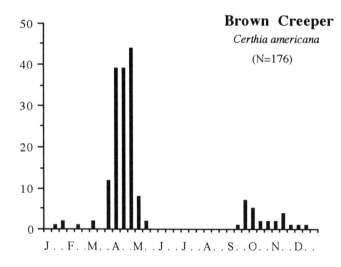

Brown Creeper
Certhia americana
(N=176)

Family Troglodytidae (wrens)

The wrens are a group of small brown birds with cocked tails. They sing energetically from the cover which they typically frequent. Five species currently occur in Washtenaw County, although the Sedge Wren is rare. The House Wren is a common summer resident known to nearly all, while the Marsh Wren is a declining species, which nests among the cattails. The tiny Winter Wren passes through quickly on migration, and the Carolina Wren ekes out a precarious existence as a permanent resident.

Carolina Wren *Thryothorus ludovicianus*

Finding code: 6
Uncommon permanent resident

Washtenaw County is on the northern edge of the range of this large wren. Since it is a permanent resident it experiences cyclic population peaks and troughs that are caused by the varying severity of successive winters. The population of Carolina Wrens in southeastern Michigan (and nearly all of the Midwest for that matter) crashed after the cold snowy winters of 1977-1978 and 1978-1979. The majority of midwestern Carolina Wrens failed to survive, leaving a few scattered pairs and individuals. In the ensuing years there were very few sightings in Washtenaw County. Starting in the mid-1980s Carolina Wrens were once again being heard. As of 1991 the Carolina Wren had re-established itself as a small part of the resident avifauna in the county; for example in just the greater Ann Arbor area there are about 15 pairs, with confirmed nests in 1990 (SHo) and 1991 (DG, JG). Territories have been scattered from Matthaei Botanical Gardens in the east to Tubbs Rd. in the west (PF).

Bewick's Wren *Thryomanes bewickii*

Not recorded during the survey period; see chapter four

House Wren *Troglodytes aedon*

Finding code: 2
Common migrant and summer resident
Early spring: 7 April (1986)
Late fall: 30 September (1980)

The bubbly song of the House Wren echoes throughout the county from late-April through September. It is a common migrant in the woods, cities, and hedgerows in every township of the county. The nesting population of this wren is amazingly large, with pairs located in virtually every city block in the county as well as an equal number of pairs in a variety of rural habitats.

Winter Wren *Troglodytes troglodytes*

Finding code: 4
Fairly common migrant
Spring dates: 29 March (1991) - 9 May (1988)
Spring maximum: 3 on 29 March 1991 in Nichols Arboretum
Fall dates: 22 September (1990) - 15 October (1989)

The Winter Wren is the smallest and most stub-tailed of the North American wrens (the Wren of Europe is the same species). While the outpouring song of this tiny bird can be heard in the northern LP and in the UP, where it nests, it is only heard occasionally in early morning on spring migration in Washtenaw County. The Winter Wren typically passes through rather quickly during the middle of April and in late September and early October. Silent birds are most commonly found around tangles, snags, and fallen logs on the forest floor. Eberwhite Woods is a fairly regular location for finding this narrow-window migrant. Occasionally Winter Wrens linger until the end of the year, having been found on four of the last 15 Ann Arbor CBCs. A record of two on 16 February 1978 in the woods adjacent to the Leslie Golf Course (MK) probably represents over-wintering birds.

Sedge Wren *Cistothorus platensis*

Finding code: 8
Rare migrant and very rare summer resident

According to numerous reports, the Sedge Wren is an increasingly uncommon nesting species in Michigan. Originally an inhabitant of wet prairies and sedge meadows, since the early 1800s it has apparently also adopted wet pastures and lush hayfields as nesting sites (ABBM). However, there are no Atlas records for Washtenaw County, although there are some for adjacent Jackson and Livingston Counties. The sparse recent records are:

1. Summer 1978 in Lodi Twp. (DH)
2. 16 September 1979 in Pittsfield Twp. (MK)
3. 23 July 1981 at the Ann Arbor Airport (RWy, BWy)
4. 18 May - 26 July 1982 with a maximum of three at the Ann Arbor Airport (RW)
5. 9 May 1983 in Manchester Twp. (MB)
6. 16 September 1986, a group of three, including one singing, near the Matthaei Botanical Gardens (JS)
7. 13 May 1989 in Northfield Twp. (RW)

Marsh Wren *Cistothorus palustris*

Finding code: 6
Uncommon migrant and summer resident
Spring arrival: 16 May (1989)
Fall departure: 5 September (1988)
Maximum: 6 on 28 June 1988 along the Huron River near Wagner Rd.

The Marsh Wren remains a fairly common species in the most extensive cattail marshes in the state. However, there are relatively few such marshes left in Washtenaw County, the largest being at the Chelsea SGA where birds can be still be seen and heard (especially in the early morning and late evening) along the reedy edges of the lake. Elsewhere the situation is more worrying. The Marsh Wren, present since 1983, now seems gone from the Wolff Road Marsh at Iron Creek Mill Pond, probably because of the purple loosestrife which has taken over the area. Numbers have been declining at the cattail marsh on the Huron River near Wagner Rd. Six were heard singing in 1988, but only two in 1991; in this case water quality in Honey Creek and human disturbance may be factors. The future status of the Marsh Wren in Washtenaw County thus seems at present to be an unsettled one. There is little evidence available of migration through the county.

Family Muscicapidae

Subfamily Sylviininae (old world warblers, kinglets, and gnatcatchers)

Golden-crowned Kinglet *Regulus satrapa*

Finding code: 1
Abundant migrant and common winter visitor
Early fall: 24 September (1980)
Late spring: 16 May (1989)
Maximum: 75 on 9 April 1980 in Nichols Arboretum

This tiny passerine is frequently found in large numbers in wooded areas in late March and early April. The Golden-crowned Kinglet nests throughout the upper LP and UP in Michigan, then reappears in October and November when many pass through the county headed south (see histogram). A small (sometimes large) number of Golden-crowned Kinglets overwinter in the county and frequently are found with wandering bands of chickadees, titmice, nuthatches and woodpeckers, although they do not typically frequent feeders.

Ruby-crowned Kinglet *Regulus calendula*

Finding code: 2
Common migrant
Spring dates: 7 April (1991) - 19 May (1990)
Spring maximum: 56 on 18 April 1982 at Nichols Arboretum
Fall dates: 22 September (1990) - 24 November (1989)
Fall maximum: 9 on 8 October 1988 at Stinchfield Woods

The Ruby-crowned Kinglet is a very common early spring and fall migrant that can be confused with some of the drably-plumaged warblers or vireos. One useful indicator is the ruby-crown's habit of flicking its wings. Large numbers of kinglets occur in Washtenaw County in April and early May, when they closely associate with Black-capped Chickadees and Yellow-rumped Warblers. During their early passage, ruby-crowns are frequently found in flocks with Golden-crowned Kinglets. However, the ruby-crown is typically later in spring and earlier in the fall than the golden-crown (see histogram). In the fall the county is again inundated with large numbers of kinglets passing through headed south. They have been found on six of the last 15 Ann Arbor CBCs, with a maximum of two birds. Additionally, there is one summer record and probable nesting attempt from 23 June 1976 (RS, UMMZ).

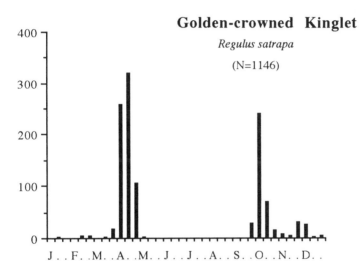

Golden-crowned Kinglet

Regulus satrapa

(N=1146)

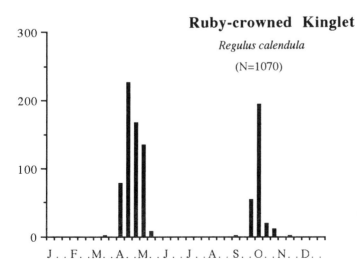

Ruby-crowned Kinglet

Regulus calendula

(N=1070)

Blue-gray Gnatcatcher *Polioptila caerulea*

Finding code: 3
Common spring migrant and fairly common summer resident
Early spring: 17 April (1982)
Late fall: 9 September (1989)
Maximum: 5 on several dates in both spring and summer

The Blue-gray Gnatcatcher is a common early to mid-spring migrant, peaking in early May. The wheezy calls of the gnatcatcher are frequently heard at the beginning of the early movement of migrant warblers. Gnatcatchers nest in reasonable numbers in wooded habitat, sometimes close to water. Fleming Creek in Matthaei Botanical Gardens is a reliable and accessible location. There is little evidence of fall migrants from other areas of the southern Lower Peninsula.

Subfamily Turdinae (thrushes)

The subfamily Turdinae contains the Eastern Bluebird, American Robin and the "brown thrushes." The first two species suffered greatly from the introduction of DDT in the late 1940s but have since recovered well. Both species are largely migratory in Washtenaw County, even though small numbers of bluebirds and robins over-winter in suitable habitat. Robins and bluebirds are relatively easy to find and identify (see species accounts). The "brown thrushes" (Veery, Wood, Hermit, Swainson's, and Gray-cheeked Thrush) are highly migratory woodland birds with quiet movements and skulking habits (unlike robins) They are justly famous for their flute-like songs. With the exception of the Hermit Thrush, which winters in the southern U.S. and Mexico, they are all neotropical migrants. All five of these species may occur in the same woodlots during the course of the spring migration but at somewhat different times: the Hermit Thrush is the first to arrive in the spring, and the Swainson's Thrush typically the last. The relative frequency of these migrants in the county seems to depend in part on whether the observer relies on song or sight identification. In the extensive woods of Nichols Arboretum, especially in early morning, all of the brown thrushes — except for the Gray-cheeked — regularly sing on spring passage. Relative frequencies based on song are: Swainson's (10), Wood (5), Veery (2), Hermit (2), and Gray-cheeked (>1). However, in the smaller and more open woodlot at Eberwhite Woods only the Wood Thrush sings regularly, the Veery sometimes and the Hermit and Swainson's rarely. Sight observations at this location would suggest the following relative frequencies: Hermit (10), Swainson's (6), Wood (2), Veery (2), and Gray-cheeked (>1). If these two sources of information are amalgamated, we can see that the Swainson's and Hermit Thrush are common on spring migration, the Wood Thrush fairly common, the Veery rather uncommon, and the Gray-cheeked Thrush rare. Some Wood Thrushes and a few Veerys remain in the county to nest, the other three passing on to the northern forests. The two summer residents are thought to be declining in Washtenaw County and elsewhere in southern Michigan. Droege (1988) documents a decline in Wood Thrush numbers averaging about 5% per year since 1966. The Veery's decline in the county could be attributed to the decrease in wet wooded areas, the Wood Thrush's to further fragmentation of woodlots and increased parasitism by cowbirds. However, all the brown thrushes are at additional risk because of cutting of forests on their tropical wintering grounds and possibly from the effects of acid rain on their boreal nesting woods.

Eastern Bluebird *Sialia sialis*

Finding code: 4
Fairly common permanent resident, reduced in winter
Maximum: 15 on 28 September 1983 at Hudson Mills

The Eastern Bluebird represents one of the best examples of the combination of human intervention and bird survival. A series of complex factors led to the precipitous decline in the Eastern Bluebird population of the eastern United States, with Washtenaw County being no exception. These farmland birds were seriously affected by the introduction of DDT, the cutting of old dead trees and stumps and competition for existing nest cavities with the aggressive European Starling. By the 1960s the Eastern Bluebird population in Washtenaw County had dwindled to its historic low. In response to this crisis, natural history organizations, Audubon Societies, park authorities, Boy Scout troops, and energetic individuals started making bluebird houses and setting up and maintaining bluebird trails. During the next 20 years the bluebird population grew steadily until in 1991 the population is again healthy, although not at pre-DDT levels. Several successful trails exist in the Ann Arbor area, such as at Matthaei Botanical Gardens and County Farm Park. Migrant birds begin to reappear in the county in late February, with most returning in March and departing in October. There has been a steady increase in numbers of over-wintering birds on the Ann Arbor CBC.

Veery *Catharus fuscescens*

Finding code: 5
Fairly uncommon migrant and fairly rare summer resident
Spring dates: 28 April (1990) - 26 May (several years)
Spring maximum: 6 on 20 May 1990 in Eberwhite Woods
Fall dates: 12 August (1979) - 30 September (several years)
Fall maximum: 2 on 4 September 1988 in Eberwhite Woods

The Veery is the most rufous and least speckled of the brown thrushes. Its song can be likened to taking a vacuum cleaner hose and spinning it round the head, first fast twice and then slower twice. The Veery is now only Code 5 on spring and fall migration, the numbers of migrant birds having dropped substantially during the last 15 years. The main Veery migration coincides with that of the warblers (mid-May and mid-September). Currently, there are only a few pairs of Veerys nesting in the county, principally in boggy wooded habitat. Recent summer records are from Bruin Lake, Embury Rd., Noggles Rd., and Sharon Hollow Nature Preserve.

Gray-cheeked Thrush *Catharus minimus*

Finding code: 6
Uncommon migrant
Spring dates: 1 May (1984) - 26 May (several years)
Spring maximum: 3 on 6 May 1984
Fall dates: 3 September (1990) - 5 October (1990)
Fall maximum: only single sightings

This moderately speckled brown thrush has always been an uncommon transient in Lower Michigan as it makes its way to and from its nesting range in Canada (Wood 1951). Early spring migrants are often quiet, and the small number that do sing tend to be heard only in the second half of May. As a clear look at the head is needed to distinguish this species from the much more common Swainson's Thrush, the numbers passing through the county may be a little higher than the rather sparse records indicate. The Gray-cheeked Thrush occurs in the same wooded habitat as the other migrant brown thrushes.

Swainson's Thrush *Catharus ustulatus*

Finding code: 3
Common migrant
Spring dates: 27 April (1983) - 29 May (1989)
Spring maximum: 11 on 16 May 1979 at Nichols Arboretum
Fall dates: 31 July (1986) - 2 October (1988)
Fall maximum: 5 on 4 September 1988 at South Seventh St., Ann Arbor

This and the following species are the two most common migrant brown thrushes in the county. Swainson's Thrushes are regular in many woodlots throughout much of May and September. During peak migration (see histogram) they can also be seen in parks, yards and gardens. Fall birds can be identified by the soft popping sound they make, like a drop of water falling into a pool. Although the Swainson's Thrush remains a common migrant, its numbers, especially on spring migration, seem to be decreasing.

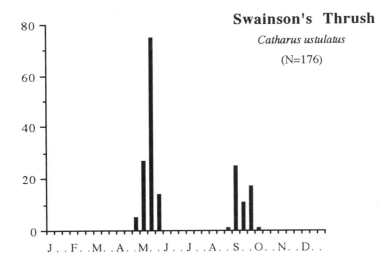

Swainson's Thrush
Catharus ustulatus
(N=176)

Hermit Thrush *Catharus guttatus*

Finding code: 3
Common migrant and fairly rare winter visitor
Spring dates: 7 April (1989) - 16 May (1979)
Spring maximum: 7 on 11 April 1990 in Eberwhite Woods
Fall dates: 23 September (1988) - 3 November (1987)
Fall maximum: 5 on several occasions in October

Of all the brown thrushes the Hermit Thrush is best able to tolerate colder weather. It winters in the southern U.S. and its breeding range includes the northern half of the state of Michigan. This is the first of the brown thrushes to arrive and the last to depart. As the histogram shows, the Hermit Thrush is common in the county in April and October. The best opportunity for hearing the justly-famous song of the Hermit Thrush is to visit Nichols Arboretum early on an April morning. Hermit Thrushes sing less regularly in other locations and at other times of the day, but silent birds can be identified by their habit of raising their rufous tails. A small number of Hermit Thrushes regularly linger in the county into December, and there are a few recent records from January and February. Over-wintering birds are most likely to be found in dense woods with flowing streams. There have been winter sightings in the last three years from Nichols Arboretum, Matthaei Botanical Gardens and the wet woods at Parker Mill County Park.

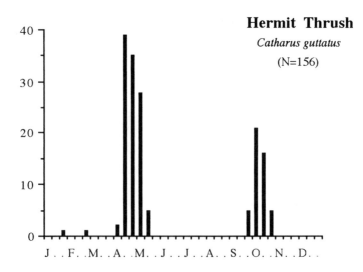

Hermit Thrush
Catharus guttatus
(N=156)

Wood Thrush *Hylocichla mustelina*

Finding code: 4
Fairly common migrant and summer resident
Spring arrival: 7 April (1981)
Fall departure: 6 October (1979)
Maximum: 14 on 14 May 1979 in Nichols Arboretum

In the last 15 years the Wood Thrush has experienced the most dramatic decline of any of the neotropical migrants in Washtenaw County. At the beginning of the survey period single-day counts in May of 6-10 birds were quite common in Nichols Arboretum; by the end counts of more than two had become rare. Comparable declines have been noted on fall migration. While this large woodland thrush can still be found nesting in certain secluded woodlots throughout the county, it is now absent from many of the places where it used to occur regularly as a summer resident.

American Robin *Turdus migratorius*

Finding code: 1
Abundant permanent resident, reduced in winter

The American Robin (Michigan's state bird) is one of the most abundant species in Washtenaw County from March to October. In the Ann Arbor area, after the House Sparrow and starling, the robin used to be the most numerous summer resident (with about 3,700 pairs) until recently overtaken by the expanding House Finch (MK). Most people rightly see robins as early harbingers of spring, as they begin to arrive in the county in early March. However, there are a few small groups of hardy birds that manage to winter in the county by changing their diets from insects and worms to berries. Naturally enough these small flocks — typically 5-15 birds, but sometimes more — tend to congregate where winter berries are plentiful, as is usually the case at Matthaei Botanical Gardens. These birds may be associated with large flocks of Cedar Waxwings and small numbers of Yellow-rumped Warblers. In winter the American Robin is probably a code 5 species.

Family Mimidae (mockingbirds, thrashers, and catbirds)

Gray Catbird *Dumetella carolinensis*

Finding code: 3
Common migrant and summer resident
Spring arrival: 4 May (1988)
Fall departure: 15 October (1989)
Maximum: 11 on 22 September 1990 at Dolph Park

The Gray Catbird is the most common of the mimids that occur in Washtenaw County. Throughout the spring and summer its cat-like mews and long strings of mimicked phrases can be heard emanating from tangles throughout the county. The catbird is equally at home in rural and urban areas. There are two records of catbirds in the winter on the Ann Arbor CBC. The most recent sighting was of an individual associated with a large flock of American Robins and Cedar Waxwings, all eating berries in dense thickets at Matthaei Botanical Gardens (17 December 1988 MK, SK).

Northern Mockingbird *Mimus polyglottos*

Finding code: 7
Fairly rare resident and visitor

There are very few county records for this operatic southern mimic. Southern Michigan is at the northern limit of its range, though records exist as far north as Whitefish Point in the Upper Peninsula. The distribution throughout the state is best described as patchy. During the early part of the survey period several birds seemed to be resident in the greater Ann Arbor area (Payne 1983), but these have been absent for years (MK). Four earlier records are from 1948-1950 (Burrows 1954). For several years a pair nested in adjacent Wayne County at the Willow Run Airport (nest located on 3 July 1988, MK, SK). Sightings of this pair may have been mistakenly credited to Washtenaw County leading to a probable breeding record (ABBM). The county records during the survey period suggest that the Northern Mockingbird is becoming increasingly rare and approaching Finding code 8. The details are:

1. 7 November 1978 at Thurston NC (LM)
2. 17 December 1978 on the Ann Arbor CBC
3. 30 December 1979 on the Ann Arbor CBC
4. 3 February 1980 at Thurston NC (AD, JJ)
5. 23 November 1980 in Ypsilanti (DBe, WBe)
6. 10 April 1981 at Gallup Park (MSm)
7. 20 December 1982 two on the Ann Arbor CBC
8. 13 March 1983 in Ypsilanti Twp. (JJ)
9. 21 May 1983 outside Nichols Arboretum (TW)
10. 22 July 1986 north side of Ann Arbor (DC)
11. 30 April 1987 at Matthaei Botanical Gardens (MK)
12. 7 May 1987 at Searles Nature Preserve (JS, VB)
13. 22 April 1989 in Lodi Twp. (SSl)
14. 2 June 1990 at the Ann Arbor Airport (BP)

Brown Thrasher *Toxostoma rufum*

Finding code: 5
Fairly uncommon migrant and summer resident
Spring arrival: 4 April (1988)
Fall departure: 21 September (1991)
Maximum: 2 on several occasions

This large mimid, which in plumage resembles a thrush, is not easy to find in Washtenaw County either as a migrant or as a summer resident. Indeed its relative scarcity is underscored by the fact that the annual average found on the May Bird Count since 1986 is under five individuals. Thrasher numbers have declined substantially in the county during the survey period. While thrashers can turn up on migration in many different kinds of habitat, as a county nesting species they seem most likely to occur in secondary growth adjacent to weedy fields. Spring males sometimes can be found singing from the tops of small trees. There are two recent winter records: 8 February 1978 and 4 January 1986 (1985 CBC).

Family Motacillidae (wagtails and pipits)

American Pipit   *Anthus rubescens*

Finding code: 7
Fairly rare migrant
Spring dates: 24 March (1979) - 5 May (1990)
Spring maximum: 7 on 24 March 1979 at an unrecorded location
Fall dates: 29 September (1989) - 27 October (1990)
Fall maximum: 35 on 27 October 1990 at Steinbach and Pleasant Lake Rds.

The American Pipit was recently recognized as a distinct species, separated from the Water Pipit (*Anthus spinoletta* of Eurasia), the name by which it had been known. This earlier name is more indicative of its typical habitat: shoreline, mudflat, bare field and short grass. The American Pipit is an irregular migrant in Washtenaw County on its way to the Arctic tundra. It is absent some years, uncommon in others. Numbers on spring migration are small, but larger flocks can sometimes be encountered in fall. Nearly all recent sightings have come from shorebirding areas.

Family Bombycillidae (waxwings)

Bohemian Waxwing   *Bombycilla garrulus*

Not seen during the survey period; see chapter four

Cedar Waxwing   *Bombycilla cedrorum*

Finding code: 3
Common permanent resident, locally abundant in the winter
Maximum: 210 on 12 January 1981 at Matthaei Botanical Gardens

The Cedar Waxwing is a common permanent resident in Washtenaw County. From September until April Cedar Waxwings occur in small to large flocks, concentrating in areas with rich berry crops such as Matthaei Botanical Gardens. During the nesting season small colonies of up to ten pairs can be found scattered throughout the county. These sites typically change from year to year. Starting in late summer Cedar Waxwings can be common along rivers and streams, feeding on flying insects.

Family Laniidae (shrikes)

Northern Shrike *Lanius excubitor*

Finding code: 7
Fairly rare migrant and winter visitor

Called the butcher bird (as are other shrike species) for its tendency to hang its dead prey from barbed wire, hawthorn spines or crotches, the Northern Shrike is a fairly rare winter visitor to the county. The Northern Shrike is a resident of the far north and does not nest in the state. As with many northern species which rarely venture into southern Michigan, Northern Shrikes are somewhat erratic in their appearance. There have been 13 records during the survey period apart from the Ann Arbor CBC. Recent non-CBC records include:

1. 19 December 1977 on Platt Rd. (MSc)
2. 30 January 1978 at Nixon and Dhu Varen Rds. (MK)
3. 7 February 1978 in the North Campus area (MK)
4. 10 December 1978 at Warren Woods (AD, JJ)
5. 8 October 1981 off Fuller Rd. (RWy)
6. 4 November 1984 in northwest Ann Arbor (MK)
7. 30 November 1984 in Ypsilanti Twp. (MK)
8. 11 January 1987 at Liberty and Wagner Rds. (DC)
9. 1 January 1989 in the Waterloo Rec Area (DBr)
10. 17 January 1989 at Huron Park (DC)
11. 14-27 February 1990 at Independence Lake (MB)
12. 15 February 1990 in Manchester Twp. (MB)
13. 8-9 February 1991 at County Farm Park (MObs)

Loggerhead Shrike *Lanius ludovicianus*

No sightings during the survey period; see chapter four

Family Sturnidae   (starlings)

European Starling *Sturnus vulgaris*

Finding code: 1
Abundant permanent resident

This noisy gregarious bird is an introduced species which first reached Washtenaw County in 1924 (Wood 1951). Since then it has adapted all too well to the mixed habitat of the county and has become equally common in urban and rural areas. Starlings gather in large flocks in the fall together with blackbirds. They nest in cavities and are often successful at taking nesting sites away from woodpeckers, bluebirds, Purple Martins and even screech owls. Starlings are accomplished mimics, and county birds imitate the vocalizations of many species, including Eastern Meadowlark (frequently), Killdeer (often) and Red-bellied Woodpecker (occasionally).

Family Vireonidae (vireos)

Vireos are visitors to Washtenaw County from Latin America, occurring here as migrants or also as summer residents. Vireos are broadly similar to warblers, but they are a little larger, somewhat slower-moving and have stouter bills. They are mostly woodland birds. Their songs tend to be sequences of slurred whistles. The Solitary and Philadelphia Vireos pass through the county on their way to and from their nesting grounds in the northern forests. The four other regular county vireos (Warbling, Red-eyed, Yellow-throated and White-eyed) nest in numbers varying from several pairs to hundreds.

White-eyed Vireo *Vireo griseus*

Finding code: 6
Uncommon and local summer resident
Spring arrival: 24 April (1979)
Fall departure: 15 September (1987)
Maximum: 6 on 6 July 1989 at Matthaei Botanical Gardens

The White-eyed Vireo is the least common of the regular vireos in the county. Unlike most vireos, which tend to be mid-tree-height to upper-canopy birds, the White-eyed Vireo is an understory skulker of scrub habitat. Although it has a distinctive song, it can be very hard to observe; and when the observer eventually does so, he or she is more likely to notice the golden spectacles rather than the white iris for which this species is named. Historically small numbers of White-eyed Vireos have occurred in Washtenaw County since 1928 when a female was discovered near Ann Arbor on 13 May (AT, UMMZ). Additional birds were discovered on 7 May 1944 (HHa), 3 May 1947 (RB), 3 May 1955 (CF, RS, DZ), a pair nest-building 12-16 May 1957 (MObs) and one bird at Nichols Arboretum 8 May 1970 (PD). In recent years there are usually a few scattered reports of this southern vireo from around the county in May. Thereafter sightings away from Matthaei Botanical Gardens are unusual. In the Gardens themselves, there is traditionally a small group of summer residents (up to four pairs) with a maximum of six singing males located on 6 July 1989 (MK). The birds are most regular in the vicinity of Fleming Creek, and there are several recent nest records.

Bell's Vireo *Vireo bellii*

Finding code: 9
Vagrant

There is a tiny nesting population of this western vireo located in Berrien County in the extreme southwest of the state. There are two records of this vagrant for Washtenaw County during the survey period and just one further historical record (27 May 1968 in Ann Arbor UMMZ), all during May:

1. 13 May 1980 in Nichols Arboretum (MK)
2. 23 May 1990 in Nichols Arboretum (TW, RWy)

Solitary Vireo *Vireo solitarius*

Finding code: 4
Fairly common migrant
Spring dates: 25 April (1990) - 20 May (1979)
Spring maximum: 7 on 12 May 1982 at Nichols Arboretum
Fall dates: 29 August (1988) - 8 October (1989)
Fall maximum: 2 on several occasions

This hooded vireo with white "spectacles" is typically the first of the family to arrive in the county in spring. As a result, during the last week of April and the first week of May the solitary is the most common vireo in the area. As a migrant, the Solitary Vireo can be found in either deciduous or coniferous woods, but during the nesting season it is typically a resident of the latter. There is one recent nesting record of this northern vireo for the county. Two adults were seen feeding a fledgling in the pines of Stinchfield Woods on 2 July 1988 (VB, JS). During fall migration the Solitary Vireo is most common around the middle of September.

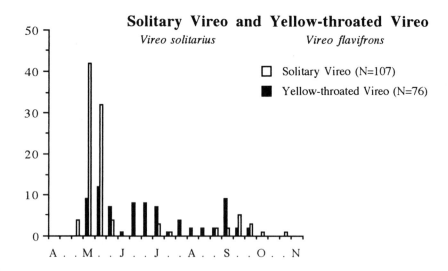

Yellow-throated Vireo *Vireo flavifrons*

Finding code: 4
Fairly common migrant and summer resident
Spring arrival: 28 April (1989)
Fall departure: 23 September (1980)
Maximum: 5 on 8 September 1991 in Nichols Arboretum

The throaty song of the Yellow-throated Vireo is heard from the treetops of woods with dense tall trees. It usually arrives around the tenth of May and departs during the first week of September. Generally, this striking vireo is an uncommon migrant, but some years it can be more frequent, such as in 1987 when 33 were recorded on the Ann Arbor May Bird Count. Small numbers spend the summer nesting in some of the county's mature deciduous woods. There are recent records from Waterloo Rec Area, Sharon Hollow Nature Preserve and Chelsea SGA. Although the ABBM findings suggest this species has been increasing in Michigan, it is by no means clear that this pattern applies to Washtenaw County.

Warbling Vireo *Vireo gilvus*

Finding code: 3
Common migrant and summer resident
Spring arrival: 26 April (1990)
Fall departure: 29 September (1980)
Maximum: 5 on 19 May 1990 at Dolph Park

This very plain species is currently the most widely distributed vireo in the county. It usually arrives in the first week of May, a few days ahead of the Red-eyed Vireo. The long song of the Warbling Vireo is frequent along tree-lined roads, streams and railroad tracks, which comprise its main nesting habitat in the county. Several pairs nest in Matthaei Botanical Gardens near the east end of the main parking lot and near the trails on the west side of the pond. The fall migration pattern of this unobtrusive species is not clear.

Philadelphia Vireo *Vireo philadelphicus*

Finding code: 6
Uncommon migrant
Spring dates: 6 May (1981) - 30 May (several years)
Spring maximum: 3 on 14 May 1988 at Nichols Arboretum
Fall dates: 25 August (1986) - 1 October (1981)
Fall maximum: 5 on 25 August 1986 at Matthaei Botanical Gardens

The Philadelphia Vireo's main breeding range is in southern Canada. In Washtenaw County it is an uncommonly recorded late spring migrant most likely to be found after 20 May. There are a number of reasons for this: Philadelphia Vireos tend to stay high in leafed-out trees: they are very similar in appearence to the Tennessee Warbler and Warbling Vireo (both common at the same time as the vireo), and their song is similar to that of the Red-eyed Vireo. Consequently, many observers are cautious about identifying Philadelphia Vireos.

Red-eyed Vireo *Vireo olivaceus*

Finding code: 2
Common migrant and summer resident
Spring arrival: 29 April (1979)
Fall departure: 16 November (1980)
Maximum: 8 on 15 May 1979 at Nichols Arboretum

While the Red-eyed Vireo remains a common migrant and summer resident throughout the state, in Washtenaw County its numbers have apparently declined somewhat during the survey period. This species' preferred summer habitat is larger tracts of deciduous woods, although it also nests in the large shade trees of older residential neighborhoods. The county habit of building homes in rural woodlots may be affecting the local population of Red-eyed Vireos, particularly because this practice provides more opportunities for Brown-headed Cowbirds to lay their eggs in Red-eyed Vireo nests. In cases where woodlots are undisturbed, the Red-eyed Vireo continues to be a common summer resident; there are usually 3-4 pairs in Eberwhite Woods.

Family Emberizidae

Subfamily Parulinae (wood-warblers)

The eastern wood-warblers comprise the subfamily Parulinae. These "butterflies of the bird world" (Peterson 1934) provide some of the most exciting — if frustrating — bird-watching that Washtenaw County has to offer. A full 37 species of warblers have been seen on migration during the survey period, although a much smaller number nest as far south as Washtenaw County. The regular nesting species (in variable numbers) are Blue-winged, Yellow and Chestnut-sided Warblers, American Redstart, Ovenbird and Common Yellowthroat. Warblers pass through in waves, frequent one day but mostly gone the next. In general, the best opportunity for seeing a large variety of these hyperactive neotropical migrants is to visit wooded habitat (especially near water) during the middle two weeks of May or during the last week of August and the first week of September. (Observers should not be put off by Peterson's notorious comment about "confusing fall warblers"; relatively few are difficult to identify and warblers are more numerous in fall.) Many of the locations described in the Site Guide will be good for warblers, but Nichols Arboretum is exceptional. For some reason the Arb has attracted large numbers of warblers for as long as birdwatchers have been walking there (Tinker 1910) and is one of the most important "migrant traps" in all of southern Michigan. Although these beautiful little birds have been undergoing serious population declines during the last 15 years, experienced birdwatchers can still find 15-20 species of warblers in the Arb on a good day.

On spring migration male warblers tend to arrive before females. These males are more conspicuous because of their songs and brighter plumages. The corresponding females follow, usually peaking 7-14 days later. Moreover, spring warblers (of both sexes) can be divided into broad classes depending on their times of arrival and peak periods in the county (see figure below). For example, Nashville Warblers are "early" and Canada Warblers are "late." In the following accounts we provide May histograms for some species which indicate or contrast these patterns. The histograms are based on Kielb's ten-year study of spring migration in Nichols Arboretum.

Information on fall warbler migration is not as complete. There are good records for September and October, providing (among other things) reliable fall departure dates. However, when this book was planned it became clear that there was a shortage of information on the early fall migration of warblers through the county. Consequently, an effort was made to find migrating warblers in August 1991; it is this effort which explains the fact that many of the early fall dates are from this year.

Spring Warbler Migration at Nichols Arboretum

	15-Apr	20-Apr	25-Apr	1-May	6-May	11-May	16-May	21-May	25-May
Blue-winged Warbler									
Golden-winged Warbler									
Tennessee Warbler									
Orange-crowned Warbler									
Nashville Warbler									
Northern Parula									
Yellow Warbler									
Chestnut-sided Warbler									
Magnolia Warbler									
Cape May Warbler									
Black-throated Blue Warbler									
Yellow-rumped Warbler									
Black-throated Green Warbler									
Blackburnian Warbler									
Pine Warbler									
Palm Warbler									
Bay-breasted Warbler									
Blackpoll Warbler									
Cerulean Warbler									
Black-and-white Warbler									
American Redstart									
Ovenbird									
Northern Waterthrush									
Connecticut Warbler									
Mourning Warbler									
Common Yellowthroat									
Hooded Warbler									
Wilson's Warbler									
Canada Warbler									

peak migration

common

uncommon

rare

isolated record *

Blue-winged Warbler *Vermivora pinus*

Finding code: 4
Fairly common migrant and summer resident
Spring arrival: 25 April (1990)
Fall departure: 28 September (several years)
Maximum: 15 on 11 May 1991 at Matthaei Botanical Gardens

The bright yellow Blue-winged Warbler is a fairly common migrant and summer resident throughout the county. As a summer resident blue-wings are most easily located in scrubby second-growth fields and are commonly associated with Yellow Warblers and Indigo Buntings. Over the last 30 years this species has virtually replaced the Golden-winged Warbler county-wide, either through competition for territories or by hybridization. Embury Rd. in Lyndon Twp. was once a seam in the hybridization zone where both species occurred and nested, but no golden-wings have been recorded in this area since 1988. The Blue-winged Warbler is most easily located at Matthaei Botanical Gardens where several pairs are regular in summer.

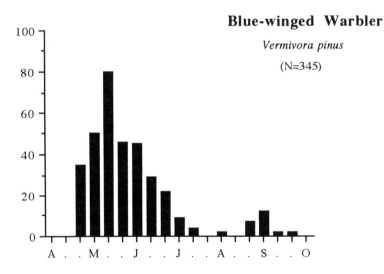

Blue-winged Warbler

Vermivora pinus

(N=345)

Golden-winged Warbler *Vermivora chrysoptera*

Finding code: 6
Uncommon migrant and rare summer resident
Spring arrival: 29 April (1981)
Fall departure: 21 September (1991)
Maximum: 3 on several occasions

The Golden-winged Warbler is now an uncommon migrant in Washtenaw County, perhaps most reliably found in Nichols Arboretum in the second half of August. This beautiful denizen of damp secondary growth has been displaced further north by the genetically-similar Blue-winged Warbler during the survey period. Its main nesting distribution is now in the northern half of the Lower Peninsula. Recent Washtenaw County records have all been migrants, with the exception of one pair in Matthaei Botanical Gardens in 1988-1989 and a possible resident male or pair in northwest Ann Arbor in 1991. The most recent summer record from Embury Rd. was in June 1988 (DBr). In the last few years Golden-winged Warblers found in the Nichols Arboretum in mid-August represent early migrants.

Brewster's Warbler

Finding code: 8
Rare migrant and summer resident

The Blue-winged - Golden-winged Warbler complex is a group of species and hybrids (Brewster's and Lawrence's Warbler) that has been well studied for many years (Parkes 1951; Berger 1958). The Brewster's is the more common hybrid produced by a Blue-winged Warbler mated with a Golden-winged Warbler, although the Brewster's plumage may also occur in the offspring of the hybrids. Recent records include three migrants from the Nichols Arboretum in Ann Arbor and a territorial male in Lyndon Twp. Several males have also been located in the Pinckney Rec Area of Livingston County where the nest of a golden-winged female was located in a territory vigorously defended by a male Brewster's in 1989 (MK, SK). The next year a female Brewster's was located nearby in the territory of a male golden-wing (RBP, LP).

1. 11 May 1980 in Nichols Arboretum (RWy, BWy)
2. 3 May 1982 in Nichols Arboretum (MK)
3. 8 May 1988 at Matthaei Botanical Gardens (JS, VB)
4. 19 May 1988 at Spring Lake (SH)
5. 16 May 1989 on Embury Rd. (MK, RWy, DC)

Lawrence's Warbler

Finding code: 9
Very rare migrant and summer resident

This is the rare hybrid produced from the Blue-winged - Golden-winged Warbler Complex (see discussion above). There are very few records from Washtenaw County:

1. 16 September 1979 near Huron Parkway, Ann Arbor (MK)
2. 8 May 1987 in the Waterloo Rec Area (HM)
3. 23 May 1990 in Superior Twp. (SP)

Tennessee Warbler *Vermivora peregrina*

Finding code: 2
Very common migrant
Spring dates: 4 May (1983) - 1 June (1983)
Spring maximum: 71 on 23 May 1983 at Nichols Arboretum
Fall dates: 25 August (1991) - 11 October (1989)
Fall maximum: 30 on 22 September 1990 in Ann Arbor

The Tennessee Warbler is a common migrant in the county; in May there are numerous records of more than 30 birds from a single location. Spring males sing their loud stuttering song from treetops county-wide, but they can be hard to find as they tend to be less active than many other warbler species. A few Tennessees nest in the UP (ABBM), but most continue on into Canada.

Orange-crowned Warbler *Vermivora celata*

Finding code: 7
Fairly rare migrant
Spring dates: 24 April (1985) - 16 May (1989)
Spring maximum: 2 on several occasions
Fall dates: 5 September (1985) - 9 October (1981)
Fall maximum: 2 on several occasions

The Orange-crowned Warbler is a common western species, but a fairly rare migrant in the eastern part of the United States. During the survey period there has only been an average of one bird each May in Nichols Arboretum (MK). This olive warbler may be a little more common in fall, where it occurs in more open habitat such as Matthaei Botanical Gardens or even in fields feeding on goldenrod (Brock 1986). Most fall sightings have occurred at the end of September or in early October. It is thus one of the latest fall warblers. There is a historical winter record from 31 January 1932 (Wood 1951).

Nashville Warbler *Vermivora ruficapilla*

Finding code: 3
Common migrant
Spring dates: 6 April (1991) - 26 May (1983)
Spring maximum: 30 on 6 May 1983 at Nichols Arboretum
Fall dates: 28 August (1991) - 12 October (1991)
Fall maximum: 6 on 2 September 1989 at Eberwhite Woods

The Nashville Warbler is a common nesting species in the upper half of the state, and a common Washtenaw County migrant. It is one of the early arriving warblers, often seen first in the last days of April. It occurs in a wide range of habitat from deep woods to bushy shrubs. The fall migration period is extended in duration with no obvious migration peaks. The latest fall record is of a bird that flew through an open window into a room at the University of Michigan where it was captured and released (JS).

Northern Parula *Parula americana*

Finding code: 6
Uncommon migrant
Spring dates: 27 April (1978) - 26 May (1983)
Spring maximum: 18 on 12 May 1990 at Nichols Arboretum
Fall dates: 28 August (1991) - 30 September (1978)
Fall maximum: 4 on 16 September 1980 at Nichols Arboretum

This small chesnut-bibbed warbler is an uncommon spring and rare fall migrant in Washtenaw County. The parula is a canopy-dwelling species, frequently found along streams or rivers and mature woods. Most of the recent records have come from Nichols Arboretum. There is only one record in the last five years from the drier habitat of Eberwhite Woods. The Northern Parula nests in *Usnea* moss (old man's beard) hanging from trees in forests in the Upper Peninsula. There are nineteenth-century reports of nesting in Washtenaw County (Barrows 1912).

Yellow Warbler *Dendroica petechia*

Finding code: 2
Very common migrant and summer resident
Spring arrival: 24 April (1978)
Fall departure: 17 October (1977)
Maximum: 13 on 3 July 1988 at Mitchell-Scarlett Woods

Aptly called the "wild canary" by non-birders (as is the goldfinch), this bright yellow warbler is a very common migrant and summer resident in Washtenaw County. May Bird Count totals have averaged over 150 individuals during the last five years. Many old fields, patches of damp bushes or marsh fringes with scrubby willows will have one or more pairs of Yellow Warblers in residence over the summer. This species is a common nest host for the Brown-headed Cowbird; however, the warbler will often build a new nest on top of the old one if a cowbird has laid an egg in it. Yellow Warblers become much harder to find after late July when the males stop singing their *sweet, sweet, sweet, I'm so sweet* songs.

Chestnut-sided Warbler *Dendroica pensylvanica*

Finding code: 3
Common migrant and uncommon summer resident
Spring dates: 28 April (1982) - 23 May (1990)
Spring maximum: 28 on 19 May 1980 at Nichols Arboretum
Fall dates: 14 August (1991) - 4 October (1981)
Fall maximum: 11 on 16 September 1980 at Nichols Arboretum

The Chestnut-sided Warbler is a widespread migrant. Chestnut-sideds are particularly common in fall, although they look very different from spring birds with their yellow crowns and white eye-rings. Nesting chestnut-sideds are widely distributed across Michigan, but are somewhat uncommon in Washtenaw County. Most county summer residents have been found in woodland edge, as at Sharon Hollow Nature Reserve (TSc), or in dense undergrowth, such as the northwest corner of Stinchfield Woods (VB, JS). These habitats are also used by the Yellow Warbler and Indigo Bunting.

Magnolia Warbler *Dendroica magnolia*

Finding code: 3
Common migrant
Spring dates: 27 April (1978) - 27 May (1983)
Spring maximum: 26 on 19 May 1984 at Nichols Arboretum
Fall dates: 29 August (1991) - 8 October (1980)
Fall maximum: 29 on 12 September 1981 at Nichols Arboretum

The sharply defined markings of the male Magnolia Warbler make it one of the easiest warblers to identify during the spring migration. With the exception of a few early spring records, this species is typical of mid-May when large numbers occur throughout the county. Magnolia Warblers nest throughout the Upper Peninsula and at scattered locations in the northern Lower Peninsula. They are very common fall migrants in Washtenaw County.

Cape May Warbler *Dendroica tigrina*

Finding code: 4
Fairly common migrant
Spring dates: 21 April (1979) - 27 May (1983)
Spring maximum: 10 on 15 May 1979 at Nichols Arboretum
Fall dates: 29 August (1991) - 8 October (1980)
Fall maximum: 6 on 11 September 1988 at Eberwhite Woods

In Quebec this warbler is known as the "paruline tigré," a name which well captures the black stripes on its yellow breast. The Cape May Warbler has an extensive spring migration period in Washtenaw County. In most years males start to appear in late April, and females linger through late May. The male has a distinctive song, but it is so high-pitched that it is out of the hearing range of some birdwatchers. The Cape May nests in small numbers in the northern parts of the state, but the main nesting range is in Canada. As in spring, the fall migration is long in duration, normally lasting through all of September. There is one winter record of a bird coming to a suet feeder (8-20 December 1983, JCa).

Black-throated Blue Warbler *Dendroica caerulescens*

Finding code: 4
Fairly common migrant
Spring dates: 30 April (1979) - 26 May (1983)
Spring maximum: 19 on 16 May 1984 at Nichols Arboretum
Fall records: 25 August (1991) - 4 October (1981)
Fall maximum: 3 on several dates

The dapper male Black-throated Blue Warbler is one of the most attractive of all the warblers. On migration black-throated blues pass through the county in mid to late May, and again in September. Unlike many species of wood warblers, they tend to forage near or close to the ground, so they can often be seen close up.

Yellow-rumped (Myrtle) Warbler *Dendroica coronata*

Finding code: 1
Abundant migrant
Spring dates : 29 March (1978) - 24 May (1983)
Spring maximum: 160 on 30 April 1979 at Nichols Arboretum
Fall dates: 22 August (1991) - 5 November (1989)
Fall maximum: 80 on 10 October 1989 at Independence Lake

Although research in Nichols Arboretum indicates that the Yellow-rumped Warbler has declined in numbers during the survey period (MK), it remains by far the most common migrant warbler in Washtenaw County. It is also the only warbler species that overwinters here, although the county population is usually very small. Large groups of yellow-rumps can often be located in trees along the Huron River and its tributaries, starting around 25 April, with migration peaking around 5 May. The early arrivals can often be found close to water, hawking for flying insects. Upon returning from its boreal nesting grounds (it is a common nesting species in the northern Lower Peninsula and in the Upper Peninsula), the Yellow-rumped Warbler can again be very common in late September and early October. In the winter the remaining yellow-rumps switch their diet to berries, especially poison ivy berries (as was the case with an unusually large winter feeding flock of 18 found at Bell Rd. along the Huron River on 11 February 1990, VB, JS). Yellow-rumped Warblers have been found on nine of the last 15 Ann Arbor CBCs.

Black-throated Gray Warbler *Dendroica nigrescens*

Not recorded during the survey period; see chapter four

Black-throated Green Warbler *Dendroica virens*

Finding code: 2
Common migrant
Spring dates: 24 April (several years) - 27 May (1983)
Spring maximum: 25 on 27 April 1979 at Nichols Arboretum
Fall dates: 22 August (1991) - 8 October (1980)
Fall maximum: 15 on 9 September 1989 at Steinbach and Ellsworth Rds.

The Black-throated Green Warbler is a common nesting species in the northern coniferous forest of Michigan. Although its numbers have fallen considerably at Nichols Arboretum during the survey period (MK), it remains one of the more common and widespread county warblers during migration. Its buzzy song is one of the first migrant warbler vocalizations that novice birdwatchers learn to recognize. Black-throated greens tend to be canopy warblers and rarely come low enough to give the observer a good view of the striking head pattern. They are one of the early warblers in spring. Most years the largest concentrations are found in the first week of May.

Blackburnian Warbler *Dendroica fusca*

Finding code: 4
Fairly common migrant
Spring dates: 27 April (1979) - 1 June (1983)
Spring maximum: 31 on 23 May 1983 at Nichols Arboretum
Fall: dates 29 August (1991) - 4 October (1980)
Fall maximum: 7 on 3 September 1980 at Nichols Arboretum

The brilliant orange throat and upper breast of the male Blackburnian makes it one of the showiest of the eastern wood-warblers. Blackburnian Warblers nest in the northern coniferous forests and pass through Washtenaw County on migration in small numbers. County migrants are most commonly seen at treetop height in mature deciduous woods.

Yellow-throated Warbler *Dendroica dominica*

Finding code: 9
Very rare spring visitor

There are reports of this southern warbler nesting in Washtenaw County around the turn of the century (Barrows 1912). There were then no nesting records in the state until 1969, and since that time a very small population has occurred regularly along tributaries of the Galien River in Berrien County (Payne 1983, ABBM). The best strategy for finding this species in southern Michigan would be to check out streams with large cottonwoods or sycamores (hence the older name Sycamore Warbler). The four county records during the survey period are tightly concentrated in mid-May and represent spring vagrants. During fall 1988, a Yellow-throated Warbler regularly visited a feeder at Grass Lake in neighboring Jackson County (DBr). Details of the county records are:

1. 17 May 1978 in Nichols Arboretum (MK)
2. 22 May 1983 in Eberwhite Woods (MP)
3. 19-21 May 1984 in Nichols Arboretum (MK, EB)
4. 18 May 1988 at Spring Lake (SH)

Pine Warbler *Dendroica pinus*

Finding code: 6
Uncommon migrant and rare summer resident
Spring arrival: 10 April (1987)
Fall departure: 7 October (1988)
Maximum: 5 on 17 April 1991 at Mitchell-Scarlett Woods

The name of this uncommon warbler precisely reflects its restricted occurrence in Washtenaw County. As a spring migrant it arrives early, most recent records coming from the second half of April when a few are occasionally found in Nichols Arboretum, Saginaw Forest, Mitchell-Scarlett Woods, or other locations with stands of pines. Fall records are patchy, perhaps partly because of identification problems. The song of the Pine Warbler is often confused with juncos in early spring and with Chipping Sparrows during the nesting season. Although the ABBM has no summer records of the Pine Warbler in Washtenaw County, there were reports of summer sightings from the survey period. All of these were from the extensive pine plantations at Stinchfield Woods, where Pine Warblers may nest, although no nests have been found. They were regularly reported there in the late 1970s (DB) and groups of three were seen in July 1988 and June 1989 (VB, JS).

Kirtland's Warbler *Dendroica kirtlandii*

Finding code: 9
Very rare migrant

This endangered species is Michigan's most famous warbler since nearly all of the estimated world population (393 singing males in 1992) nests in a restricted area in the northern Lower Peninsula. Nationally, records of migrating Kirtland's Warblers are very few. From 1875 through 1954 there were only 12 records of Kirtland's Warbler from the county (Burrows 1954). Although Washtenaw County would appear to be on the direct migration path, there are only two survey period reports:

1. 12 May 1982 in Matthaei Botanical Gardens (RW)
2. 24 May 1984 in Nichols Arboretum (EB)

Prairie Warbler *Dendroica discolor*

Finding code: 8
Rare migrant and summer resident

The Prairie Warbler is a bird of sandy, shrubby upland. Throughout Michigan it is in serious decline as both a migrant and a nesting species. In Washtenaw County it is now of less than annual occurrence. Most of the records are of migrants, but three singing males have been found on territory during the last five years:

1. 13 September 1977 in Nichols Arboretum (MK)
2. 14 September 1978 in Pittsfield Twp. (MK)
3. 12 May 1980 in Nichols Arboretum (MK)
4. 10 August 1980 in Nichols Arboretum (MK)
5. 4 May 1982 in Saginaw Woods (MK)
6. May 1987 in the Waterloo Rec Area (MObs)
7. 11 June 1989 two singing males in the Waterloo Rec Area (MK)
8. 27 April 1990 in Miller Park (RWy, BWy, EB)

Palm Warbler *Dendroica palmarum*

Finding code: 4
Fairly common spring migrant, uncommon fall migrant
Spring dates: 27 April (several years) - 16 May (1980)
Spring maximum: 14 on 5 May 1979 at Nichols Arboretum
Fall dates: 19 September (1979) - 13 October (1990)
Fall maximum: only single individuals

This mostly terrestrial, tail-bobbing warbler is most commonly seen in late April and the first week in May. On spring migration the bog-nesting Palm Warbler seems largely restricted to the open edges of streams and rivers. Dexter Mill Pond is one of the more reliable locations. Small numbers of Palm Warblers are found in late September and early October (in more varied habitat) as they head to the southern U.S., the Caribbean and Mexico, where many winter in the thick coastal scrub. There was one early winter record from 2 December (TW, RWy) from the early 1970s.

Bay-breasted Warbler *Dendroica castanea*

Finding code: 3
Common migrant
Spring: 1 May (1981) - 1 June (1983)
Spring maximum: 67 on 24 May 1983 at Nichols Arboretum
Fall dates: 20 August (1991) - 6 October (1982)
Fall maximum: 18 on 16 September 1980 at Nichols Arboretum

The Bay-breasted Warbler is one of the most abundant warbler migrants in Washtenaw County in mid-late May. These warblers show up at a time when most of the trees have leafed out; therefore they are sometimes difficult to observe even though they usually appear in fairly large numbers. Bay-breasted Warblers reappear in the county in late August through mid-September. In the fall all of the Bay-breasted Warblers, including the adult males, have molted into a drab greenish plumage, easily confused with the fall plumage of the Blackpoll Warbler (two species that would never be confused in the spring). An excellent discussion on the separation and identification of these two species can be found in the *A Field Guide to Advanced Birding* by Kenn Kaufman (1990).

Blackpoll Warbler *Dendroica striata*

Finding code: 5
Fairly uncommon migrant
Spring dates: 2 May (1983) - 30 May (1984)
Spring maximum: 7 on 25 May 1981 at Nichols Arboretum
Fall dates: 22 August (1991) - 2 October (1980)
Fall maximum: 6 on 21 September 1991 at Matthaei Botanical Gardens

The black-capped spring blackpoll is a fairly uncommon migrant in the second half of May. The situation in fall is somewhat uncertain because of the difficulty in distinguishing this species from the Bay-breasted Warbler. However, most bay-breasts have passed through before blackpolls appear toward late September. According to Payne (1983:49), "Blackpolls move eastward through Michigan in the fall and then southward from New England." Consequently, blackpolls are numerous in fall migration to the north of Washtenaw County (RBP). Recent local records corroborate this with few fall sightings.

Cerulean Warbler *Dendroica cerulea*

Finding code: 6
Uncommon migrant and summer resident
Spring arrival: 29 April (1982)
Fall departure: 28 September (1981)
Maximum: 5 on 15 May 1987 at McClure and Loveland Rds.

This small warbler reaches the northern limit of its breeding range in southern Michigan. As both a migrant and a resident it frequents the canopy of tall deciduous woods; as a result the cerulean is more often heard than seen. Although uncommon, it is fairly regular in Nichols Arboretum in the first ten days of May, and in Eberwhite Woods in the middle of the month. Small numbers of summer residents occur in the Waterloo Rec Area, especially along Loveland and McClure Rds. There are very few fall records, probably because most have passed through by early August; in other words, before observers have started to look for fall warblers.

Black-and-white Warbler *Mniotilta varia*

Finding code: 3
Common migrant
Spring dates: 8 April (1982) - 28 May (1989)
Spring maximum: 22 on 14 May 1989 in Nichols Arboretum
Fall dates: 14 August (1991) - 2 October (1988)
Fall maximum: 5 on 28 September 1990 in Eberwhite Woods

Because the Black-and-white Warbler forages along branches and up the trunks of trees (unlike nuthatches, which will go down trunks as well as up), it can migrate before the trees start to leaf out. Consequently, this unusual warbler is widespread in the county during the last week of April and the first week of May. The male's thin song is often likened to a squeaky bicycle wheel. The fall migration is more protracted than that of most warbler species. Although the ABBM has "probable" nesting records for this species from southern Livingston County, and there are earlier records from Oakland and Wayne Counties (Payne 1983), there is no evidence of the Black-and-white Warbler as a summer Washtenaw resident during the survey period. However, there is a record of a nest with eggs from 18 May 1949 at Half Moon Lake, where a singing male was present in summer until at least 1954 (Burrows 1954).

American Redstart *Setophaga ruticilla*

Finding code: 2
Common migrant and uncommon summer resident
Spring arrival: 6 May (1982)
Fall departure: 6 October (1982)
Maximum: 45 on 4 September 1989 in Nichols Arboretum

The American Redstart is one of the most numerous migrating warblers in the county. Redstarts are late spring arrivals with few seen before 10 May. During the rest of May and through much of September they can be very common. Relatively small numbers of American Redstarts remain to nest in Washtenaw County, the great majority passing further north. Occasional summer residents can be seen along the Huron River upstream of Ann Arbor (especially from a canoe) and in some of the moist woodland areas of the westernmost townships, such as the Sharon Hollow Nature Preserve.

Prothonotary Warbler *Protonotaria citrea*

Finding code: 9
Very rare spring visitor

Southern Michigan is at the northern limit of the nesting range of this southern warbler, with most recent records coming from the southwest corner of the state (ABBM). Prothonotaries occured in the county almost annually from 1946 to 1950 in late May and June (Burrows 1954), but since then they have been very scarce. This golden-yellow bird frequents swamps, streams and pools with clear water. The only survey period records are of short-stay spring visitors:

1. 14 May 1987 at the M-14 Ann Arbor School lands (BWy, ESh)
2. 13-14 May 1989 two at Dolph Park (CC), one relocated the next day (BP, VB, JS)

Worm-eating Warbler *Helmitheros vermivorus*

Finding code: 8
Rare spring visitor

The Worm-eating Warbler is a rare visitor to Nichols Arboretum in Ann Arbor. Because of its drab coloration, head markings, and skulking behavior, the Worm-eating Warbler is easily confused with a sparrow. Prior to the survey period there were four records from Nichols Arboretum: 6 May 1966 (HT, TCl, DLi), 21 April 1967 (PD), 27 April 1970 (PD), and May 1973 (RD, GD). Worm-eating Warblers are most often found along the hillsides facing the inner valley of the Nichols Arboretum, or in the Rhododendron Glen, although several have been located in the *Warbler Hot-spot*. In the spring of 1991 a male sang from high in the trees for several days, indicating that he was on territory.

1. 11 May 1978 in Nichols Arboretum (EB)
2. 5 May 1981 in Nichols Arboretum (DB, MK)
3. 27 April 1983 in Nichols Arboretum (MK)
4. 4-7 May 1984 in Nichols Arboretum (MObs)
5. 23-24 April 1985 in Nichols Arboretum (JM, SM, MK, RWy) (on the 24th there may have been two birds present)
6. 8-17 May 1991 in Nichols Arboretum (MObs)

Ovenbird *Seiurus aurocapillus*

Finding code: 3
Common migrant and fairly uncommon summer resident
Spring arrival: 25 April (1982)
Spring maximum: 10 on 20 May 1984 in Nichols Arboretum
Fall departure: 1 October (several years)
Fall maximum: 4 on 1 October 1990 in Eberwhite Woods

The Ovenbird is a common, though decreasing, migrant and summer resident throughout most of Michigan. This is a bird of the forest floor, where it builds its nest on the ground; it is usually first detected by its increasingly loud *teacher, teacher, teacher* call. Both migration periods in Washtenaw County are relatively protracted. Ovenbirds are fairly uncommon summer residents in the county (Finding code 5) and are mostly restricted to mature woods. These woods can be quite variable, for Ovenbirds summer on the largely open floor of the pines at Stinchfield Woods as well as in denser habitat at places like Sharon Hollow Nature Preserve.

Northern Waterthrush *Seiurus noveboracensis*

Finding code: 6
Uncommon migrant
Spring dates: 17 April (1982) - 21 May (1981)
Spring maximum: 2 (several dates)
Fall dates: 8 August (1977) - 8 September (1977)
Fall maximum: 2 (several dates)

This large, terrestrial, tail-bobbing warbler is most frequently encountered along streams and pond edges throughout the county. Small numbers occur early in May and are frequently detected by either their loud, ringing song or a sharp *chip* emanating from the water's edge. Most records are from along the Huron River (Huron metroparks, Island Park and Nichols Arboretum in Ann Arbor, or by canoeing the river). Other good spots to locate these birds in the spring are along Fleming Creek in Matthaei Botanical Gardens, Dolph Park and Waterloo Rec Area. In the fall many waterthrushes may pass through undetected, as they are very early migrants. The nearest nesting population of both this species and the Louisiana Waterthrush's are in the Highland Rec Area and Indian Springs Metropark in nearby Oakland County. In these unusual situations at the northern edge of the Louisiana's and southern edge of the Northern Waterthrush's ranges the two species nest in close proximity in the same woods.

Louisiana Waterthrush *Seiurus motacilla*

Finding code: 8
Rare migrant and summer resident

Although the Louisiana Waterthrush is very similar to the Northern Waterthrush in appearance, behavior and habitat, its distribution is much more southerly and only a few birds venture as far north as Michigan. There are survey period nest records from Sylvan Twp. in 1979 and 1980 (RHa) but no confirmations since then, although singing birds were found during May and June in the mid-1980s along the Washtenaw and Livingston County lines (MK). All but one of the migrant records are from spring, and some may represent "overshooting" wanderers.

1. 2-3 May 1981 in Nichols Arboretum (MK)
2. 16 April 1981 at Sharon Hollow Nature Preserve (SH)
3. 8 May 1982 in Nichols Arboretum (MK)
4. 29 April - 2 May 1984 in Nichols Arboretum (MObs)
5. 5 May1985 at Osborne Mills (MObs)
6. 16 May 1986 in Lyndon Twp. (MK)
7. 15 May 1987 two in Lyndon Twp. (MK, TWi, HM)
8. 6 September 1987 at Matthaei Botanical Gardens (JS, VB)
9. 1 May 1988 two at Sharon Hollow Nature Preserve (TV)
10. 12 May 1990 at M-14 Ann Arbor School lands (RWy)

Kentucky Warbler *Oporornis formosus*

Finding code: 8
Rare migrant

The southern Kentucky Warbler is one of the rarest Michigan nesting species, with only two "probable" reports during the ABBM survey. The more general picture in southern Michigan of occasional birds overflying their normal range and then returning south is borne out in Washtenaw County by the short-stay May records listed below, although there is one nest record from Loveland Rd. in the Waterloo Rec Area on the Washtenaw - Jackson County line from a territory occupied during 1979-1983 (Baker 1984) where four young fledged on 28 June 1982 (DB, RBP) and a record on 25 April 1955 in Ann Arbor (MD, MZ, UMMZ), However, there is nothing in the literature to explain the three September records.

1. 14 May 1977 in Nichols Arboretum (RWy)
2. 17 May 1978 in Nichols Arboretum (RWy)
3. 8 May 1979 two in Nichols Arboretum (RWy, PS)
4. 10 September 1979 in Nichols Arboretum (MK)
5. 13 May 1980 in Nichols Arboretum (RWy)
6. 27 May 1981 in the Waterloo Rec Area (DB)
7. 23 September 1981 at Matthaei Botanical Gardens (MK)
8. May 1982 in the Waterloo Rec Area (TW)
9. 22 May 1984 in Nichols Arboretum (RWy)
10. 12 September 1985 in Nichols Arboretum (MK)

Connecticut Warbler *Oporornis agilis*

Finding code: 7
Fairly rare spring migrant
Spring dates: 5 May (1980) - 30 May (several years)
Spring maximum: 2 (several dates)

The elusive Connecticut Warbler is not common as a migrant anywhere in the United States. Its nesting range is along the central U.S. - Canada border, with a small and local population in northern Michigan (ABBM). Statewide, probably the most reliable location for finding this warbler is Nichols Arboretum, where at least one or two birds are heard (and more rarely seen) nearly every year during the second half of May. All of the county records except one come from this site, and the early spring date of 5 May 1980 (MK, BWy) is the only one from the first half of the month. There are no fall records during the survey period. The historical spring maximum of four (21 May 1975 AM, LM) was also from Nichols Arboretum. Historically, the earliest sighting was 2 May 1906 (Wood and Tinker 1934), and fall records range from 21 August 1950 (EBu) through 1 October 1917 (Wood and Tinker 1934).

Mourning Warbler *Oporornis philadelphia*

Finding code: 6
Uncommon migrant
Spring dates: 7 May (1979) - 7 June (1983)
Spring maximum: 2 on several dates
Fall dates: 4 September (1988) - 28 September (1989)
Fall maximum: only individuals

The Mourning Warbler nests across Michigan, except in the southernmost two tiers of counties (ABBM). Even so, it is uncommon in Washtenaw County on migration, with average annual totals of around five individuals. Spring males sing a loud *chirry, chirry, chorry chorry*, from dense undergrowth. Mourning Warblers are typically very late migrants, peaking the last ten days in May, which may partly explain the paucity of records. In both spring and fall migration, Mourning Warblers may turn up in a variety of shrubby habitats and, unlike the previous species, are not closely associated with Nichols Arboretum. There are nesting records for Livingston County (Payne 1983) and Oakland County (RPB), but apparently none for Washtenaw County.

Common Yellowthroat *Geothlypis trichas*

Finding code: 2
Very common migrant and summer resident
Spring arrival: 28 April (several years)
Fall departure: 6 October (1989)

The comical black mask and *witchity, witchity, witchity* song are the main identifying features of this common migrant and summer resident. The Common Yellowthroat is the second most common nesting warbler in the county, only outnumbered by the Yellow Warbler. Recent May Bird Counts have averaged a little over a hundred birds. Yellowthroats can be found in almost every county habitat that contains vegetation above damp soil, such as cattail marshes, swampy areas, lush grass, and stream edges. Yellowthroats rarely occur in the woodland habitat frequented by many migrating warblers.

Hooded Warbler   *Wilsonia citrina*

Finding code: 7
Fairly rare migrant and rare summer resident
Spring-summer dates: 23 April (1985) - 7 July (1979)
Maximum: 4 in late May 1982 in Lyndon Twp.

The Hooded Warbler is an uncommon spring migrant and rare summering species in the county. Surprisingly this southern warbler is most common as an early migrant in late April and early May, with most records from Nichols Arboretum and the Waterloo Rec Area. Prior to the survey period is an even earlier record of a bird in Nichols Arboretum on 14-15 April 1969 (PD). As a summer resident there have been records of two or three males annually at Matthaei Botanical Gardens (HM, MK) with an adult feeding fledged young located 7 July 1979 (HM, TWi); they are fairly regular at Bird Hills Park (RBP), and a singing male spent the early summer of 1989 at Stinchfield Woods (MObs). There were no fall records for this species during the survey period.

Wilson's Warbler   *Wilsonia pusilla*

Finding code: 4
Fairly uncommon migrant
Spring dates: 30 April (1981) - 23 May (1981)
Spring maximum: 5 on 20 May 1988 at Dolph Park
Fall dates: 20 August (1988) - 25 September (1981)
Fall maximum: 7 on 15 September 1980 at Nichols Arboretum

The Wilson's Warbler nests mainly in Canada in riparian thickets of shrubs and small trees, and in the western U.S. There is one nest record from Chippewa County, Michigan (ABBM). On migration it tends to occupy similar habitat, where it stays hidden in the undergrowth. Two of the more reliable locations for this species are Dolph Park and Matthaei Botanical Gardens, where such habitat can be found. County records during the survey period suggest that it is not as common as generally believed, being close to a code 5 species.

Canada Warbler *Wilsonia canadensis*

Finding code: 4
Fairly common migrant
Spring dates: 2 May (1983) - 29 May (1984)
Spring maximum: 14 on 29 May 1983 in Nichols Arboretum
Fall dates: 18 August (1991) - 12 September (1981)
Fall maximum: 4 on 12 September 1981 at Nichols Arboretum

The necklaced Canada Warbler is a fairly common late May migrant in a wide variety of habitats, peaking around May 22. When it occurs in wooded habitat it is likely to stay in the understory. The nearest nesting record is for the Edwin George Reserve in Livingston County just north of the county line, so the possibility of the Canada Warbler summering in Washtenaw County cannot be ruled out. In the fall the Canada Warbler is once again a fairly common migrant in the early part of the migration.

Yellow-breasted Chat *Icteria virens*

Finding code: 7
Fairly rare spring migrant and summer resident

The Yellow-breasted Chat is the largest of the warblers and is a species of extensive scrubby fields. As Washtenaw County is close to the northern edge of its nesting range, it is both rare and tends to fluctuate in numbers, perhaps reflecting the May weather in the region (ABBM). In recent years most records have come from the Ann Arbor area or from the southwest corner of the county. Throughout the survey period there are only three fall records:

1. 18 September 1979 in Nichols Arboertum (MK)
2. 27 August 1980 in Nichols Arboretum (MK)
3. 6 May 1982 in Nichols Arboretum (MK)
4. 14 May 1985 at Matthaei Botanical Gardens (MK)
5. 9 June 1985 at Iron Creek Mill Pond (MB)
6. 25 June 1985 along Embury Rd. (MK)
7. 7 July 1986 one east of Mitchell-Scarlett Woods (DC)
8. 16 May 1987 at Independence Lake (SH)
9. 10 June 1987 at Whelan Lake (MB)

    10. 15 May 1988 at Sharon Hollow Nature Preserve (MObs)
    11. 25 May 1988 in Augusta Twp. (MK, RWy, TWi, RP)
    12. 16 June 1989 in Brown Park (DC)
    13. 6 July 1989 at Mitchell-Scarlett Woods (MK)
    14. 17 May 1990 along Liberty Rd. west of Ann Arbor (DC)
    15. 17 May 1990 at Columbia Lake (MB)
    16. 31 May 1990 at Whelan Lake (MB)
    17. 15 September 1990 in the Ann Arbor area (ESh)
    18. 12 May 1991 at Whelan Lake (MB)

Subfamily Thraupinae (tanagers)

Summer Tanager *Piranga rubra*

Finding code: 9
Very rare spring visitor

The closest area to Washtenaw County where this southern species is regularly located is at Oak Openings Metropark near Toledo, Ohio. It is not known to nest in Michigan (ABBM); the small number of annual records seem to be mostly of spring vagrants wandering north of their usual range. This species frequents tall mature woods, especially beech-maple or oak. The *pit-a-ti-tick* call of the Summer Tanager is quite different from the *tick-burr* call of the much more common Scarlet Tanager. The only two county sightings during the survey period are of females from the same month from the Ann Arbor area, so the possibility that they represent the same bird cannot be eliminated:

    1. 11 May 1983 a female in Nichols Arboretum (MK)
    2. 24 May 1983 a female in Eberwhite Woods (MP)

    The only record of an adult male predates the survey period and is from 8 May 1969 (BM) and relocated on 12 May (MObs) in Nichols Arboretum (UMMZ), with an earlier record of an unsexed bird from 13 May 1951 in Ann Arbor (Burrows 1954).

Scarlet Tanager *Piranga olivacea*

Finding code: 4
Fairly common migrant and fairly uncommon summer resident
Spring arrival: 5 May (1981)
Spring maximum: 6 on 5 May 1981 at Nichols Arboretum
Fall departure: 21 September (1991)

The aptly named Scarlet Tanager is a fairly common spring migrant in areas with tall trees and woods bordering streams and rivers. In spring and early summer the tanagers' throaty song and *tick-burr* call broadcast their arrival. These woodland birds can be difficult to observe, despite the brilliant red and black plumage of the male. Relatively small numbers of tanagers nest in the county, mostly in mature deciduous woods or along the heavily wooded stretches of the major rivers. There are remarkably few fall records for the Scarlet Tanager, partly because it leaves early for Central and South America, and also because most females and immatures slip quietly through unobserved.

Subfamily Cardinalinae (cardinals, grosbeaks, and allies)

Northern Cardinal *Cardinalis cardinalis*

Finding code: 1
Abundant permanent resident

The bright-red Northern Cardinal is a very common permanent resident in southern Michigan, but is much less common in the northern part of the state as it reaches the limits of its range. The Northern Cardinal was not always a resident of the county; the first record was on 14 June 1884, and the first nest was discovered in Ann Arbor on 24 May 1903 (Wood and Tinker 1910). In Washtenaw County it is widely distributed in most open habitats. It is particularly common in residential areas, where it nests in bushes and shrubs and readily comes to birdfeeders. As with many other species the cardinal is parasitized by the Brown-headed Cowbird in Washtenaw County. Typically, the earliest nests in late March and early April are free of cowbird eggs. Mid-season nests in late May and early June are heavily parasitized by cowbirds, and adult cardinals are sometimes accompanied by cowbird fledglings to feeders. The third or late-season nests in late June and July are once again mostly free of cowbird interference.

Rose-breasted Grosbeak *Pheucticus ludovicianus*

Finding code: 3
Common migrant and summer resident
Spring arrival: 20 April (1988)
Fall departure: 1 October (1980)
Maximum: 15 on 21 September 1991 at Matthaei Botanical Gardens

The Rose-breasted Grosbeak is a common migrant and resident in Washtenaw County. The brightly colored male is unmistakable in the field, while the female's streaky brown plumage can easily be missed as she blends into the surrounding foliage. The female actually resembles a giant female Purple Finch with an oversized bill. In the spring grosbeaks are commonly seen at woodland fringes, where they are also common during the breeding season. The *krink* chip note, resembling the squeak of a rusty hinge, is often the first indication that this beautiful woodland fringe species is present.

Black-headed Grosbeak *Pheucticus melanocephalus*

Finding code: 10
Vagrant

Only the second county record for this western vagrant occurred during the survey period in Nichols Arboretum in Ann Arbor. A male was observed on 30 April 1980 (DB) and relocated on 1 May (MK). Subsequent efforts at finding this bird were unsuccessful. The first record for this vagrant was on 25 March 1963 in Ann Arbor (UMMZ).

Indigo Bunting *Passerina cyanea*

Finding code: 2
Common migrant and summer resident
Spring arrival: 11 May (1991)
Fall departure: 24 September (1981)
Maximum: 10 on several dates in May

The indigo-blue of the male Indigo Bunting is a common sight from early May through late August. The female can often be missed since her plumage is a soft muted brown, and she tends to skulk in the undergrowth, unlike the male who sings from high perches. As a migrant the Indigo Bunting commonly occurs in a wide variety of habitats in the county. During the nesting season male buntings are common songsters in all scrubby secondary woods, wooded fields, and roadsides. In fall migration the Indigo Bunting is surprisingly uncommon, considering its abundance in the spring and summer.

Dickcissel *Spiza americana*

Finding code: 9
Very rare summer visitor

The Dickcissel's main range is in the Central Plains, and its occurrence in Michigan is irregular (except perhaps in Berrien County in the southwest corner of the state). Every few years a sudden range expansion occurs, as in the drought years of 1988 and 1989 when Dickcissels spread as far east as southern Ontario. However, even in such years this grassland species remains rare in Washtenaw County. There are only four records during the survey period:

1. 7 June 1978 in Manchester Twp. (RW)
2. 24 June 1988 at Zeeb and Jackson Rds. (SH)
3. 16-22 June 1989 at Sharon Hollow and Herman Rds. (MB, RW)
4. 17 August 1989 in Manchester Twp. (RW)

Subfamily Emberizinae

Rufous-sided Towhee *Pipilo erythrophthalmus*

Finding code: 4
Fairly common migrant and summer resident
Spring arrival: 9 April (1988)
Fall departure: 18 October (1981)
Maximum: 6 on 21 May 1989 at Searles Nature Preserve

The Rufous-sided Towhee is a fairly common resident in scrubby second-growth fields scattered across the county, where its distinctive *drink-your-tea* song can be heard from April through summer. Towhees can also be found, especially on migration, scratching leaf litter on the woodland floor. Occasional individuals linger into winter; there are six Ann Arbor CBC records during the last 15 years. There is also one record of the Spotted Rufous-sided Towhee (the western race): a male came to a feeder in Northfield Twp. for one day (13 January 1988 RI, UMMZ).

Sparrows

About a dozen species of native North American sparrows can be found in Washtenaw County during the year. Only the Song Sparrow is a regular permanent resident, and even its numbers appear to be much reduced in winter. There are several species which nest in the county during the summer but spend the cold months further south; these include Chipping, Field, Vesper, Savannah and Swamp Sparrows. Another group passes through the county to and from their nesting grounds further north; the commoner members of this group are Fox, White-throated and White-crowned Sparrows. Finally, the American Tree Sparrow is a winter visitor from its summer territory in the Arctic.

If time of year is one useful clue to identifying sparrows, others are habitat, behavior and song. Chipping Sparrows prefer residential areas, Savannah Sparrows drier fields and Swamp Sparrows cattail marshes. Sparrows also vary in behavior: Grasshopper Sparrows are skulkers, while the Vesper Sparrow often sing from open perches. Most northern sparrows (Fox, Lincoln's, White-throated and White-crowned) have attractive musical songs, whereas the grassland sparrows produce insect-like buzzes. Sparrows can also be usefully divided into groups, as indicated by their genus.

For example, the *Spizella* sparrows are small and round-headed with rusty caps, small bills and unstreaked breasts. In contrast, the *Melospiza* sparrows are larger with longer tails and rarely congregate in groups or parties, although migratory groups of Song Sparrows are a noticeable exception.

Beginning birders — with some reason — tend to dismiss sparrows as amorphous and impossible "LBJs" (little brown jobs). However, sparrows are an interesting and significant component of the county's avifauna and should not be lightly dismissed. With perseverance, most individual sparrows can be identified.

Bachman's Sparrow *Aimophila aestivalis*

Not seen during the survey period; see chapter four

American Tree Sparrow *Spizella arborea*

Finding code: 2
Very common winter visitor
Fall arrival: 4 October (1985)
Spring departure: 13 May (1989)
Maximum: 65 on 15 January 1989 at Chelsea SGA
This *Spizella* sparrow with a central stickpin on a clear breast is a common winter visitor to the county. Small flocks spend the winter foraging in hedgerows, roadsides and open areas bordering woods, sometimes in association with Dark-eyed Juncos. Most of these northern sparrows arrive in November, and they are largely gone by mid-April. As a result, there is very little overlap seasonally with the similar Chipping Sparrow.

Chipping Sparrow *Spizella passerina*

Finding code: 2
Very common migrant and summer resident
Spring arrival: 10 April (1988)
Fall departure: 30 October (1988)
Maximum: 28 on 2 July 1988 in Stinchfield Woods

The Chipping Sparrow is the late spring and summer version of the American Tree Sparrow, differing from its winter counterpart in having a white eyebrow and lacking a central breast spot. This small sparrow nests throughout Michigan. In Washtenaw County it is particularly common in areas of lawns studded with occasional trees, shrubs and especially pines. It is found in suburbia, in cemeteries and in park-like areas around buildings. It also nests in drier woodlots such as Stinchfield Woods and in woodland edges. By mid-September most Chipping Sparrows have departed south, while those few that remain have molted into winter plumage, lacking the familiar rufous cap.

Clay-colored Sparrow   *Spizella pallida*

Finding code: 10
Extremely rare migrant

Aside from a small population in the Port Huron SGA, the Clay-colored Sparrow nests in north-central Michigan and to the west of the state. There is one fall record from the beginning of the survey period for the Clay-colored Sparrow on 15 October 1978 in Pittsfield Twp. (MK).

Field Sparrow   *Spizella pusilla*

Finding code: 3
Common migrant and summer resident
Spring arrival: 24 March (1989)
Fall departure: 3 December (1988)
Maximum: 9 on 3 July 1988 at Ford and Dixboro Rds

This is a rural sparrow of low thickets and "old field," where it can be heard singing its mechanical bouncing ping-pong ball song. Unlike the other *Spizella* sparrows in the county, it has a pink bill. The Field Sparrow nests throughout southern Michigan, but is uncommon in the Upper Peninsula. County Farm Park and places of similar habitat are good areas for finding these attractive little birds. The Field Sparrow has a tendency to linger into the winter, and it has been recorded in very low numbers on five of the last 15 CBCs. However, there are no February records.

Vesper Sparrow *Pooecetes gramineus*

Finding code: 5
Fairly uncommon migrant and summer resident
Spring arrival: 13 March (1988)
Fall departure: 21 October (1989)
Maximum: 12 on 14 July 1979 in Ypsilanti Twp.

The Vesper Sparrow is larger than the *Spizella* sparrows and shows conspicuous white outer tail feathers in flight, like a junco. It is most likely to be found singing from a hedgerow perch on a roadside bush, but is nowhere common or reliable except perhaps in the southwest corner of the county. The status of this sparrow in Washtenaw County is somewhat uncertain. Some observers believe that it is becoming increasingly hard to find, while others maintain that it is holding its own in reasonable numbers. The ABBM map shows little evidence of nesting vespers in the greater Detroit area, and this species may be threatened by the creeping suburbanization in the county. There is also evidence that it does not thrive in areas of intensive agriculture.

Lark Sparrow *Chondestes grammacus*

Not seen during the survey period; see chapter four

Savannah Sparrow *Passerculus sandwichensis*

Finding code: 3
Common summer resident in agricultural areas
Spring arrival: 21 April (1990)
Fall departure: 21 October (1989)
Maximum: 12 on 30 September 1979 at the Ann Arbor Landfill

The pale lightly-streaked Savannah Sparrow is largely restricted to areas of open cultivated farmland, such as in Freedom Twp., where it can be the commonest sparrow. It is essentially a ground-dwelling bird, so observers should listen for its distinctive insect-like song and then look for the yellow lores between the bill and eye. Although the Savannah Sparrow nests widely to the north of Washtenaw, there is surprisingly little evidence of migration.

Grasshopper Sparrow   *Ammodramus savannarum*

Finding code: 6
Uncommon and local summer resident
Spring arrival: 11 May (1987)
Fall departure: 8 October (1980)
Maximum: 6 on 22 June 1985 in Webster Twp.

This small flat-headed sparrow is an unobtrusive inhabitant of dry hayfields. Its typical song consists only of a short chip followed by a long buzz. As the finding code suggests, the Grasshopper Sparrow is today very local in Washtenaw County, since its habitat has been reduced by modern agricultural practices. The early harvest of hay and wheat may inadvertently destroy eggs and young. In recent years, more reliable locations have been Ann Arbor Airport, Steinbach Rd. south of Pleasant Lake Rd. and other locations in the westernmost tier of townships.

Henslow's Sparrow   *Ammodramus henslowii*

Finding code: 8
Rare migrant and summer resident

Like the previous species, the Henslow's is a secretive grassland sparrow, but it tends to prefer more weedy fields where it may nest in small loose colonies. The last known such colony in the county was off Noggles Rd. in Manchester Twp., but no birds have been found there since 1988 (MB). Although perhaps never common in lower Michigan, the Henslow's Sparrow has experienced a serious decline during the last 20 years, perhaps as a result of more farm machinery, fertilizers and pesticides and of the growth of abandoned fields. However, the fact that there were no reports of Henslow's Sparrow in the county in 1990 or 1991 does not mean that it is likely lost to the county as a nesting species. It is notoriously difficult to find, partly because of its secretive nature and minimalist *sli-dick* song and partly because of its habit of switching nesting locations from year to year. The survey period records are:

1. 23 July 1981 three at Ann Arbor Airport (RWy, BWy)
2. 20 May - 16 August 1982, a maximum of three at the Ann Arbor Airport (RW)
3. 20 August 1985 at Wellwood and Sharon Hollow Rds. (MB)
4. 28 April - late June 1986 two along Noggles Rd., Manchester Twp. (MB)
5. 11 June 1986 in Lyndon Twp. (EC)
6. 1 July 1987 on Noggles Rd. (MB)
7. June and July 1988 two along Noggles Rd., Manchester Twp. (MB)
8. 8 July 1988 in the Waterloo Rec Area (RW)
9. 7 October 1989 along Zeeb Rd. (JS, VB)

Fox Sparrow *Passerella iliaca*

Finding code: 5
Fairly uncommon migrant
Spring dates: 14 March (1988) - 13 May (1982)
Maximum: 10 on 31 March 1988 at Dolph Park
Fall dates: 23 September (1989) - 26 November (1989)
Maximum: 4 on 17 October1988 in Eberwhite Woods

The Fox Sparrow is the largest and reddest of all the county sparrows, hence its name. In migration it tends to forage on the ground in dense underbrush or in tangles on the floor of mature woods. In these situations it can be confused with the Hermit Thrush, which has a similar migration pattern. Annually small numbers of Fox Sparrows are found feeding at the base of feeders situated close to brushy cover. Limited numbers of this narrow-window migrant pass through the county on their way to and from their breeding grounds in northern Canada. On occasion spring birds give voice with their melodious fluting song.

Song Sparrow   *Melospiza melodia*

Finding code: 2
Common resident, reduced in winter
Maximum: 16 on 13 October 1991 at County Farm Park

The Song Sparrow is a ubiquitous nesting species in Michigan except for a few offshore islands (ABBM). In Washtenaw County the Song Sparrow can easily be found in almost any habitat apart from heavily built-up areas and the interior of mature woodlots. Indeed, its sprightly song is as common in spring and summer in residential areas as it is outside towns and villages. The county population of this common bird is considerably reduced in winter; nevertheless an annual average of about 30 has been recorded on recent Ann Arbor CBCs.

Lincoln's Sparrow   *Melospiza lincolnii*

Finding code: 7
Rare spring and fairly rare fall migrant
Spring dates: 11 May (1987) - 17 May (1989)
Spring maximum: 3 on 14 May 1989 at Nichols Arboretum
Fall dates: 23 September (1990) - 16 October (1985)
Fall maximum: 5 on 23 September 1990 at Matthaei Botanical Gardens

The natty Lincoln's Sparrow is known to be an extreme "skulker." This, plus the fact that it tends to be silent on migration, may explain the paucity of spring records. This scarcity would otherwise be hard to explain, since this sparrow nests in reasonable numbers in the northern part of the state. In fact, the Lincoln's Sparrow is most likely to be seen in the fall, when occasional individuals or small groups migrate south through the county, typically at the end of September or in early October. There is a single record (21 December 1983) from the Ann Arbor CBC (RW).

Swamp Sparrow *Melospiza georgiana*

Finding code: 4
Fairly common migrant and summer resident
Spring arrival: 9 March (1989)
Fall departure: 2 January (1985)
Maximum: 7 on 16 July 1988 at Iron Creek Mill Pond

The rufous-capped Swamp Sparrow might be more aptly named the "marsh sparrow," since it is closely associated with cattail marshes in Washtenaw County. Here it can often be heard singing its slow trill. Although most Swamp Sparrows head south in the fall, a small number attempt to over-winter, mostly along the Huron River (an average of five have been recorded on the last 15 CBCs). However, with the exception of a bird that over-wintered at a feeder in Dexter (1991-1992, PH), the Swamp Sparrow withdraws from the county during the coldest months of the year.

White-throated Sparrow *Zonotrichia albicollis*

Finding code: 1 (on migration)
Common to abundant migrant and uncommon in winter
Spring dates: 6 March (1986) - 16 May (1988)
Spring maximum: 125 on 28 April 1981 at Nichols Arboretum
Fall dates: 17 September (1988) - 5 November (1988)
Fall maximum: 13 on 5 October 1991 in Eberwhite Woods

Of all the Code 1 birds, this species is probably the least likely to be known to county residents, unless they have noticed it scratching in the earth in their backyards. More typically, this chunky terrestrial sparrow can be found — sometimes in large numbers — foraging on the woodlot floor. Although a few birds over-winter, large numbers depart, making it possible to establish migration dates (see histogram). In spring and even in fall, White-throated Sparrows will sing their ethereal song of four or five long whistled notes (ascending *or* descending), which reminds some people of the Canadian national anthem, *Oh Canada,* and others of *Old Sam Peabody.*

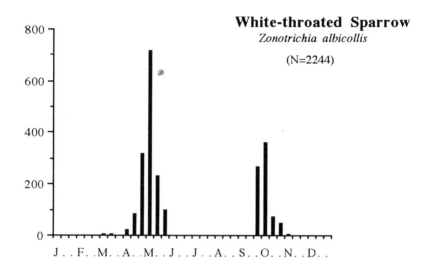

White-throated Sparrow
Zonotrichia albicollis

(N=2244)

White-crowned Sparrow *Zonotrichia leucophrys*

Finding code: 4
Fairly common migrant
Spring dates: 26 April (1979) - 19 May (1990)
Spring maximum: 5 on 14 May 1988 on Waters Rd.
Fall dates: 6 October (1988) - 12 November (1989)
Fall Maximum: 27 on 15 October 1989 in Manchester Twp.

This large handsome sparrow breeds further north in Canada than the preceding species, and so tends to arrive later. It is also much less common. On spring passage it seems to be an extremely narrow-window migrant, typically found only in the middle two weeks of May (see histogram). Migrating white-crowns occur in more open scrubby areas than white-throats and are regular at County Farm Park in October. There is one record of an overwintering bird at Matthaei Botanical Gardens in 1980-1981 (MK).

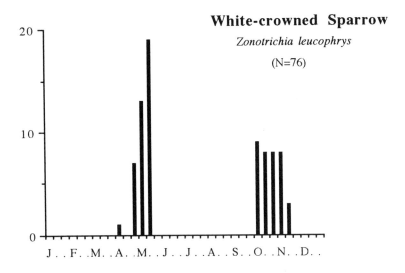

White-crowned Sparrow
Zonotrichia leucophrys
(N=76)

Harris' Sparrow *Zonotrichia querula*

Not seen during the survey period; see chapter four

Dark-eyed Junco *Junco hyemalis*

Finding code: 2
Common winter visitor
Fall arrival: 26 September (1989)
Spring departure: 13 May (1989)
Maximum: *c.* 250 on 17 January 1985 at Noggles and English Rds.

The pert Dark-eyed Junco breeds in the northern forests from central Michigan to the tree limit in Canada and winters in greatest numbers further south. Typically it arrives in Washtenaw County in October and leaves in April. During this period these ground-dwelling birds are common on bare ground or in grass near cover, in roadside bushes, along fencerows and under feeders. Before departure male juncos may also sing from treetops.

Southern Michigan is part of the northern edge of the junco's wintering range and research has shown that males tend to winter further north than females (Ketterson and Nolan 1979). It is not surprising that in Washtenaw County wintering males outnumber the drabber females by at least 4 to 1.

Lapland Longspur   *Calcarius lapponicus*

Finding code: 9
Very rare and irregular winter visitor

Lapland Longspurs summer in the low arctic tundra and winter in the northern United States. Longspurs are birds of extensive open ground, where they may occasionally mingle with the more common Horned Larks and Snow Buntings. During the survey period there were only three reports of this species in Washtenaw County:

1. 4 February 1978 west of Ann Arbor (TW, DB)
2. 2 January 1988, 45 on the Ann Arbor CBC
3. 17 December 1989 at Steinbach and Dexter-Chelsea Rds. (DC)

Snow Bunting   *Plectrophenax nivalis*

Finding code: 6
Uncommon winter visitor
Fall arrival: 7 November (1988)
Winter departure: 26 January (1989)
Maximum: 155 on 26 January 1989 in Manchester Twp.

Like the preceding species, the Snow Bunting is a winter wanderer in southern Michigan, sometimes occurring in large flocks. However, buntings are considerably more common than longspurs; for example, they have been recorded on seven of the last 15 CBCs. The best locations for finding winter Snow Buntings in Washtenaw County are on manured tilled fields in agricultural areas. In flight they are easily recognizable because of their flashing white wings.

Subfamily Icterinae (blackbirds and orioles)

Bobolink *Dolichonyx oryzivorus*

Finding code: 4
Fairly common migrant and summer resident
Spring arrival: 26 April (1979)
Fall departure: 11 September (1978)
Maximum: 78 on 16 August 1982 near Dexter

The Bobolink's occurrence is variable in Washtenaw County. Some years they are widely distributed in their restricted habitat of hay and alfalfa fields, but other years they are local and hard to find. Recent annual May Bird Count totals have varied from 15 to 70. Bobolinks in the county often prefer fields that are sloping or have grassy knolls, above which the striking black, white and gold males cruise and hover as they sing their gurgling-bouncing-bubbling songs. Early cutting of hay and alfalfa is thought to reduce nesting success (ABBM) and may be impacting the county population.

Red-winged Blackbird *Agelaius phoeniceus*

Finding code: 1
Abundant migrant and summer resident
Early spring: 21 February (1983)
Late fall: 1 December (1991)
Maximum: *c.* 50,000 on 13 October 1985 north of Dhu Varren Rd.

The red-wing is undoubtedly one of the most abundant species in the county. Starting in late February and early March the first males begin to appear. The best habitats are filled first, with cattail marshes bursting out with the familiar *o-ga-lee* song. In late April the females begin to arrive, and by late May pairs occupy roadside ditches, open streambanks and fallow fields throughout the county. Nesting takes place starting in May, with flocks of juvenile birds evident by late June and early July. By late August large feeding flocks and large communal roosts shared with other blackbirds and starlings begin to form. During September and October these communal roosts can reach thousands of birds. The maximum number represents part of one of these great communal roosts which totaled over

110,000 and was estimated as the birds departed the roost at 7:30 a.m. Red-wings have been tallied on nine of the last 15 Ann Arbor CBCs, with a maximum of 70 birds, indicating that a few individuals attempt to over-winter.

Eastern Meadowlark *Sturnella magna*

Finding code: 3
Common migrant and summer resident
Spring arrival: 17 March (1988)
Fall departure: 5 November (1989)
Maximum: 11 on 21 October 1989 in eastern Freedom Twp.

The fluting song of the Eastern Meadowlark is a common sound in the grassland areas of Washtenaw County. Often the handsome male meadow-lark can be seen singing from fenceposts or utility wires. The practice of early mowing of hay fields has less affected meadowlarks since they nest earlier than other hay-field species. Meadowlarks often migrate in small flocks, typically in April and October. The song of this species is fre-quently imitated by the European Starling, so downtown or suburban "meadowlarks" are very probably starlings. For reasons that are unclear, the winter status of this species has changed dramatically during the last 30 years. Between 1962 and 1976, 93 Eastern Meadowlarks were recorded on the Ann Arbor CBC, but only seven were found throughout the survey period. The most recent report of wintering Eastern Meadowlarks was of two birds on 29 January 1989 at Easton and Steinbach Rds. (BS).

Western Meadowlark *Sturnella neglecta*

Finding code: 8
Rare migrant and summer resident

The ABBM data show that during the Atlas period this species was sparsely distributed across the state with lower numbers found in the east. The most reliable location in Washtenaw County is traditionally the Ann Arbor Airport, but Western Meadowlarks are not found there every year. In the field the two species of Meadowlark can only be separated by song — presumably for this reason there is no evidence of fall migration. The survey period records are as follows:

1. 27 June 1982 at Washtenaw County Community
   College (EC, ECo)
2. 10 May 1983 at Ann Arbor Airport (RW)
3. 12 March 1986 in northwest Ann Arbor (MK)
4. 10-18 April 1987 at the Ann Arbor Airport (SH, DC)
5. 14 May 1987 at 5 Mile and Earhart Rds. (MK, HM, TWi)
6. 13-20 May 1990 on Schneider Rd. (MObs)
7. 18 May 1990 southwest of Ann Arbor (MK, RWy, DC, DB)
8. 2 June 1990 at the Ann Arbor Airport (BP)

Yellow-headed Blackbird *Xanthocephalus xanthocephalus*

Finding code: 9
Rare vagrant

The Yellow-headed Blackbird is only found nesting in Michigan in a few of the larger marshes located along the Great Lakes shorelines. There have been two verified county observations of this unusual but striking migrant during the survey period:

1. 27 July 1981 two females or immatures in a blackbird
   roost along Huron Pkwy. (MK)
2. 19 May 1991 a male near Dan Hoey Rd., Dexter (RW)

Rusty Blackbird *Euphagus carolinus*

Finding code: 5
Uncommon migrant
Spring dates: 18 March (1989) - 3 May (1981)
Spring maximum: 20 on 9 April 1988 at Chelsea SGA
Fall dates: 2 October (1984) - 21 November (1977)
Maximum: 36 on 1 December 1991 at Trinkle Road Marsh

The histogram shows that the Rusty Blackbird is an early spring and late fall migrant through Washtenaw County, typically in small flocks of three to 20 birds. On migration it frequents swamps and open wet wooded areas and can therefore be missed unless the observer searches this habitat at the appropriate times of the year. A few birds occasionally linger into early winter; Rusty Blackbirds have been recorded on three of the last 15 Ann Arbor CBCs.

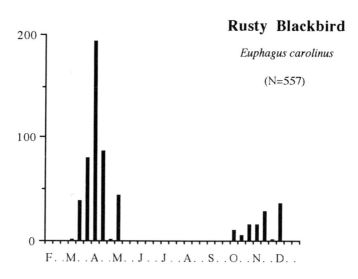

Rusty Blackbird

Euphagus carolinus

(N=557)

Brewer's Blackbird *Euphagus cyanocephalus*

Finding code: 8
Rare migrant

This common western blackbird has been expanding its range eastward and now occurs in Michigan as an uncommon nesting species, mostly in the northern half of the state (ABBM). The few county records, as well as those published in the *Jack Pine Warbler* from neighboring counties, suggest that the Brewer's Blackbird is a very early migrant (late February - early March). This fact, plus the difficulty of distinguishing it from the Rusty Blackbird, probably explains its high code status. Closer inspection of early blackbird flocks should add to the number of records for this species in the county:

1. 20 March 1977 five at the Ann Arbor Airport (TW)
2. Week of 25 October 1978 at an Ann Arbor feeder (AD, JJ)
3. 31 March 1981 at Montibeller Twp. Park (RW)
4. 23 February 1983 southwest of Ann Arbor (MK)
5. 12 March 1985 two in Chelsea SGA (RW)
6. 27 February 1988 in Manchester Twp. (MB)

Common Grackle *Quiscalus quiscula*

Finding code: 1
Abundant migrant and common summer resident
Early spring: 3 March (1988)
Late fall: 18 November (1989)
Maximum: *c.* 7,500 on 3 October 1979 going to roost at Glacier Way and Huron Parkway

The Common Grackle is the largest and most glossy of the county black-birds. The grackle typically arrives in the county at the same time as the American Robin in early March and remains until October. Grackles are widely distributed in many habitats throughout the county. They often nest in conifers in residential areas and are sometimes common lawn birds and feeder visitors. As with the other blackbirds they gather in large fall flocks. Small numbers have been recorded on 13 of the last 15 Ann Arbor CBCs.

Brown-headed Cowbird *Molothrus ater*

Finding code: 2
Common migrant and summer resident
Early spring: 17 March (1990)
Late fall: 1 December (1990)
Maximum: *c.* 1,500 on 3 October 1979 going to roost at Glacier Way and Huron Parkway

Well known for its novel reproductive behavior of laying eggs in the nests of other bird species, this blackbird is widely distributed in many habitats across the county. Small groups and individual pairs of both sexes are common starting in May. Some of the more common local host species include: Willow Flycatcher, Wood Thrush, Red-eyed Vireo, Yellow War-bler, Northern Cardinal, Indigo Bunting, Field Sparrow and Chipping Sparrow.   Small feeding groups start to appear towards mid-July, and large migratory flocks are in evidence by September. These birds remain into early winter in small numbers and have been observed on 12 of the last 15 Ann Arbor CBCs.

Orchard Oriole *Icterus spurius*

Finding code: 6 (in May)
Uncommon spring visitor, fairly rare summer resident
Spring arrival: 7 May (1988)
Fall departure: 16 August (1981)
Maximum: 2 on several occasions

The chestnut and black Orchard Oriole reaches the northern limit of its nesting range in southern Michigan. Small numbers reach Washtenaw County as spring migrants in May (fewer than ten records per year), some of which may be overshooting visitors who then withdraw south. However, most years there are one or two records of nesting pairs of Orchard Orioles from locations scattered across the county. Matthaei Botanical Gardens is the most reliable site. There are but a handful of July reports, and only two in August, corroborating the ABBM finding that the Orchard Oriole is largely gone from the state by August.

Northern Oriole *Icterus galbula*

Finding code: 3
Common migrant and summer resident
Spring arrival: 29 April (1989)
Fall departure: 17 September (1989)
Maximum: 9 on 5 May 1981 at Nichols Arboretum

Despite the brilliant coloring of the male, the Northern Oriole is a hard-to-see bird of tall deciduous trees. Northern Orioles are common in Washtenaw County in shade trees in residential areas, in parks, and along wooded roads and the woodland edge. Here the females build their woven hanging nests. The resident population is joined in May and late August by migrants.

Family Fringillidae (fringilline and cardueline finches)

Subfamily Carduelinae (cardueline finches)

Pine Grosbeak *Pinicola enucleator*

Finding code: 8
Very rare winter visitor

The Pine Grosbeak is a species of the far north, nesting well beyond Michigan. During the winter this species is a common visitor to the Upper Peninsula and a rare visitor as far south as Washtenaw, Wayne and Oakland Counties. The most recent sightings have been:

1. 29 December 1977 at Washtenaw Community College (S)
2. 31 December 1977 at Warren Woods (AD, JJ)
3. 14 Janary 1978 35 at Washtenaw Community College (TWi)
4. 29 January 1978 three in Nichols Arboretum (RWy)
5. 5 January 1986 seven on the Ann Arbor CBC (KH)

Purple Finch *Carpodacus purpureus*

Finding code: 5
Fairly uncommon winter visitor
Fall arrival: 11 September (1990)
Spring departure: 7 May (1991)
Maximum: 30 in December 1988 at a feeder at Spring Lake

The Purple Finch is one of the more common of the winter finches to visit Washtenaw County. These wandering winter birds begin to appear in October and are sometimes common on the Ann Arbor CBC. Small numbers of Purple Finches remain in the county into early April. There is one nest record for Washtenaw County, an adult at a nest on 12 May 1952 (AB). With the new resident status of the House Finch, there has been a great deal of confusion about the identity of the finches occuring at feeders in the winter and spring. Examination of the head and breast plumage can distinguish the two species. The female Purple Finch has a striking eye-stripe (which is absent in the House Finch), and the males have no brown streaking on their flanks or bellies (which is present in the male House Finch). The two species can also be distinguished by song.

House Finch *Carpodacus mexicanus*

Finding code: 1
Abundant permanent resident

The House Finch is a native western North American species. House Finches were introduced in the eastern U.S. when they were released on Long Island, New York in the 1940s. They first reached Michigan in 1972, and Washtenaw County in 1982 (Payne 1983). The first confirmed nesting of the House Finch in the county was in 1983 (RBP, UMMZ). Between 1982 and 1990 the population of House Finches exploded in the county, especially in urban areas such as Ann Arbor. By 1990 there were over 4,000 pairs in Ann Arbor alone (MK). This bright songster is now among the most common of birds throughout the county. While it is believed to be a common nest-site competitor with the House Sparrow, there is no evidence that the House Finch has had a negative impact on any species in the Ann Arbor area (MK). It appears that some portion of the House Finch population may wander or migrate in the late fall and early winter, since the winter population appears to be much smaller.

Crossbills

The two crossbill species, red and white-winged, are rare winter and spring visitors to Washtenaw County. These gypsies roam continent-wide. While small numbers of both species nest in the northern LP and throughout the UP, their occurrence is sporadic, highly irruptive, and unpredictable. As survey period records indicate, they are rarely seen in the county, a fact corroborrated by the historical data. There were only six records of Red Crossbills during 1908-1951 and three records of white-wings from 1883-1945 (Wood 1951; Burrows 1954); between 1960 and 1963 a number of Red Crossbills occurred near Ann Arbor (Payne 1987). Again, between 1969 and 1973 there were incursions of both crossbill species into Washtenaw County (WAS). Birdwatchers sighting their first crossbills are often surprised at their small size — slightly larger than a House Finch and decidedly smaller than either an Evening Grosbeak or Northern Cardinal.

As with most winter finches, flocks tend to contain fewer brightly-colored males than the predominant female-like plumaged individuals. This is probably due to delayed plumage maturation in first-year adult males, as well as the presence of juvenile birds.

Red Crossbill *Loxia curvirostra*

Finding code: 8
Rare winter visitor

The all-crimson Red Crossbill has a circumpolar distribution, occurring in coniferous forests on the three northern continents. In Washtenaw County it occurs rarely. Because of large variation in bill size, vocalization, and its spotty distribution, many different races of the Red Crossbill have been described (Monson and Phillips 1981; Payne 1983, 1987; Dickerman 1987). In Europe at least three species of red-colored crossbills are recognized based on the same variations that occur in the North American species (Perrins 1987). When a birdwatcher sees Red Crossbills careful notes should be taken regarding both vocalizations and bill size. Since there are nest records in the state for every month of the year (ABBM) and county records from July 1972 (MObs) and June 1973 (SM), the occurrence of Red Crossbills in May in appropriate nesting habitat raises the possibility they have nested in the county.

1. 21 November 1981 15 at Saginaw Forest (EP)
2. 23 December 1984 six on the Ann Arbor CBC
3. 6 January 1985 six at Stinchfield Woods (DB)
4. 3 December 1986 at Spring Lake (SH)
5. 25 May 1988 28 at Stinchfield Woods (MK, RWy, TWi, RP)
6. 12 November 1990 eight on Noggles Rd. (MB)
7. 21 December 1990 four at Cavanaugh Lake (MSm)

White-winged Crossbill *Loxia leucoptera*

Finding code: 9
Very rare winter visitor

The White-winged Crossbill is quickly distinguished from the species above by the presence of two white wing-bars and the warbling nature of its song. The White-winged Crossbill is the rarest of the winter finches to occur in the county during the survey period. The only records are:

1. 8 November 1977 in Matthaei Botanical Gardens (RO)
2. 20 December 1980 22 on the Ann Arbor CBC
3. 20 December 1981 six on the Ann Arbor CBC
4. 19-21 February 1983 two at Arborcrest Cemetery (TW, MK)

Common Redpoll *Carduelis flammea*

Finding code: 6
Uncommon winter visitor
Fall arrival: 14 September (1977)
Spring departure: 29 March (1978)
Maximum: *c.* 200 on several occasions

The Common Redpoll is typically the last of the winter finches to appear in Washtenaw County. The greatest number of sightings are between 15 January and 12 March. This small finch is sometimes common at feeders during years when large numbers over-winter in the county. More typically there are only scattered reports of two or three birds coming to feeders.

Hoary Redpoll Carduelis *hornemanni*

Finding code: 9
Rare winter visitor

There are two survey period sightings of the pale Hoary Redpoll in Washtenaw County. This last sighting coincided with the last major invasions of redpolls into southern Michigan.

1. 16 January 1978 on north campus, University of Michigan (LM, EC)
2. Fall 1982 one in a flock of *c.* 200 Common Redpolls at a feeder near Iron Creek Mill Pond (MB)

Pine Siskin *Carduelis pinus*

Finding code: 4
Fairly common migrant and winter visitor, rare summer resident
Fall arrival: 12 October (1991)
Spring departure: 16 May (1990)
Maximum: *c.* 110 on 23 January 1989 at Barton Pond

The thin-billed Pine Siskin is a resident of the northern parts of Michigan and is usually encountered in Washtenaw County only as a migrant or winter visitor. As with other winter finches, the siskin is an irruptive species. Even so, there are always a few siskins in Washtenaw County in winter (hence the finding code of 4), although these small populations increase considerably in invasion years. The last such year was 1988-1989 when several flocks of 60-70 birds were reported. There have been suggestions that following winters with large numbers some siskins may stay and nest in the southern part of the state (ABBM). However, Hinshaw (1980) found no such correlation, and the available records indicate no increase in siskins nesting in Washtenaw County following the 1989 irruption. It is therefore likely that other factors are involved, such as cool spring weather. Pine Siskins nested on or near the University of Michigan campus 1976-1982 (Payne 1983); more recent sightings of fledged nestlings or females with brood patches are listed below:

1. May 1986 a female with brood patch banded at UMMZ (SK)
2. May 1989 adults with fledged young on feeders at School of Public Health, University of Michigan, Ann Arbor (MK, GH)
3. May 1990 adults with fledged young on University of Michigan central campus (MK)

American Goldfinch *Carduelis tristis*

Finding code: 1
Common resident, abundant migrant and winter visitor

The American Goldfinch, another species referred to as the "wild canary," is a common permanent resident throughout the county. It is equally at home in cities and towns as along tree-lined country roads and scrubby fields. The goldfinch is a late-summer nesting species, with many nests found in late July and August. Large flocks (30-60 birds) gather in the fall and remain together through the winter visiting well-stocked feeders. As with other finches these winter feeding flocks wander, visiting a variety of food sources on a daily or weekly routine. In years with little snowfall, or an abundant natural food supply, goldfinches will rarely be seen at feeders, though the feeders may be well stocked with favorite foods.

Evening Grosbeak *Coccothraustes vespertinus*

Finding code: 7
Fairly uncommon winter visitor
Fall arrival: 8 September (1983)
Spring departure: 16 May (1987)
Maximum: 24 on 15 December 1989 at Spring Lake

This large yellow and black finch nests from the upper half of the Lower Peninsula north into Canada. Evening Grosbeaks are gregarious noisy birds. The nomadic nature of this species results in years with very few grosbeaks and others of invasion magnitude. The last big invasion was in the late 1970s, when Evening Grosbeaks could be seen at feeders throughout the county, both in urban and rural settings. Unusally, there was a scattering of spring records in 1987-1988. There have been no sightings of this beautiful winter nomad since late December 1989. Survey period records are:

1. 1 February 1978 ten in northwest Ann Arbor (MK)
2. 17 December 1978 55 on the Ann Arbor CBC
3. 30 October 1979 northeast Ann Arbor (TWi)
4. 20 December 1980 on the Ann Arbor CBC
5. 12 November 1981 nine on Scio Church Rd. (EP)
6. 9 October 1981 in Nichols Arboretum (MK)
7. 18 December 1982 five on the Ann Arbor CBC
8. 8 September 1983 at a feeder in Ypsilanti (WBe, DBe)
9. 18 December 1983 nine on the Ann Arbor CBC
10. 23 November 1985 eight in northwest Ann Arbor (DC)
11. 5 January 1986 37 on the Ann Arbor CBC
12. 15 December 1986 two at Spring Lake (SH)
13. 15 April 1987 three at the Searles Nature Preserve (RW)
14. 13 May 1987 north campus, University of Michigan (MK)
15. 16 May 1987 on central campus, University of Michigan (MK)

16. 16 April 1988 six at Spring Lake (SH)
17. 15 November 1989 three at Searles Nature Preserve (RW)
18. Starting 15 December 1989 24 at Spring Lake (SH, JH)

Family Ploceidae (weavers)

House Sparrow *Passer domesticus*

Finding code: 1
Abundant resident

The introduced House Sparrow is a common resident throughout the county. In the larger urban areas it is quite abundant. It is believed by some that competition with the invading House Finch may reduce the number of House Sparrows. Studies in Ann Arbor (Kielb unpublished data) indicate that after ten years of increasing competition with House Finches there has been no discernible change in the House Sparrow population, with over 40,000 pairs present.

Chapter Four

Additional Species

This short chapter consists of three parts. Section A discusses species for which there are only old (pre-survey period) records. Section B deals with species that we have concluded are best treated as hypothetical and so are not part of the official county list. Section C briefly notes county sightings of some of the exotic or escaped birds which have been found in the wild.

In Section A we describe the well-documented species that were recorded in the county before the 1977-1991 survey period but have not been seen since. One of these, the Passenger Pigeon, has been extinct for several decades; another, the Greater Prairie-Chicken, has been extirpated from the state of Michigan. Still others, such as the Barn Owl, Bewick's Wren and Lark Sparrow, have virtually disappeared over the last forty years as Michigan species. Most of the others are true vagrants, often straying far from their normal range. This group even includes two visitors from Eurasia: the Eurasian Wigeon and the Tufted Duck. There remain a few species that are either rare migrants through the Great Lakes Region, such as the Buff-breasted Sandpiper, or birds that are extremely hard to locate, such as the Yellow Rail.

Section B continues the accounts by discussing genuine North American species for which there are only somewhat unsatisfactory records for Washtenaw County. In some cases the species may well have been present in the area covered by this book, but we have opted for a fairly conservative approach to exceptional sightings. Examples of these "hypotheticals" would be Gyrfalcon and Whimbrel.

Finally, in Section C we note a selection of records of species that are "exotic" or "escaped," or otherwise thought not to be an established part of Michigan avifauna. Various free-flying parakeets and exotic waterfowl fall into this category. These notes are intended to be illustrative rather than exhaustive.

Section A: Accepted Species Not Seen after 1976

Red-throated Loon   *Gavia stellata*

The Red-throated Loon breeds in the Canadian tundra and on migration is more often recorded on the Great Lakes (particularly at Whitefish Point) than on smaller inland waters. There are four reported Washtenaw County sightings this century, three of spring migrants and one summer record of an injured bird (Wood 1951:18). According to Burrows (1954:2) there were no records between 1940 and 1953, and we have traced none since.

American White Pelican   *Pelecanus erythrorhynchos*

There is a single county record of this southern vagrant. According to Wood, "D. B. Reynolds observed an individual near Ann Arbor on August 28, 1938" (1951:24).

Eurasian Wigeon   *Anas penelope*

This duck is a fairly regular vagrant from Europe to the eastern United States. There are two county records of presumably the same bird in the Ann Arbor area on 28 April and 9 May 1945 (Riggs 1946). In April 1990 one was seen for several days in eastern Jackson County (MObs).

Tufted Duck   *Aythya fuligula*

"An adult male was shot on Whitmore Lake on the Washtenaw- Livingston county line during the fall duck hunting period by C. Melling, who later brought it to the University Museum for identification" (JPW 52:82). These events occurred during October 1973. As Payne (1983:12) notes, the possibility of this bird being an escapee cannot be ruled out; however, there are several other records of this old world stray in the Great Lakes Region, and the balance of probabilities suggests a genuine vagrant.

Oldsquaw *Clangula hyemalis*

Burrows (1954) lists six spring records between 1930 and 1952, with a maximum of two birds on 12 April 1945 at Independence Lake (HHa and class). Since then, we have traced only one further report: eight were seen on 13 April 1968 (SMi) on the Huron River near Ann Arbor (JPW 46:87). This big-water duck still remains a possibility in spring on the larger lakes in the county.

Surf Scoter *Melanitta perspicillata*

The only county record this century of this pelagic duck is of one shot at South Lake on 25 October 1941 by Claude Ritz (Wood 1951:89). More recent sightings have been made in adjacent counties: three on 4-12 May 1966 near Adrian across the southern border in Lenawee County (HT) and one in 1974 to the north in Livingston County (JPW 53:103).

Barrow's Goldeneye *Bucephala islandica*

There is a single county record for this North Atlantic visitor to the Great Lakes Region. One was found on the Huron River near Ann Arbor on 25 February 1951 (WG) (JPW 29:43).

American Swallow-tailed Kite *Elanoides forficatus*

Only one twentieth-century county record for this southern vagrant has been traced. A specimen was collected in the Ypsilanti area on 4 October 1924 and is preserved in UMMZ (Payne 1983:15).

Gray Partridge *Perdix perdix*

This is an introduced game bird which apparently spread into southern Michigan from introductions in Ohio and Indiana around 1916-1917 (Wood 1951:142). Wood mentions that specimens were collected in Washtenaw County. It does not appear to have lasted long as a county or state resident.

Greater Prairie-Chicken *Tympanuchus cupido*

Originally a resident of the state, the Greater Prairie-Chicken, never common in Washtenaw County, was extirpated from the state in the early 1980s (Payne 1983:19). The few historical county records from Washtenaw County were all from Manchester and Sharon Twps. in the southwest corner of the county, the last a bird heard by L. Walkinshaw on 21 May 1940 (Burrows 1954:33).

Yellow Rail *Coturnicops noveboracensis*

This small marshbird has the daunting reputation of being one of the most elusive species in all of North America. The Yellow Rail continues to summer in the UP in areas of extensive sedge marshes such as at Seney NWR. However, there are only two known county records, and both of them are old: a spring record from 19 April 1925 and one for fall on 29 September 1908 (Burrows 1954:36). Three birds "ticking" at night were found in Jackson County along Reithmiller Rd. on 16 May 1989 (DC, MK, RWy). At least one of these birds remained until 18 May (HM, RP).

King Rail *Rallus elegans*

This large rail has been listed as endangered in Michigan since 1987, presumably after Rabe (1986) found only 26 King Rails in an extensive survey of Michigan shoreline marshes. The last known county record is the following: "On December 11, 1957, I approached to within ten feet of a King Rail at the northern end of Geddes Pond, Ann Arbor, Washtenaw County. It was able to run and fly well" (Kirby 1959:159). There are several earlier records including three of adults with broods in 1918, 1925 and 1936 (Burrows 1954:35).

Piping Plover *Charadrius melodus*

The diminutive Piping Plover is now on the Federal and Michigan lists of endangered species. Its decline to only a handful of nesting pairs has been principally attributed to a heavy increase in human activity on its traditional breeding grounds — secluded Michigan beaches. Even when its population was much larger, the Piping Plover was probably a rare migrant away from the shores of the Great Lakes. The only county record comes from Whitmore Lake, where one was observed by M.B. Trautman on 7 September 1937 (Wood 1951:161).

Buff-breasted Sandpiper *Tryngites subruficollis*

There are no records in the survey period for this rare migrant, although two birds were seen on 24 August 1976 at the Ann Arbor Airport (TW). This species is known to frequent extensive areas of short grass on migration, and surveys of the county's proliferating golf courses might produce further observations of this rarity.

Red Phalarope *Phalaropus fulicaria*

The pelagic Red Phalarope occurs only exceptionally on inland waters. A specimen of this species was collected from Whitmore Lake on 6 September 1937 by M. B. Trautman. The back of the specimen label states "first seen in Washtenaw County" (R. Payne, personal communication).

Iceland Gull *Larus glaucoides*

There is a single county record for this northern white-winged gull: one was seen on 13 March 1949 (DZ) "supported with full details" (JPW 27:119).

Common Tern *Sterna hirundo*

The Common Tern is a declining species in Michigan, particularly threatened by the increase in the population of Ring-billed Gulls (ABBM). It nests principally on coastal islands in the major lakes. As far as we can discover, there have been no county records since one was seen by HHa and class, on 8 May 1949 (Burrows 1954:51). Norman Wood saw a migrating flock of 50 on 30 August 1937 in the Ann Arbor region (Wood 1951:216).

Least Tern   *Sterna antillarum*

There is only one county record for this southern tern. One was seen on 9 June 1954 in Ann Arbor (RZ) (Zimmerman and Van Tyne 1959:27).

Passenger Pigeon *Ectopistes migratorius*

The story of the rapid decline and sudden extinction of the Passenger Pigeon is well enough known, and the last recorded Michigan specimen was taken in 1898. The early authorities all describe this species as being abundant in the state in the nineteenth century. According to Wood, "There are several reports from old residents of southeastern Michigan that the Passenger Pigeon nested in Washtenaw and Wayne Counties" (1951:224).

Barn Owl *Tyto alba*

The Barn Owl probably no longer nests in Michigan. The last record was 28 June 1983 in Monroe County (MK) (ABBM). Among the reasons commonly given for its disappearance are the decline in its grassland habitat and predation by Great Horned Owls. The latest county records of living birds were 8 May 1969 at North Campus, University of Michigan (CF, UMMZ), and 24 August 1976 on Main St., Ann Arbor (WAS). There is also a road-kill specimen from Dexter dated 14 July 1970 (UMMZ). There were reports of a pair in Milan in May 1973 (MObs) and in a granary in Clinton, just south of the county's southern boundary, into the 1970s (MB).

Gray Jay *Perisoreus canadensis*

The Gray Jay is an uncommon permanent resident in the Upper Peninsula. There are a few records of occasional birds wandering south, especially in winter. The only county record is "one seen near Ann Arbor, Washtenaw County, in December 1975" (Payne 1983:39).

Black-billed Magpie *Pica pica*

This western species is a rare vagrant to Michigan. The single county record is of an adult male taken near Ann Arbor on 6 December 1955 (KZ) and identified at UMMZ (Payne 1983:39).

Common Raven *Corvus corax*

In Michigan the raven is a bird of northern forests, which it requires for nesting. Human persecution and logging in the second half of the nineteenth century almost eliminated the Common Raven from the state's avifauna. Since the 1940s its population has been recovering and spreading southward in the northern Lower Peninsula (ABBM). The only Washtenaw County records this century are of a dead bird found on 11 January 1932 (Wood 1951:302) and "one individual (seen well and close) flushed from field near intersection of Saline-Ann Arbor Rd. and Wagner Rd. in March 1975" (DH). Given its current expansion, it is possible that further county observations will be made in the future.

Bewick's Wren *Thryomanes bewickii*

There are at least seven county records for the Bewick's Wren, including a 1922 nesting report. However, this wren has become increasingly rare in southern Michigan, and elsewhere east of the Mississippi, during the last two decades. The most recent Washtenaw County record is of one observed in Ann Arbor on 18 April 1970 (WR) (JPW 48:82).

Bohemian Waxwing *Bombycilla garrulus*

Only three county records have been traced for this erratic winter visitor to Michigan. The first record is from 23 October 1915 (Tinker and Wood 1916). The second was observed as follows: "A flock of 18 was noted at Ann Arbor by N. A. Wood and several other observers from mid-January to March 14, 1922" (Wood 1951:353). The most recent record is of a single individual found by W. Faust and others in Ann Arbor during November 1971 (JPW 50:17).

Loggerhead Shrike *Lanius ludovicianus*

According to Burrows (1954:97-98), the predatory Loggerhead Shrike was a regular, if uncommon, migrant and summer resident in the county until at least the late 1940s. We have traced no county records since 1952. Today this shrike is either an endangered or threatened species throughout the Great Lakes Region. During the atlas period (1983-1988) only nine confirmed nesting pairs were discovered throughout Michigan (ABBM). The causes of the Loggerhead Shrike's precipitous decline in the northern part of its range are not fully understood.

Black-throated Gray Warbler *Dendroica nigrescens*

An individual of this western species was discovered by W.R. Solomon in Nichols Arboretum on 30 April 1958, and collected by Norman L. Ford on the following day (Zimmerman and Van Tyne 1959:47). This is the only county record. There are very few records for the state.

Bachman's Sparrow *Aimophila aestivalis*

A singing male of this southern species was observed in Ann Arbor 23-24 April 1948 (WL, CW, HT, JV) (Zimmerman and Van Tyne 1955:59).

Lark Sparrow *Chondestes grammacus*

A small nesting colony of Lark Sparrows existed in the northwestern corner of the county at least from 1942 to 1952. For example, three Lark Sparrows were found (HHa and class) on 8 May 1948 in the Waterloo Recreation Area (JPW 26:175). Today no nesting populations are known in Michigan; the nearest regular location is at Oak Openings Metropark west of Toledo, Ohio.

Harris' Sparrow *Zonotrichia querula*

There are three county records of this visitor from the northern Great Plains: one on 16 May 1957 in Ann Arbor (MObs), one on 2 January 1965 on the Ann Arbor CBC (HT) and another on 18 October 1974 in Nichols Arboretum (CM) (JPW 53:30).

Section B: Hypothetical Species

In this section we discuss genuine North American species for which there are only somewhat unsatisfactory records for Washtenaw County. In coming to these decisions we have relied on several sources: written commentaries by major authorities, examination of specimens in UMMZ, the opinions of local experts and our own judgment. Classifying a record as "hypothetical" does not necessarily imply that the observer might not have seen the claimed rarity; it merely indicates that a lack of adequate documentation precludes full acceptance of the record in question.

There are a number of nineteenth-century county records (including several from Covert's 1881 list) for which the specimens are now lost and which later authorities (Wood 1906; Barrows 1912; Wood 1951) have found, for various reasons, to be questionable. Among these are claimed sightings for Sabine's Gull, Labrador Duck, Whooping Crane, Black Rail, Black-necked Stilt, Long-billed Curlew, Smith's Longspur, Blue Grosbeak and Northern Hawk Owl. Like our predecessors we consider the county status of these species to be (at best) hypothetical. Further, the 1911 record for a Northern Gannet in the "Ann Arbor region" reported in Wood and Tinker (1934) in fact refers to a specimen collected at Hamburg Lake in southern Livingston County. We now review the status of five further species.

Gyrfalcon   *Falco rusticolus*

The single county record for this large falcon from the far north is of a white-phase bird in Saline Twp. reported on 9 December 1974 (UMMZ). As the record is based on notes written down from a telephone call (R. Payne, personal communication), it seems best to consider this record questionable.

Whimbrel   *Numenius phaeopus*

Charles Steinbach reported a group of 15 Whimbrel on 1 October 1983 from Dexter Mill Pond. This would be an exceptional county sighting for this rare Michigan migrant, as nearly all southern records come from the Great Lakes shorelines. We are therefore hesitant to accept this record as a confirmed sighting without independent corroboration.

Long-billed Dowitcher   *Limnodromus scolopaceus*

Distinguishing the two dowitcher species in the field is known to be extremely difficult (Wilds and Newlon 1983). Since there are reports in Wood (1951:195) of parties of dowitcher species being seen in the county in the fall, it is possible that some may have been long-billed. However, there are no museum specimens of Long-billed Dowitchers from the county (Phil Chu, personal communication), and all recent observations of dowitchers (see chapter three) are thought to be short-billed. Hypothetical status thus seems appropriate.

Western Kingbird   *Tyrannus verticalis*

Jeff Renner reported seeing a Western Kingbird in Ann Arbor on 20 October 1988. Unfortunately, efforts by other birders to find this western vagrant were unsuccessful. After much discussion, we eventually decided to exclude the Western Kingbird from the main species list because of incomplete documentation.

Le Conte's Sparrow *Ammodramus leconteii*

Le Conte's Sparrow is a very local summer resident in sedge habitat in the Upper Peninsula (ABBM). While it has been found on fall migration in Jackson County (Wood 1951:483), we have traced no records of this potential county migrant. Further, according to Wood (1951:482), the old specimen in UMMZ labeled "Ann Arbor, May 1894" may be of mistaken provenance.

Section C: Exotic and Escaped Species

Many birds have been imported into the United States for a wide variety of reasons: as pets, game birds or ornamental species for parks and lakes. From time to time, such introduced species become established, as is the case with the county's scattered population of Mute Swans. In other cases, introductions may be short-lived. In 1913, Henry Ford released a number of European Goldfinches in Detroit. A possible descendant of these birds was collected in Ann Arbor in 1926 (Wood 1951:522).

From time to time exotic birds escape from confinement or are deliberately set free. Of these the Monk Parakeet is listed both by Payne (1983) and ABBM as a scarce resident in Michigan. However, we prefer to consider this import from South America currently as an exotic species. Monk Parakeets were sighted in Ann Arbor with some regularity from 1977 to 1980 (MObs), but have not been reported since. There is one nest record from Oakland County in 1983 (ABBM) but thereafter no state nesting records and very few sightings. The status of the Monk Parakeet as a wild species in southern Michigan is uncertain. A Black-headed Parakeet seen on the Medical Campus at the University of Michigan in July 1987 (MK) is clearly an escapee, as was the Swinhoe's Pheasant found on Central Campus (JH). Survey period sightings of exotic waterfowl in Washtenaw County include four Brazilian Ducks with native species on Iron Creek Mill Pond in October 1987 (VB, JS) and two sightings of Egyptian Geese in northeast Ann Arbor (MK, BWy, RWy, RW). The status of the Muscovy Duck is somewhat more problematic. Introduced to Gallup Park and sometimes kept as a farmyard animal, feral Muscovy Ducks have been noted in various parts of the county (MObs). They breed in the wild and also hybridize with the Mallard. They may eventually become a recognized part of the county's avifauna.

Chapter Five

Seasonal Distribution

The final chapter of the book provides a visual summary in bar-graph format of the current status of most of the birds in Washtenaw County. We have excluded, with one or two exceptions, all birds with finding codes of 9 or 10, since the occurrence of such high code birds is not predictable. The bar-graph information is based on an *average* year and does not take into account exceptional events such as abnormal weather conditions or occasional invasions by irruptive species.

The bar-graphs themselves are plotted over the 12 months from January to December. The interpretation of the graph lines is given in a key at the top of each page.

Solitary Sandpiper

nested (1977-1991)	*	very common/abundant ▅	uncommon —
probably nested (1977-1991)	?	common ▬	rare - - - -
nest record prior to 1977	o		

		Jan	Feb	Mar	Apr	May	June	July	Aug	Sep	Oct	Nov	Dec
Common Loon	o												
Pied-billed Grebe	*												
Horned Grebe													
Double-crested Cormorant													
American Bittern	o												
Least Bittern	o												
Great Blue Heron	*												
Great Egret													
Green-backed Heron	*												
Black-crowned Night-Heron													
Tundra Swan													
Mute Swan	*												
Snow Goose													
Canada Goose	*												
Wood Duck	*												
Green-winged Teal													
American Black Duck	*												
Mallard	*												
Northern Pintail													
Blue-winged Teal	*												
Northern Shoveler													
Gadwall													
American Wigeon													
Canvasback													
Redhead													
Ring-necked Duck													
Greater Scaup													
Lesser Scaup													
Common Goldeneye													
Bufflehead													
Hooded Merganser													
Common Merganser													
Red-breasted Merganser													
Ruddy Duck													
Turkey Vulture	*												
Osprey													
Bald Eagle													
Northern Harrier	o												
Sharp-shinned Hawk													
Cooper's Hawk	*												
Northern Goshawk													
Red-shouldered Hawk	o												
Broad-winged Hawk	*												
Red-tailed Hawk	*												
Rough-legged Hawk													

		Jan	Feb	Mar	Apr	May	June	July	Aug	Sep	Oct	Nov	Dec
Golden Eagle												
American Kestrel	*											
Merlin												
Peregrine Falcon												
Ring-necked Pheasant	*											
Ruffed Grouse	*											
Northern Bobwhite	*											
Wild Turkey	?											
Virginia Rail	*											
Sora	*											
Common Moorhen	*											
American Coot	*											
Sandhill Crane	*											
Semipalmated Plover												
Killdeer	*											
Greater Yellowlegs												
Lesser Yellowlegs												
Solitary Sandpiper												
Spotted Sandpiper	*											
Upland Sandpiper	*											
Semipalmated Sandpiper												
Least Sandpiper												
Baird's Sandpiper												
Pectoral Sandpiper												
Dunlin												
Short-billed Dowitcher												
Common Snipe	?											
American Woodcock	*											
Bonaparte's Gull												
Ring-billed Gull												
Herring Gull												
Caspian Tern												
Forster's Tern												
Black Tern	o											
Rock Dove	*											
Mourning Dove	*											
Black-billed Cuckoo	?											
Yellow-billed Cuckoo	*											
Eastern Screech Owl	*											
Great Horned Owl	*											
Snowy Owl												
Barred Owl	?											
Long-eared Owl	o											
Short-eared Owl	o											

		Jan	Feb	Mar	Apr	May	June	July	Aug	Sep	Oct	Nov	Dec
Northern Saw-whet Owl													
Common Nighthawk	*												
Whip-poor-will	?												
Chimney Swift	*												
Ruby-throated Hummingbird	*												
Belted Kingfisher	*												
Red-headed Woodpecker	*												
Red-bellied Woodpecker	*												
Yellow-bellied Sapsucker													
Downy Woodpecker	*												
Hairy Woodpecker	*												
Northern Flicker	*												
Olive-sided Flycatcher													
Eastern Wood-Pewee	*												
Yellow-bellied Flycatcher													
Acadian Flycatcher	*												
Alder Flycatcher													
Willow Flycatcher	*												
Least Flycatcher	*												
Eastern Phoebe	*												
Great Crested Flycatcher	*												
Eastern Kingbird	*												
Horned Lark	*												
Purple Martin	*												
Tree Swallow	*												
Northern Rough-winged Swallow	*												
Bank Swallow	*												
Cliff Swallow	*												
Barn Swallow	*												
Blue Jay	*												
American Crow	*												
Black-capped Chickadee	*												
Tufted Titmouse	*												
Red-breasted Nuthatch	*												
White-breasted Nuthatch	*												
Brown Creeper													
Carolina Wren	*												
House Wren	*												
Winter Wren													
Sedge Wren	?												
Marsh Wren	*												
Golden-crowned Kinglet	*												
Ruby-crowned Kinglet	o												
Blue-gray Gnatcatcher	*												
Eastern Bluebird	*												

		Jan	Feb	Mar	Apr	May	June	July	Aug	Sep	Oct	Nov	Dec
Veery	*												
Gray-cheeked Thrush													
Swainson's Thrush													
Hermit Thrush													
Wood Thrush	*												
American Robin	*												
Gray Catbird	*												
Northern Mockingbird	?												
Brown Thrasher	*												
American Pipit													
Cedar Waxwing	*												
Northern Shrike													
European Starling	*												
White-eyed Vireo	*												
Solitary Vireo	*												
Yellow-throated Vireo	*												
Warbling Vireo	*												
Philadelphia Vireo													
Red-eyed Vireo	*												
Blue-winged Warbler	*												
Golden-winged Warbler	?												
Tennessee Warbler													
Orange-crowned Warbler													
Nashville Warbler													
Northern Parula	o												
Yellow Warbler	*												
Chestnut-sided Warbler	*												
Magnolia Warbler													
Cape May Warbler													
Black-throated Blue Warbler													
Yellow-rumped Warbler													
Black-throated Green Warbler													
Blackburnian Warbler													
Yellow-throated Warbler													
Pine Warbler	?												
Prairie Warbler	o												
Palm Warbler													
Bay-breasted Warbler													
Blackpoll Warbler													
Cerulean Warbler	*												
Black-and-white Warbler	o												
American Redstart	*												
Worm-eating Warbler													
Ovenbird	*												
Northern Waterthrush													

nested (1977-1991)	*	very common/abundant ▓	uncommon ────
probably nested (1977-1991)	?	common ▬▬	rare -----
nest record prior to 1977	o		

		Jan	Feb	Mar	Apr	May	June	July	Aug	Sep	Oct	Nov	Dec
Louisiana Waterthrush	*												
Kentucky Warbler	*												
Connecticut Warbler													
Mourning Warbler													
Common Yellowthroat	*												
Hooded Warbler	*												
Wilson's Warbler													
Canada Warbler													
Yellow-breasted Chat	*												
Scarlet Tanager	*												
Northern Cardinal	*												
Rose-breasted Grosbeak	*												
Indigo Bunting	*												
Rufous-sided Towhee	*												
American Tree Sparrow													
Chipping Sparrow	*												
Field Sparrow	*												
Vesper Sparrow	*												
Savannah Sparrow	*												
Grasshopper Sparrow	*												
Henslow's Sparrow	?												
Fox Sparrow													
Song Sparrow	*												
Lincoln's Sparrow													
Swamp Sparrow	*												
White-throated Sparrow													
White-crowned Sparrow													
Dark-eyed Junco													
Lapland Longspur													
Snow Bunting													
Bobolink	*												
Red-winged Blackbird	*												
Eastern Meadowlark	*												
Western Meadowlark	?												
Rusty Blackbird													
Brewer's Blackbird													
Common Grackle	*												
Brown-headed Cowbird	*												
Orchard Oriole	*												
Northern Oriole	*												
Pine Grosbeak													
Purple Finch	o												
House Finch	*												
Red Crossbill	?												
White-winged Crossbill													

nested (1977-1991)	*	very common/abundant ▬		uncommon ——										
probably nested (1977-1991)	?	common ▬		rare - - - - -										
nest record prior to 1977	o													

		Jan	Feb	Mar	Apr	May	June	July	Aug	Sep	Oct	Nov	Dec
Common Redpoll													
Pine Siskin	*												
American Goldfinch	*												
Evening Grosbeak													
House Sparrow	*												

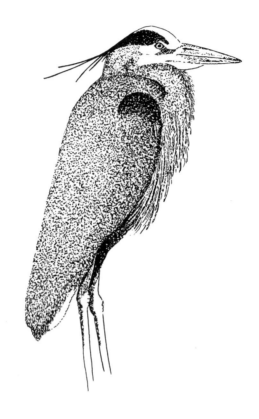

Great Blue Heron

Appendix

1992 Addenda

Least Bittern	Additional sightings:15 August at Thurston Pond (MObs) and at a small pond at Dhu Varren and Nixon Rds. (JB)
Little Blue Heron	Additional sighting: an adult 15-20 August at Thurston Pond (MObs)
Green-backed Heron	New early spring date: 19 April (VB, JS)
Northern Shoveler	New late spring date: 22 May (VB, JS)
Gadwall	New late spring date: 25 April (VB, JS)
Ring-necked Duck	New early fall date: 8-31 August (VB, JS)
Bufflehead	New late spring date; 9 May (VB, JS)
Osprey	Summer record: 19 July at Iron Creek Mill Pond (MB)
Rough-legged Hawk	New late spring date: 19 April (VB, JS)
Broad-winged Hawk	New maximum: 54 on 19 April over Nichols Arboretum (RN)
Sanderling	Additional record: 15 August at M-14 - Water Treatment Pond (VB, JS)
Caspian Tern	Additional records: 15 August (2)(VB, JS, MK), 16 August (4) (BP)
Cliff Swallow	New colony on the Maiden Lane Bridge: summer (RBP, LP)

White-eyed Vireo	New nest records: two adults and five nestlings on 20 June at Noggles Rd. (MK, SK) and a nest at Matthaei Botanical Gardens (UMMZ)
Lawrence's Warbler	Additional record: one on 13 May at Iron Creek Mill Pond (DM)
Black-throated Green Warbler	New early fall date: 25 July (VB, JS, SF)
Blackburnian Warbler	New late spring date: 10 June (RW)
Pine Warbler	Additional summer record: two singing males on 4 July in Stinchfield Woods (VB, JS)
Bay-breasted Warbler	New late spring date: 3 June (VB, JS)
Prothonotary Warbler	Additional sighting: 5 May in Nichols Arboretum (DC)
Worm-eating Warbler	Additional sighting: 2-14 May in Nichols Arboretum (MObs)
Kentucky Warbler	Additional records: Singing male 3-19 June at Bird Hills Park (MObs); 27 May Nichols Arboretum (MK)
Yellow-breasted Chat	Additional records: 20 June two males off Noggles Rd. (MObs); one 7-15 July at Matthaei Botanical Gardens (BB, DC)
Western Meadowlark	Additional record: 9 May off Waters Rd. (VB, JS)

Bibliography

American Ornithologists' Union. 1983. *Check-list of North American Birds*, 6th ed. Lawrence, KS: American Ornithologists' Union.

Baker, D. T. 1984. Kentucky Warbler nesting in Michigan. *Jack-Pine Warbler* 62:26.

Baker, D., T. Wells, and R. Wykes. 1982. *A Guide to Birdfinding in Washtenaw County and Surrounding Areas*. Ann Arbor: Washtenaw Audubon Society.

Barrows, W. B. 1912. *Michigan Bird Life*. Michigan Agricultural College.

Batts, H. L., Jr. 1955. A simple study in winter bird ecology. *Jack-Pine Warbler* 33:115-26.

_____. 1961. Nesting success of birds on a farm in Southern Michigan. *Jack-Pine Warbler* 39:72-83.

Beard, E. B. 1944. Ann Arbor organizes bird club. *Jack-Pine Warbler* 22: 143-44.

Berger, A. J. 1948. Early nesting and cowbird parasitism of the goldfinch in Michigan. *Wilson Bulletin* 60:52.

_____. 1950. Nesting of the Yellow-breasted Chat at Ann Arbor, Michigan. *Jack-Pine Warbler* 28:14.

_____. 1951. The cowbird and certain host species in Michigan. *Wilson Bulletin* 63:26-34.

_____. 1951. Changes since 1910 in the breeding population of the Alder Flycatcher, Least Flycatcher, Redstart, and Cardinal in Ann Arbor. *Jack-Pine Warbler* 29:52-55.

_____. 1951. Notes on the nesting season of the Catbird. *Jack-Pine Warbler* 29:115-18.

_____. 1955. Six-storied Yellow Warbler nest with eleven Cowbird eggs. *Jack-Pine Warbler* 33:84.

_____. 1956. Two albinistic Alder Flycatchers at Ann Arbor, Michigan. *Auk* 73:137-38.

_____. 1956. Barn Swallow and Rough-winged Swallow nesting under bridges. *Jack-Pine Warbler* 34:10.

_____. 1956. Prairie Horned Lark nest notes. *Jack-Pine Warbler* 34:69-72.

_____. 1957. Nest behavior of the House Sparrow. *Jack-Pine Warbler* 35:86-92.

_____. 1958. The Golden-winged - Blue-winged Warbler Complex in
   Michigan and the Great Lakes area. *Jack-Pine Warbler* 36:37-73.
_____. 1967. Traill's Flycatcher in Washtenaw County, Michigan.
   Jack-Pine Warbler 45:117-23.
Berger, A. J., and P. B. Hofslund. 1950. Notes on the nesting of the Alder
   Flycatcher (*Empidonax trailii*) at Ann Arbor, Michigan. *Jack-Pine
   Warbler* 28:7-11.
Berger, A. J., and D. F. Parmelee. 1952. The Alder Flycatcher in
   Washtenaw County, Michigan: Breeding Distribution and cowbird
   parasitism. *Wilson Bulletin* 64:33-38.
Bircham, P. M. M. 1989. *The Birds of Cambridgeshire.* Cambridge:
   Cambridge University Press.
Brewer, R., G. A. McPeek, and R. J. Adams, Jr. (editors). 1991. *The Atlas
   of Breeding Birds of Michigan.* East Lansing: Michigan State
   University Press.
Brock, K. J. 1986. *Birds of the Indiana Dunes.* Bloomington: Indiana
   University Press.
Burrows, E. 1954. The birds of Washtenaw County. Unpublished manu-
   script, on file at University of Michigan Museum of Zoology.
Covert, A. B. 1881. Natural History, birds. In *The History of Washtenaw
   County, Michigan,* 173-93. Chicago: Chas. C. Chapman and Co.
Craighead, J. J., and F. C. Craighead, Jr. 1956. *Hawks, Owls and Wildlife.*
   Harrisburg, PA: Stackpole Co. and the Wildlife Management
   Institute Reprint. 1969. New York: Dover Publications.
Culbert, R. 1989. Birds of Saginaw Forest. *Washtenaw County Bird Survey*
   2 (4).
Cuthbert, N. L. 1963. *The Birds of Isabella County, Michigan.* Ann Arbor,
   MI: Edwards Brothers.
De Benedictis, P. A. 1984. Blue-winged / Golden-winged Warbler com-
   plex. *Birding* 16:205-7.
Dennis, J. V. 1981. *Beyond the Bird Feeder.* New York: Alfred A. Knopf.
Dickerman, R. W. 1987. The "Old Northern" subspecies of Red Crossbill.
   American Birds 41:189-94.
Droege, S. 1988. *Analysis of Changes in Bird Populations from 1966-1987
   for Michigan.* Laurel, MD: USFWS Office of Migratory Birds.
Evers, D. C. 1992. *A Guide to Michigan's Endangered Wildlife.* Ann Arbor:
   University of Michigan Press.
George, J. L. 1952. Birds of a southern Michigan farm. M.S. thesis,
   University of Michigan.
Godfrey, W. E. 1986. *The Birds of Canada.* Ottawa, ON: National
   Museums of Canada.
Gruson, E. S. 1972. *Words for Birds.* New York: Quadrangle Books.

Hann, H. W. 1937. Life History of the Oven-bird in southern Michigan. *Wilson Bulletin* 49:145-237.

Haymen, P., J. Marchant, and T. Prater. 1986. *Shorebirds*. Boston: Houghton Mifflin Co.

Hinshaw, J. 1980. Pine Siskin nesting records for southern Michigan. *Jack-Pine Warbler* 58:34-35.

Jollie, M. 1976. A contribution to the morphology and phylogeny of the Falconiformes, Part I. *Evolutionary Theory* 1:285-98.

Jollie, M. 1977. A contribution to the morphology and phylogeny of the Falconiformes, Part II. *Evolutionary Theory* 2:115-208.

Kaufman, K. 1990. *A Field Guide to Advanced Birding*. Boston: Houghton Mifflin Co.

Kelley, A. H. 1978. *Birds of Southeastern Michigan and Southwestern Ontario*. Bloomfield Hills, MI: Cranbrook Institute of Science.

Kenaga, E. E. 1983. *Birds, Birders, and Birding in the Saginaw Bay Area*. Midland, MI: Chippewa Nature Center.

Ketterson, E. D., and V. Nolan. 1979. Seasonal, annual, and geographic variation in sex ratio of wintering populations of Dark-eyed Juncos (*Junco hyemalis*). *Auk* 96:532-36.

Kielb, M. A. 1989. The fall migration of the Ruby-throated Hummingbird at Holiday Beach in Southeastern Ontario. *The Northwind* 4 (1):3-4.

_____. 1990. Spring sightings at Nichols Arboretum, Ann Arbor, Michigan, 1979-1989. *Washtenaw County Bird Survey* 3 (1).

Kilham, L. 1983. *Life History Studies of Woodpeckers in Eastern North America*. Cambridge: Publication of the Nuttall Ornithological Club No. 20.

Kirby, R. 1959. Some fall and winter Michigan bird records. *Jack-Pine Warbler* 37:159-60.

Kraut, R. (editor). 1990. *Footloose in Washtenaw*. Ann Arbor: The Ecology Center of Ann Arbor.

Ligon, J. D. 1967. *Relationships of the Cathartid Vultures*. Occasional Papers of the Museum of Zoology, University of Michigan No. 651.

Monson, G., and A. Philips. 1981. *Annotated Checklist of the Birds of Arizona*. Tucson, AZ: University of Arizona Press.

Moore, J. E. 1945. Five Barn Owlets. *Jack-Pine Warbler* 23:95-104.

O'Reilly, R. A., Jr. 1954. An invasion of southern Michigan by Brown-capped Chickadee. *Jack-Pine Warbler* 32:79-82.

Parkes, K. C. 1951. The genetics of the Golden-winged X Blue-winged Warbler complex. *Wilson Bulletin* 63:5-15.

Payne, R. B. 1983. *A Distributional Checklist of the Birds of Michigan*. Miscellaneous Publications Museum of Zoology, University of Michigan No. 164.

_____. 1987. *Populations and Type Specimens of a Nomadic Bird: Comments on the North American Crossbills Loxia pusilla Gloger 1834 and Crucirostra minor Brehm 1845.* Occasional Papers of the Museum of Zoology, University of Michigan. No. 714.

Peet, M. M. 1908. An ecological study of the birds of the Ypsilanti Bayou. *Report of the Michigan Academy of Science, Arts, and Letters* 10:162-96.

Perrins, C. 1987. *Birds of Britain and Europe.* Austin, TX: University of Texas Press.

Peterson, R. T. 1934. *A Field Guide to the Birds.* Boston: Houghton Mifflin Co.

_____. 1987. Those tricky Alder and Willow Flycatchers. *Birding* 19:14-16.

Potter, P. E. 1966. Birding areas in Michigan: The Ann Arbor area. *Jack-Pine Warbler* 44:91-93.

Rabe, M. L. 1986. King Rail census, 1986: Population status and habitat utilization. Michigan DNR.

Riggs, C. D. 1946. European Widgeon record for Washtenaw County, Michigan. *Jack-Pine Warbler* 24:102.

Root, T. 1988. *Atlas of Wintering North American Birds.* Chicago: University of Chicago Press.

Sibley, C. G., and J. Ahlquist. 1983. The phylogeny and classification of birds based on the data of DNA-DNA hybridization. *Current Ornithology* 1:245-93.

_____. 1986. Reconstructing bird phylogeny by comparing DNAs. *Scientific American* 252:82-92.

Sturgeon, M. T. 1946. Arctic Three-toed Woodpecker on the Michigan State Normal College Campus Ypsilanti, Michigan. *Jack-Pine Warbler* 24:30.

Swales, J. 1989. Shorebird observations in the county, 1988-89. *Washtenaw County Bird Survey* 2 (3).

Terres, J. 1980. *The Audubon Encyclopedia of North American Birds.* New York: Alfred A. Knopf.

Tinker, A. D. 1910. The birds of School Girl's Glen, Ann Arbor, Michigan. *Michigan Geological and Biological Survey* 1:35-66.

_____. 1911. Spring migration in Michigan. *Wilson Bulletin* 23:28-34.

Tinker, A. D., and N. A. Wood. 1916. Fall migration records (1906-1915) at Ann Arbor, Michigan. *Wilson Bulletin* 28:122-27.

Veit, R. R., and L. Jonsson. 1984. Field identification of smaller sandpipers within the genus *Calidris. American Birds* 38:853-76.

Walkinshaw, L. H. 1978. *Birds of the Battle Creek, Calhoun County, Michigan Area.* Ann Arbor, MI: University Microfilms International.

Washtenaw County Fragile Lands. 1981. Ann Arbor. Washtenaw County
Metropolitan Planning Commission.
Whitney, B., and K. Kaufman. 1985. The *Empidonax* challenge: Looking
at *Empidonax*, Part I. *Birding* 17:151-58.
_____. 1985. The *Empidonax* challenge: Looking at *Empidonax*,
Part II. *Birding* 17:277-87.
_____. 1986. The *Empidonax* challenge: Looking at *Empidonax*,
Part III. *Birding* 18:153-59.
_____. 1986. The *Empidonax* challenge: Looking at *Empidonax*,
Part IV. *Birding* 18:315-27.
_____. 1987. The *Empidonax* challenge: Looking at *Empidonax*,
Part V. *Birding* 19:7-15.
Wilds, C., and M. Newlon. 1983. The identification of the Dowitchers.
Birding 15:151-66.
Wilson, B. V. 1947. The Western Meadowlark in Michigan. *Jack-
Pine Warbler* 25:3-12.
Wood, N. A. 1903. Some rare Washtenaw County warblers. *Bulletin of the
Michigan Ornithological Club* 4:81.
_____. 1906. Twenty-five years of bird migration at Ann Arbor,
Michigan. Michigan Academy of Science. Eighth Annual Report.
_____. 1908. Notes on the spring migration at Ann Arbor, Michigan.
Auk 35:10-15.
_____. 1951. *The Birds of Michigan*. Miscellaneous Publications
Museum of Zoology, University of Michigan. No. 75.
Wood, N. A., and O. M'Creary. 1905. An unusual bird wave. *Bulletin of
the Michigan Ornithological Club* 6:1.
Wood, N. A., and A. D. Tinker. 1910. Notes on some of the rarer birds of
Washtenaw County, Michigan. *Auk* 27:129-41.
_____. 1934. *Fifty Years of Bird Migration in the Ann Arbor Region of
Michigan 1880-1930*. Occasional Papers of the Museum of
Zoology, University of Michigan. No. 280.
Zimmerman, D. A., and J. Van Tyne. 1959. *A Distributional Checklist of
the Birds of Michigan*. Occasional Papers of the Museum of
Zoology, University of Michigan. No. 608.

Index

Numbers in **bold** refer either to main species accounts or to site descriptions.

Tanager,
  Scarlet, 8, 25, 29, 43, 198, **199**
  Summer, 27, **198**
Teal,
  Blue-winged, 45, 49, 71, 75, **77**
  Green-winged, **75**
Tern,
  Black, 24, 31, 32, 52, **124**
  Caspian, 13, 40, **122-23**, 247
  Common, 123, **232**
  Forster's, 23, 24, **123**
  Least, 123, **232**
Thrasher, Brown, **167**
Thrush,
  Gray-cheeked, 160, 161, **162**
  Hermit, 27, 32, 39, 41, 160, 161,
    164, 207
  Swainson's, 160, 161, 162, **163**
  Wood, 30, 43, 160, 161, **165**, 217
Thurston Pond Nature Center, 13, **40**,
  44, 167, 247
Titmouse, Tufted, 10, 39, **152**, 153,
  158
Towhee,
  Rufous-sided, 36, **202**
  Spotted, 202
Trinkle Road Marsh, 17, 44, **49**, 66,
  68, 74, 77, 78, 79, 92, 101, 102,
  215
Turkey, Wild, 29, 48, **99**
Turnstone, Ruddy, **110**

Veery, 25, 43, 51, 57, 160, 161, **162**
Vireo,
  Bell's, 38, **171**
  Philadelphia, 33, 170, **174**
  Red-eyed, 8, 36, 170, 173, **174**,
    217
  Solitary, 48, 170, **172**
  Warbling, 170, **173**, 174
  White-eyed, 11, 25, 26, 33, 35,
    38, 170, **171**, 248

Yellow-throated, 22, 29, 30, 43,
  170, **173**
Vulture, Turkey, 6, 53, **69-70**

Warbler,
  Bay-breasted, 176, **188**, 189, 248,
  Black-and-white, 176, **189-90**
  Black-throated Blue, 53, 176, **183**
  Black-throated Gray, 184, **234**
  Black-throated Green, 176, **184-
    85**, 248
  Blackburnian, 176, **185**, 248
  Blackpoll, 176, **188-89**
  Blue-winged, 29, 32, 33, 43, 175,
    176, **177**, 178, 179
  Brewster's, 38, **178-79**
  Canada, 175, 176, **197**
  Cape May, 176, **183**
  Cerulean, 10, 27, 51, 176, **189**
  Chestnut-sided, 43, 48, 175, 176,
    182
  Connecticut, 38, 176, **194**
  Golden-winged, 27, 33, 52, 176,
    177, **178**, 179
  Hooded, 10, 11, 23, 38, 48, 51,
    176, **196**
  Kentucky, 23, **193-94**, 248
  Kirtland's, **186-87**
  Lawrence's, 178, **179**, 248
  Magnolia, 176, **182**
  Mourning, 27, 38, 176, **195**
  Myrtle (see Yellow-rumped)
  Nashville, 175, 176, **180**
  Orange-crowned, 25, 176, **180**
  Palm, 25, 176, **187-88**
  Parula (see Parula, Northern)
  Pine, 48, 176, **186**, 248
  Prairie, 51, **187**
  Prothonotary, 25, 26, **190-91**, 248
  Tennessee, 174, 176, **179**
  Wilson's, 26, 176, **196**
  Worm-eating, 38, **191**, 248